Advancing Qualitative Methods in Criminology and Criminal Justice

D1145654

For several decades qualitative research has been under-represented in criminological and criminal justice research. This collection is intended to promote the understanding of qualitative research designs and to encourage their use among those seeking answers to questions about crime and justice. To this end top qualitative scholars have been assembled to provide their insights on the topic. A wide range of expert contributors delve into topics such as, the state of qualitative methods in the discipline, the potential ethical and physical hazards of engaging in ethnographic research, how to make sense of and interpret participants' stories, innovative ways to collect data, the value of using mixed methods to understand crime and justice issues, effective strategies for teaching fieldwork, and the inherent rewards of a career spent speaking with others. This book will be an ideal introduction for students and scholars of Criminal Justice, Criminology, and Sociology, regardless of whether their primary methodology is qualitative or quantitative.

This book was originally published as a special issue of the *Journal of Criminal Justice Education*.

Heith Copes is Associate Professor of Criminal Justice at the University of Alabama at Birmingham, USA. His research interests include criminal decision-making as it relates to various types of illegal behavior including drug distribution, automobile theft and identity theft. His research has been published in a variety of journals, including *Social Problems*, the *British Journal of Criminology*, *Deviant Behavior* and *Justice Quarterly*.

WITHDRAWN

2 3 APR 2023

Advancing Qualitative Methods in Criminology and Criminal Justice

Edited by
Heith Copes

Routledge
Taylor & Francis Group

LONDON AND NEW YORK

First published 2012
by Routledge
2 Park Square, Milton Park, Abingdon, Oxon, OX14 4RN

Simultaneously published in the USA and Canada
by Routledge
711 Third Avenue, New York, NY 10017

Routledge is an imprint of the Taylor & Francis Group, an informa business

First issued in paperback 2013

This book is a reproduction of the *Journal of Criminal Justice Education*, Volume 21, Issue 4. The Publisher requests to those authors who may be citing this book to state, also, the bibliographical details of the special issue on which the book was based.

Trademark notice: Product or corporate names may be trademarks or registered trademarks, and are used only for identification and explanation without intent to infringe.

British Library Cataloguing in Publication Data
A catalogue record for this book is available from the British Library

ISBN13: 978-0-415-78311-8 (hbk)
ISBN13: 978-0-415-84586-1 (pbk)

Typeset in Helvetica
by Taylor & Francis Books

Disclaimer
The publisher would like to make readers aware that the chapters in this book are referred to as articles as they had been in the special issue. The publisher accepts responsibility for any inconsistencies that may have arisen in the course of preparing this volume for print.

Contents

Notes on Contributors

John J. Brent is a doctoral student in the Sociology and Criminal Justice Department at the University of Delaware, USA. His current research interests include criminal justice theory, criminological trends of late-modernity, and the cultural contexts of crime. He is co-author of *Theorizing Criminal Justice: Eight Essential Orientations* (2010) with Peter B. Kraska.

Heith Copes is an associate professor in the Department of Justice Sciences at the University of Alabama at Birmingham, USA. His research interests include qualitative methods, auto theft, and the intersections of criminal motivation and experiential aspects of the offending experience.

Dean A. Dabney is an associate professor in the Department of Criminal Justice at Georgia State University, USA. He received his doctorate in sociology from the University of Florida in 1997. His scholarly interests include the organizational culture within law enforcement agencies, forms of deviance and/or criminal behaviours that occur in organizational settings, and qualitative research methods.

Thomas J. Holt is an assistant professor in the School of Criminal Justice at Michigan State University, USA. His research focuses on cybercrime and the ways that technology and the Internet facilitate deviance. He has published in journals such as *Crime and Delinquency, Deviant Behavior*, and the *Journal of Criminal Justice*. He is also the editor of the book *Crime On-line: Correlates, Causes, and Context*, published by Carolina Academic Press

Scott Jacques is assistant professor of Criminal Justice at the University of Cincinnati, USA. In addition to his interest in theorizing criminological method, he also studies victimizations of and social control by drug dealers. His work has been published in journals such as *Criminology, Crime & Delinquency, Journal of Research in Crime & Delinquency*, and *Justice Quarterly*.

Peter B. Kraska is a professor and graduate program director in the Criminal Justice Department at Eastern Kentucky University, USA. His interests include mixed methods research, criminal justice theory, and various trends associated with late modernity, such as the military/criminal justice blur. His latest book is a comprehensive research methods text titled, *Criminal Justice and Criminology Research Methods* (Pearson).

James W. Marquart is the dean of the School of Economic, Political and Policy Sciences at the University of Texas-Dallas, USA, and a professor of criminology. He has long-term research and teaching interests in prison organizations, capital punishment, criminal justice policy, and research methods. His current research involves an analysis of the long-term effects (i.e., prison violence, racially motivated attacks, and gang-related violence) of the in-cell racial integration policies in the California and Texas prison systems.

J. Mitchell Miller is a professor in the Department of Criminal Justice at the University of Texas at San Antonio, USA. A former editor of the *Journal of Crime & Justice* and the *Journal of Criminal Justice Education*, he maintains a broad research agenda oriented around justice system program evaluation, criminological theory development, drugs and crime, and alternative fieldwork.

Robert G. Morris, Ph.D., is an assistant professor of criminology at the University of Texas at Dallas, USA. He studies the etiology of technology driven crime with a specific interest in fraud (crimes of trust) and cybercrime as well as contemporary issues in criminal justice, such as corrections administration and inmate misconduct. His recent work has appeared in *Crime and Delinquency*, *Criminal Justice and Behavior*, the *Journal of Criminal Justice, Deviant Behavior*, and other peer-reviewed outlets.

Mark R. Pogrebin is a professor of criminal justice and public affairs in the School of Public Affairs at the University of Colorado at Denver, USA. He has conducted numerous field studies in the areas of police undercover work, tragic events and emotion management, African-American policewomen, women jailers, psychotherapists' deviant behavior with clients, women in prison and on parole, the strategic uses of humor among police, gun use and violence of convicted felons, and re-entry obstacles for parolees. He has published six books and numerous journal articles and has had over 35 of his articles reprinted in anthologies.

Lois Presser is associate professor of sociology at the University of Tennessee, USA. Her research concerns discourses of power, powerlessness, justice, and injustice. She is the author of *Been a Heavy Life: Stories of Violent Men* (2008). Currently she is developing a theory of harmful action.

Sveinung Sandberg, Ph.D., is a postdoctoral research fellow at the Department of Sociology and Human Geography at the University of Oslo, Norway. In 2009 he published the book *Street Capital: Black Drug Dealers in a White Welfare State* (with Willy Pedersen). Research interests include illegal drugs, drug dealing, violence, subculture theory, and discourse analysis.

Richard Tewksbury is professor of justice administration at the University of Louisville, USA. He is a former editor of *Justice Quarterly* and of the *American Journal of Criminal Justice*. His research centers on issues of identity construction and management among deviants and stigmatized criminal offenders, sex, sexuality and sex offending and pedagogical issues in criminal justice. He is both an advocate for and practitioner of alternative fieldwork approaches.

Richard Wright is Curators' Professor in the Department of Criminology and Criminal Justice at the University of Missouri – St. Louis, USA, and Editor-in-Chief of the *British Journal of Sociology*. He has co-authored several books based on qualitative data obtained from offenders (*Burglars on Burglary*, 1984; *Burglars on the Job*, 1994; *Armed Robbers in Action*, 1997; *Street Justice*, 2006) and also co-edited *The Sage Handbook of Fieldwork* (2006).

Introduction

Advancing Qualitative Methods in Criminal Justice and Criminology

Heith Copes

Criminology has a long history of using qualitative methods to understand the perspective of offenders and those who seek to deter, punish and/or rehabilitate them. In fact, examples of qualitative criminology can be found as early as the mid-nineteenth century when Mayhew was chronicling the lives of the London poor. In the early part of the twentieth-century quantitative and qualitative scholars at the University of Chicago worked side-by-side to produce some of the most important insights into crime and justice. The body of literature produced by eliciting the accounts of law-violators and those who sanction these people has provided great insights into our understanding of crime and justice. By letting participants "speak for themselves" we get to hear the motives and decisions of those in the criminal underworld and to see the daily lives of those who work within the various components of the criminal justice system. Additionally, qualitative methods are well suited for developing and evaluating crime control programs (Decker, 2004). Knowing how offenders enact their crimes, perceive criminal opportunities, and manage potential risks can be the bedrock for designing and implementing successful crime prevention programs.

Despite the insights gained from quantitative and qualitative methodologies, contemporary scholars still squabble over which is best (e.g., Higgins, 2009; Tewksbury, 2009; Worrall, 2000). In his introduction to the special issue on quantitative methods appearing in the *Journal of Criminal Justice Education* Pratt (2010, p.1) addresses succinctly the fruitlessness of this argument, "the qualitative-quantitative dichotomy strikes many as, at best, an empty debate and, at worst, utterly foolish—much like debating whether a hammer or a monkey-wrench is better." While I agree with the sentiment of Pratt's statement, I also understand why those in the minority (i.e., qualitative researchers) often take a defensive stance on the issue. Due to misunderstandings about appropriate data collection and analysis strategies, qualitative research is often held to inappropriate standards for sampling and generalizability, seen as merely descriptive, and had its contributions devalued (Miller, 2005). For instance, in a recent review of my work (with Lynne Vieraitis) involving interviews with 59 identity thieves conducted among willing participants in Federal prisons across the nation, a reviewer commented that the results were simply "anecdotal" and critiqued the fact that we had no statistical or graphic presentations of the data (see Miller, 2005 for similar stories). Apparently, little thought was given to the fact that no generalizeable sampling frame feasibly could be constructed or to the reality that *a priori* construction of a survey would not have accurately, let along fully, captured rich information on motives, life stories, and modus operandi that was gained by interviewing.

Most criminological and criminal justice researchers agree that the research question should drive the method. In practice, however, the majority of scholars either ignore this basic assumption or only ask questions they can answer statistically. A review of research published in criminology and criminal justice journals shows that scholars (at least in the United States) have gravitated to quantitative methods (DiChristina, 1997; Kleck, Tark, & Bellows, 2006; Tewksbury, DeMichle, & Miller, 2005). In a recent content analysis of articles that appeared in the top fifteen journals in the field[1] from 2000 to 2009 my co-authors and I sought to assess how much (or how little) qualitative methods were used in the research presented in these journals (Copes, Brown, & Tewksbury, 2011). This undertaking was informative. A mere 3.69% were classified as ethnographic.[2] While I assumed these journals favored quantitative designs, I did not realize how much this was the case. This finding lends credence to the claim that qualitative methods are under-represented and that the field is at risk of becoming one-dimensional. Many of those who are beginning careers with an interest in qualitative methods surely catch on to the prevailing strategies and adjust their work strategies accordingly. If for no other reason than to remind criminology and criminal justice scholars that qualitative strategies remain useful, this edited collection is sorely needed.

The goal of this volume is not to argue that qualitative methods are superior to quantitative ones. Instead, its purpose is to promote the use and understanding of sound qualitative research designs and to encourage their use among those seeking answers to questions about crime and justice. The target audience for this book includes those whose research repertoire emphasizes qualitative methods and those who have little experience with such methods but who see value in qualitative approaches and seek to learn about them. Should these articles inspire readers to undertake ethnographic work of their own then so much the better.

To this end some of the top qualitative scholars in the field have authored articles in this collection. The articles that appear provide insights into the state of qualitative methods in the discipline (Tewksbury, Dabney, & Copes), the potential ethical and physical hazards of engaging in ethnographic research (Holt; Jacques & Wright; Pogrebin), how to make sense of and interpret narratives (Presser; Sandberg), innovative ways to collect data (Holt; Miller & Tewksbury), the value of using mixed methods to understand crime and justice issues (Brent & Kraska), effective strategies for teaching fieldwork (Morris & Marquart), and the inherent rewards of a career spent speaking with others (Pogrebin).

The people who have contributed to this collection all have enhanced our understanding of crime and the justice system through the use of ethnographic methods. Each has answered the call to promote his or her preferred research methodology. I encourage others who have already engaged in ethnographic research to do the same and to be more vocal about the strengths (and weaknesses) of this methodological style. As a "marginalized" community within the discipline it is our responsibility to advocate for ethnographic research as valuable and important, to recruit and educate a new generation of scholars, and to address the lack of understandings about ethnographic research that permeates the mainstream of the discipline. To accomplish these goals it would be beneficial for those who engage in qualitative methods to pass on their skills to students, to make a stronger presence at academic conferences (perhaps by organizing special sessions), to apply for state and federal funding to support qualitative data collection, and to seek out editorial positions of academic journals in the field. By making ourselves and our research a larger and more visible presence within the discipline we can work to ensure that ethnographic research does not wither away or stagnate. It is my hope that the articles included in this collection will help enliven and promote this methodological design.

1 Rankings were based on Sorensen, Snell and Rodriguez (2006) and Sorensen (2009).
2 We used the term "ethnographic research" to refer to research that drew upon text-based data collected through fieldwork, semi-structured or unstructured interviews, focus groups, or some combination of these techniques.

REFERENCES

Becker, H. (1966). Outsiders: Studies in the sociology of deviance. New York: Free Press.

Bernasco, W. (2010). Offenders on offending: Learning about crime from criminals. Portland, OR: Willan.

Copes, H., Brown, A., & Tewksbury, R. (2011). A content analysis of ethnographic research published in top criminology and criminal justice journals from 2000-2009. Journal of Criminal Justice Education, DOI: 10.1080/10511253.2010.519714.

Cromwell, P. (2010). In their own words: Criminals on crime. New York: Oxford.

Decker, S. (2004). Using offender interviews to inform police problem-solving, Guide No. 3. Problem-Oriented Guides for Police, Problem Solving Tool Series. Washington, D.C.: Office of Community Oriented Policing Services, U.S. Department of Justice.

DiChristina, B. (1997). The quantitative emphasis in criminal justice education. Journal of Criminal Justice Education, 8, 181-199.

Higgins, G. 2009. Quantitative versus qualitative methods: Understanding why quantitative methods are predominant in criminology and criminal justice. Journal of Theoretical and Philosophical Criminology, 1, 23-37.

Kleck, G., Tark, J., & Bellows, J. J. (2006). What methods are most frequently used in research in criminology and criminal justice? Journal of Criminal Justice, 34, 147-152.

Miller, J. (2005). The status of qualitative research in criminology. Proceedings from the National Science Foundation's Workshop on Interdisciplinary Standards for Systematic Qualitative Research. Retrieved July 19, 2010, from http://www.wjh.harvard.edu/nsfqual/ Millerpercent20Paper.pdf.

Pratt, T. (2010). Special issue on quantitative methods for criminal justice and criminology. Journal of Criminal Justice Education, 21, 103-104.

Sorensen, J., Snell, C., & Rodriguez, J. J. (2006). An assessment of criminal justice and criminology journal prestige. Journal of Criminal Justice Education, 17, 297-322.

Sorensen, J. (2009). An assessment of the relative impact of criminal justice and criminology journals. Journal of Criminal Justice, 37, 505-511.

Tewksbury, R. (2009). Qualitative versus quantitative methods: Understanding why qualitative methods are superior for criminology and criminal justice. Journal of Theoretical and Philosophical Criminology, 1, 38-59.

Tewksbury, R., DeMichele, M. T., & Miller, J. M. (2005). Methodological orientations of articles appearing in criminal justice's top journals: Who publishes what and where. Journal of Criminal Justice Education, 16, 265-279.

The Prominence of Qualitative Research in Criminology and Criminal Justice Scholarship

Richard Tewksbury, Dean A. Dabney and Heith Copes

Most criminologists would agree that the discipline favors quantitative methodologies over qualitative ones. The present study seeks to revisit and expand past assessments on the prominence of qualitative research appearing in criminology and criminal justice (CCJ) publication outlets. Our inquiry is divided into two parts. First we consider the frequency with which empirical studies based upon qualitative methods and analyses were published in top CCJ journals from 2004 to 2008. Second, we add a new avenue of inquiry to the discussion by assessing the frequency with which qualitative methods and analyses are being used in doctoral dissertations produced within the US CCJ PhD programs during the same five-year timeframe. Overall, our findings support the claim that qualitative research continues to represent only a small proportion of published research in the field. We seek to contextualize this empirical observation within the existing debate on the role of methods and theory in CCJ scholarship.

Despite the "common knowledge" in the field that quantitative methods are the norm, and the recognition that "theory construction is a largely qualitative endeavor" where "qualitative researchers primarily build and advance theories" (Worrall 2000, pp. 358–359), there have been surprisingly few attempts to document or specify the prominence of qualitative scholarship in criminology and criminal justice (CCJ) relative to scholarship derived from quantitative methods and analysis. The field tends to take for granted that qualitative researchers are hard at work producing well-conceived and well-executed inductive research that might serve to formulate and expand theoretical propositions from the ground up. So too we do assume that the fruits of these labors are making their way into print and that senior qualitative researchers are passing along their skills and insights to the next generation of junior scholars who will continue the ball rolling. The purpose of this article is to determine the prominence of qualitatively derived scholarship, report on the persons and institutions that produce this scholarship, and to reflect upon the role this work plays in the advancement of the causes and consequences of criminal behavior. To do this we conduct a systematic examination of published work in the field, including scholarly articles and dissertations.

In the first study of the use of varying methodological approaches in the field, Tewksbury, DeMichele, and Miller (2005) reviewed all 725 articles published in five leading CCJ journals for the five-year period of 1998-2002.[1] They report that of all articles appearing in the journals, 6.3% employed a qualitative methodology. Quantitatively oriented articles accounted for the majority (73.1%) of all the published articles in the sample.[2] Of the five reviewed journals, they found that *Justice Quarterly* had the largest proportion of qualitative articles (10.9%), followed by *Criminology* (8.2%), *Journal of Criminal Justice* (7.2%), *Journal of Research in Crime and Delinquency* (2.5%), and *Criminal Justice and Behavior* (0.7%).

In a similar, but smaller, study Kleck, Tark, and Bellows (2006) reviewed the research designs and data collection and analysis techniques used in all empirical articles appearing in seven leading CCJ journals during 2001 and 2002.[3] This study reported that across all seven journals, 4.5% of the 375 reviewed articles employed qualitative data analysis.[4] Notably, two of the journals in this study (*Journal of Criminal Law and Criminology*, and not surprisingly *Journal of Quantitative Criminology*) published no articles employing qualitative data analysis. As in the Tewksbury et al. (2005) study, *Justice Quarterly* had the largest compliment (8.6%) of qualitative articles, followed by *Criminology* (6.3%), *Journal of Research in Crime and Delinquency* (6.1%), and *Crime and Delinquency* (5.5%).

More recently, Buckler (2008) expanded the focus to include three regional journals. He added *American Journal of Criminal Justice* (published by the Southern Criminal Justice Association), *Western Criminology Review* (published by the Western Society of Criminology) and the *Southwest Journal of Criminal Justice* (published by the Southwestern Association of Criminal Justice) to a list that included *Criminology, Justice Quarterly, Journal of Research Crime and Delinquency, Crime and Delinquency,* and *Journal of Criminal Justice,* but

---

1. The journals included by Tewksbury et al. (2005) were *Criminology, Journal of Criminal Justice, Justice Quarterly, Journal of Research in Crime and Delinquency,* and *Criminal Justice and Behavior.*

2. Additionally, articles presenting a theoretical argument or discussion (and no original data analysis) accounted for seven percent of all articles; other categories of methodological analysis in the sample included evaluation studies (5.2%), methodological discussions (5.1%), mixed methods (1.4%), legal analysis (1.0%), meta analyses (0.6%), and historical analyses (0.3%).

3. Kleck et al. (2006) reviewed the journals *Criminology, Journal of Research in Crime and Delinquency, Journal of Criminal Justice, Justice Quarterly, Journal of Criminal Law and Criminology, Crime and Delinquency,* and *Journal of Quantitative Criminology.* Note that there is considerable overlap between these journals and those reviewed as part of the Tewksbury et al. (2005) study, namely Kleck et al. (2006) include four of the five journals from the Tewksbury et al. (2005) study, omitting only *Criminal Justice & Behavior* and adding three new journals.

4. Of the total sample, qualitative data collection (not analysis) was employed by some articles. Informal interviews were used in 7.6% of all articles and direction observation was employed in 6.2% of all articles. However, the data gathered via these methods were subsequently used in quantitative analyses.

also Buckler limited his analysis to those articles appearing in the 2003-2007 volumes of these journals. Two interesting findings emerged from this study. First, in most cases, the percentage of articles in the top journals classified as qualitative were higher than the numbers reported by Tewksbury et al. (2005) and Kleck et al. (2006). For instance, Buckler reported that 11.7% of articles in *Criminology* were qualitative, compared to 8.2% for Tewksbury et al. (2005) and 6.3% in Kleck et al. (2006). Also, for the 2003-2007 volumes, Buckler reported 12.1% of articles in *Crime and Delinquency* were qualitative compared to Kleck et al.'s (2006) finding of 5.5% for the 2001-2002 timeframe. However, in other cases, Buckler's findings suggest that the prominence of qualitative work receded at some publication outlets. For example, the qualitative representation in *Justice Quarterly* decreased from 10.9% and 8.6% respectively in the earlier Tewksbury et al. and Kleck studies to 6.6% in the Buckler inquiry.

Buckler's findings suggest only marginal differences in the prominence of qualitative articles in top-tier journals compared to the regional journals that he chose to include in his analysis. Whereas the top-tier journals all published no more than 12.1% of articles reporting some qualitative findings, the three regional journals realized slightly higher percentages with 14.3%, 13.6%, and 13.8% of articles, respectively, reporting qualitative findings. However, we note that it is difficult to make direct comparisons between the findings of the Buckler study and of those that came before it, as Buckler did not classify articles as exclusively quantitative or qualitative, but rather, "for an article to be considered as qualitative, the researcher had to report a finding through a narrative format that did not convert the finding into numerical data" (p. 387). Therefore, any article employing mixed methods in which at least one finding was reported in narrative format was counted as qualitative; this was a much broader definition than that used by Tewksbury et al. (2005) or Kleck et al. (2006) and likely resulted in larger percentages.

Overall, it appears that qualitative research is a clear minority within CCJ publications. It has been suggested that heavy emphasis on quantitative scholarship results in an impact on the development of the discipline. For example, Tewksbury et al. (2005) concluded that

> by using such heavily quantitative language criminal justice and criminology are becoming less able to communicate with system administrators and practitioners. The use of advanced statistical techniques, producing highly fruitful findings in their own right, has the potential to limit the audience for criminal justice and criminological research findings. ... Although there is a pragmatic drive pushing crime and justice studies and research, there is a significant need to advance theoretical discussions. As this study reveals, there is little article space given to scholars conducting theoretical development in the top U.S. journals. (p. 277)

This under-representation of qualitative work leads us to ask: is there a bias among editors and reviewers that makes it difficult to get these manuscripts accepted? Are there fewer researchers who chose this type of design? Are people not being trained in rigorous qualitative methods? In discussing the review process of her recent qualitative research, Jody Miller (2005) quoted reviewers as describing the manuscript as "journalistic" and "based on hearsay." Such reviews suggest a misunderstanding of qualitative research. That said, there is evidence to suggest that the editors of the top CCJ journals are not biased against qualitative research in favor of its quantitative counterpart. Buckler (2008) reported on interviews conducted with 10 current or past editors of criminal justice journals (five of whom are/were editors of top-tier journals). When discussing the content of the journals they edit, these editors suggested that "very few qualitative oriented manuscripts are submitted for review" (p. 391). Editors of top-tier journals estimated that no more than 15% of submitted manuscripts employ qualitative analyses, while editors of lower-tier journals estimated between 10% and 50% of received manuscripts are qualitative in nature. Nonetheless, while acknowledging that their journals do primarily publish quantitative articles, Buckler also reported that "all the editors expressed that they would like to see more qualitative research published in academic journals" (p. 395).

If few CCJ scholars are submitting qualitative articles to the discipline's journals, the question arises of whether there are scholars being trained in qualitative methods. In his assessment of the content of 10 commonly used research methods' textbooks in criminal justice undergraduate and graduate programs, Sever (2001) reported that 7.3% of the total pages in these books were devoted to discussions of qualitative research. This compared to 9.1% of the textbook pages addressing quantitative research methods. However, it is important to note that Sever (2001) derived these calculations from a sample of texts that included Berg's *Qualitative Research Methods for the Social Sciences*. This text alone accounted for 25% of the total qualitative method discussion pages across the entire sample. If re-calculated without the Berg text, the average percent of pages in the remaining nine texts drops to 5.8%.

At the doctoral level of CCJ education DiChristina (1997) reported that, across the 16 doctoral programs reviewed in 1995, only one program required a qualitative method course compared to 15 programs that required a quantitative method course (and 13 required at least two quantitative method courses). More recently, Buckler (2008) reported that across the 25 PhD-granting CCJ programs operating in 2006, only four programs required a qualitative method course. And, he found that only 10 other doctoral programs offered any elective courses in qualitative methods. Therefore, in 11 doctoral CCJ programs (44%) there were no opportunities for students to take coursework in qualitative methods and in only four of the 25 (16%) programs can we be sure that all students were exposed to at least one qualitative research methods' class during their doctoral education. Buckler (2008, p. 401) concluded that "one reason for the quantitative/qualitative divide is that qualitative methods are not frequently taught, illustrated and legitimized by doctoral degree granting criminology and criminal justice programs."

7

The present study seeks to add to the ongoing scholarly conversation about the prominence of qualitative methods in two important ways. First, in surveying the prominence of published qualitative research, we adopt a broader and more up-to-date sampling strategy, one that incorporates recent volumes from a larger number of American-based CCJ journals as well as several prominent international peer-reviewed outlets. We also collected data on a comprehensive set of variables, allowing for analysis of the authors' background and institutional affiliations. This approach provides a more informed understanding of the sources of qualitative research and the conduits through which the scholarship is being disseminated. Second, we review all doctoral dissertations produced in the timeframe by the US CCJ programs to provide insight into the pipeline of qualitative researchers and scholarship taking shape to fuel future published materials. Collectively, these data sources allow for an important contemporary pulse check on the qualitatively informed knowledge base of the discipline and capacity to alter said knowledge base in the immediate future.

Methods

Sample Selection

Two samples are used in the present study. The first sample is of articles published in the most prestigious American and international CCJ journals. The second sample is of individuals earning a doctoral degree in criminology or criminal justice. The first sample for the study is composed of all articles published between 2004 and 2008 in 16 American-based and three internationally based CCJ journals. The list of American journals was derived from the CCJ journal prestige rankings provided by Sorensen, Snell, and Rodriguez (2006). We selected the top 15 CCJ domestic journals in the prestige rankings Sorensen et al. (2006) derived from surveys with more than 1,000 members of the Academy of Criminal Justice Sciences and the American Society of Criminology. While these rankings do not reflect citation counts, circulation rates, or other measures of scholarly impact or scope, they arguably encompass those publication outlets that scholars target for their own research and/or turn to when seeking to consume the research of their peers. Of these 15 journals, two were excluded from the current study because they were either explicitly targeted at a particular methodological orientation (*Journal of Quantitative Criminology*) or actually an annual publication rather than a true journal (*Advances in Criminological Theory*). The 13 journals included in the current analysis are *Crime and Delinquency, Criminal Justice and Behavior, Criminology, Criminology and Public Policy, Deviant Behavior,*[5] *Journal of Criminal Justice, Journal*

---

5. It is important to note that when identifying the methodological orientation of articles in *Deviant Behavior* only those articles that explicitly address crime, criminals, criminal justice processes, or actors were included in the data. All articles focused on non-criminal or non-criminal justice topics (e.g., sexual deviance, student cheating, etc.) were excluded from the data.

of Criminal Law and Criminology,[6] *Journal of Interpersonal Violence, Journal of Research in Crime and Delinquency, Justice Quarterly, Law and Human Behavior, Law and Society Review,* and *Theoretical Criminology*. In addition, we included three non-American journals that were not included in Sorensen et al.'s study. These journals are the *British Journal of Criminology, Canadian Journal of Criminology and Criminal Justice,* and *Australian and New Zealand Journal of Criminology*. These outlets were included because of the common assumption that international journals are more welcoming of qualitative research and also as a means of adding an international dimension to the ongoing environmental scan of the publishing landscape.

We concentrated our journal-based inquiry on a five-year interval, amassing all content published in volumes containing a publication date from 2004 through 2008. The content was arrayed in 380 issues spanning a total of 95 journal volumes.[7] With respect to content, only "full" articles are included in the data under consideration here. Editorials, research notes, commentaries, and presidential addresses are excluded from the analysis. The final dataset thus includes 2,493 published articles (2,092 articles in the US journals and 401 in the non-US journals).

The second sample is composed of all 420 dissertations that were successfully defended to satisfy doctoral degree requirements in CCJ from the 33 institutions/departments granting such degrees between the same 2004 and 2008 interval. The doctoral degree-granting institutions were identified by those included in the Association of Doctoral Programs in Criminology and Criminal Justice.[8] Individuals and their dissertations were identified through a search in ProQuest Digital Dissertations. All individuals with a dissertation categorized with the subject code "criminology" were identified, and their dissertations were reviewed to identify if they graduated with a degree in CCJ (if not, they were excluded from the sample) and to identify the data and analytic methods used in the dissertation.

Data Collection

All data collection was conducted by members of the authorship team. Works within both the article and the dissertation samples were reviewed carefully one at a time. For each, attention was focused on the abstracts, methods, and result sections in order to identify those articles that relied on both qualitative modes of inquiry and analysis. Articles or dissertations using what is conventionally deemed a qualitative mode of inquiry such as face-to-face interviews or

6. We only included articles that appeared in the criminology, and not the criminal law, section.
7. We included articles published in general issues as well as special or thematic issues, some of which involved a guest editor. None of the special issues revolved around themes that precluded or prescribed articles derived by qualitative means.
8. Although included in the sample, it should be noted that four doctoral degree-granting programs (George Mason University, Old Dominion University, University of Arkansas-Little Rock, and University of South Carolina) are relatively new and did not have any successfully defended dissertations during this time period.

social observation but that proceeded to report only numeric findings or that subjected the data to statistical analyses were not coded as qualitative. In order to be coded as qualitative, a study had to rely on a qualitative mode of inquiry and also subject the resulting data to an interpretive or thematic means of analysis. Note that the mere presence of statistical findings was not the litmus test for exclusion, rather the critical factor was whether or not a thematic or interpretive treatment of the data was present. Using these selection criteria, only those articles and dissertations that all authors unanimously agreed were qualitative in orientation were coded as qualitative.

Uniform templates were developed to systematically gather those data points that were deemed relevant to the present inquiry. With respect to the qualitative journal articles, variables included the journal name, year of publication, and number of authors. We tallied these qualitative articles relative to non-qualitative articles in each journal. We also collected information on the authors of each of these qualitative papers, which included name, university, country, position/rank, and department. To determine the rank of the author at the time of publication we looked to the author biographies, if provided. Positions included 1 = full professor; 2 = associate professor; 3 = assistant professor; 4 = instructor; 5 = student; 6 = other; 7 = non-academic. For the non-US positions we equated them with the comparable US rank; thus, lecturer = 3; senior lecturer and reader = 2; professor = 1.

To determine the types of departments that house those who publish qualitative research, we coded departments as follows: 1 = criminology/criminal justice; 2 = health sciences; 3 = political science; 4 = psychology; 5 = social sciences; 6 = social work; 7 = sociology; 8 = non-academic. Universities have considerable diversity with respect to the names of departments. Therefore it was necessary to group departments into fewer categories. We chose to combine all criminology, criminal justice, justice sciences, and justice administration into the same category (criminology/criminal justice). Those classified in health sciences consisted of family medicine, health promotion, health services, life and health sciences, nursing, public health, and surgery. The social science departments included behavioral sciences, human development, law, pan African studies, social policy, social science and policy, and women's studies.

A separate template was developed to gather data on the sample of qualitative dissertations. Here, data points included the date the degree was earned as well as the name of the candidate, his or her dissertation chair, degree-granting institution, and department.

Data Analysis

We begin by discussing the percentage of qualitative articles that were published in the 16 journals that we sampled. We then change the unit of analysis to describe characteristics of the authors of these qualitative articles. Finally, we turn to a description of dissertations, which includes the percentage of qualitative dissertations and the departmental characteristics of the authors. Analyses of the distribution of qualitative articles, the characteristics of the authors, and the methodological breakdown of dissertations are based on univariate statistics.

Findings

Published Qualitative Articles

Overall, the data in the present study show that representation of qualitatively oriented articles in the top US CCJ journals remains very low. Referring to Table 1, note that of the 2,092 articles appearing in the 2004-2008 volumes of the 13 domestic journals under study here, only 5.74% rely on qualitative data modes of inquiry and analysis techniques. Looking only at the three non-US journals a different pattern emerges. Of the 401 articles published in the 2004-2008 volumes of these journals, 27.2% of them used qualitative methods and analyses.

An interesting dichotomy emerges when we disregard the geographic origin of the publication. Ten of the 16 journals in our sample (*Journal of Criminal Law & Criminology, Journal of Interpersonal Violence, Criminology, Crime & Delin-*

Table 1 Journals' inclusion of qualitative articles

Journal	Total articles	Qualitative	Percent (%)
Deviant Behavior	74	23	31.08
Theoretical Criminology	97	19	19.58
Law & Society Review	128	18	14.06
Journal of Criminal Law & Criminology	17	1	5.88
Journal of Interpersonal Violence	470	25	5.31
Criminology	157	7	4.45
Crime & Delinquency	126	5	3.97
Journal of Criminal Justice	273	11	4.03
Journal of Research in Crime/Delinquency	84	3	3.57
Justice Quarterly	112	4	3.57
Criminology & Public Policy	66	1	1.51
Law & Human Behavior	195	2	1.02
Criminal Justice & Behavior	277	1	0.36
Total	2,092	120	5.74
International Journals			
British Journal of Criminology	235	88	37.44
Canadian Journal Criminology & C.J.	87	14	16.09
Australian & New Zealand Journal of Crimiminology	79	9	11.39
Total	401	111	27.68

quency, Journal of Criminal Justice, Journal of Research in Crime & Delinquency, Justice Quarterly, Criminology & Public Policy, Law & Human Behavior, and *Criminal Justice & Behavior*) had less than six percent of their articles published during the five-year period as qualitatively oriented pieces. However, five journals (*Deviant Behavior, Theoretical Criminology, British Journal of Criminology, Canadian Journal of Criminology and Criminal Justice,* and *Law & Society Review*) exceeded 14% of published articles being of a qualitative nature. These five journals are clearly different regarding their publication of qualitatively oriented articles. The three international journals had relatively high rates of qualitative articles—over one-third of articles published in the *British Journal of Criminology* were qualitative. Viewed a different way, we note that the number of qualitatively oriented articles published in the 2004-2008 volumes of the *British Journal of Criminology* (n = 88) exceeds the sum total (n = 60) of qualitative articles published in the aforementioned 10 journals during that same five-year time period. While there may be some legitimate and obvious reasons for this situation (see below), it is clear that the majority of qualitatively oriented scholarship on crime- and justice-related topics is being generated by a few selected peer-reviewed journals. In short, these are the places that CCJ scholars have found success at publishing qualitative research.

Not only are some journals home to a significantly greater proportion of qualitative work than the other journals assessed, but also it is notable that three journals (*Criminal Justice and Behavior, Law and Human Behavior,* and *Criminology and Public Policy*) have exceptionally low rates of qualitative articles in their pages. Referring again to Table 1, note that each of these three journals contains fewer than two percent of their articles reporting qualitative findings. And, in raw numbers, across these three journals a total of only four qualitative articles appeared in print during the five years of this study. Rather obviously, these are not outlets that add to our stock of knowledge about crime- and justice-related topics via qualitatively oriented inquiry. This situation is likely attributable to input (a lack of submissions) and/or throughput (attrition during the editorial review process) factors. For example, the low numbers for *Criminal Justice and Behavior* and *Law and Human Behavior* journals might be a byproduct of their connections to the psychology discipline. Both journals have long had a psychologist as editor and have editorial boards with a sizable compliment of scholars from this discipline. *Criminal Justice and Behavior* is sponsored by the American Association for Correctional and Forensic Psychology while *Law and Human Behavior* is the journal of the American Psychology-Law Society (AP-LS), a division of the American Psychological Association. Input factors might be shaped by the journal's charge, for example, the masthead for *Criminal Justice and Behavior* states that the journal "seeks contributions examining psychological and forensic aspects of juvenile and criminal justice systems." Both input and throughput factors seem obvious for these journals given the quantitative emphasis among psychologists. The picture is less clear for *Criminology and Public Policy.*

Characteristics of Qualitative Articles and Authors

Overall, there were 362 separate authors of qualitative articles published in the sampled journals. Examination of characteristics of the qualitative articles shows that across the sample there is a mean of 2.41 authors per article. Fully 71.2% of the articles have multiple authors. As shown in Table 2, there is variation, ranging from 1 to 3.00 in the mean number of authors per article across the journals. In addition, there was considerable variation in the type of department in which authors were housed and the number of co-authors. Those in health sciences (3.68), psychology (3.26), and non-academics (3.25) had the three highest means for number of authors. Those in sociology and criminal justice had means closer to two. This likely reflects the nature of collaboration in the fields. Moreover, while it is likely that authorship teams would employ divisions of labor that would result in the qualitative inquiry being assigned to a subset of the team members, these data do suggest that there is a reasonable pool of CCJ-oriented scholars in the field who are well versed in qualitative methods and analysis.

To investigate this issue of qualitative authorship capacity further, we examined the number of articles published by each of the 362 authors. The results indicated that for the five-year period only 11 authors had three or more publications appear in our sample of 16 journals, five of which had four, and one had seven. As such, while it is common for highly productive scholars to publish numerous quantitative articles in a year, this does not seem to be the case among the population of individuals publishing qualitative research in top peer-reviewed outlets. Perhaps the relatively long time that is required to do

Table 2 Mean number of Authors per qualitative articles

Journal	Mean number
Deviant Behavior	1.78
Theoretical Criminology	1.21
Law & Society Review	1.11
Journal of Criminal Law & Criminology	1.00
Journal of Interpersonal Violence	2.76
Criminology	2.71
Crime & Delinquency	2.00
Journal of Criminal Justice	1.91
Journal of Research in Crime/Delinq	1.66
Justice Quarterly	2.25
Criminology & Public Policy	1.00
Law & Human Behavior	1.50
Criminal Justice & Behavior	3.00
British Journal of Criminology	1.70
Canadian Journal Criminology & C.J.	2.14
Australian & New Zealand Journal of Criminology	1.22
Total	2.41

Table 3 Home departments of unique authors of qualitative articles

Department	N^1	Percent (%)
Criminology/Criminal Justice	116	33.7
Social Science	66	19.2
Sociology	65	18.9
Non-Academic	31	9.0
Psychology	31	9.0
Health Science	19	5.5
Social Work	11	3.2
Political Science	5	1.5
Total	344	100

[1]Departmental information was missing on 18 individuals.

ethnographic research limits the quantity of articles being produced (Buckler 2008; Pogrebin 2010). While reflecting on his experiences conducting and publishing qualitative research, Pogrebin (2010) stated his data collection often took longer than a year to complete and that on average he was able to publish about two articles per project. Quantitative articles, on the other hand, often draw upon secondary data, which reduces or eliminates time for the data collection phase and can often produce multiple papers using different combinations of variables or analysis techniques.

Next we turn our attention to the home base of operations for qualitative CCJ scholars. Table 3 shows that of the qualitative articles published in the 16 journals, one-third (33.7%) of the authors hold organizational affiliations in CCJ departments.[9] Social science department members are the second most populous in the sample, representing 19.2% of the authors, followed closely by individuals from sociology departments that constitute 18.9% of the authors. Slightly less than one in 10 of the authors (nine percent) claim a non-academic affiliation and the remainder of the authors hold affiliations in assorted other academic units. Even though CCJ departments house the largest percentage of authors, nearly two-thirds of authors are still housed elsewhere. While publishing one's work in our selected sample of CCJ journals is but one way to disseminate scholarship (books, journals from other disciplines, and research reports represent other options), at first blush these data raise the possibility that non-CCJ departments (e.g., sociology) are training and mentoring the next generation of qualitative CCJ researchers.

Table 4 shows the country in which the authors of these qualitative articles work. The first column reports the distribution for the entire sample, the second column shows the distribution for only the 13 American journals, and the third column presents the distribution for the three international journals.

9. Due to the stability in department affiliation (only one author changed department type) we include information only on unique authors as to not bias the results in favor of those who published multiple articles.

Table 4 Country of origin for authors of qualitative articles

Country	Percent of authors for all articles (%)	Percent of authors in the US journals (%)	Percent of authors in international journals
USA	47.4	75.3	13.3
UK	27.6	10.0	48.9
Canada	12.0	5.9	20.6
Australia	6.2	3.7	10.0
Israel	1.0	0.9	1.1
Hong Kong	1.0	1.8	–
France	0.7	–	1.7
Germany	0.7	–	1.7
Canary Islands	0.7	1.4	–
Brazil	0.5	–	1.1
Norway	0.5	0.5	0.6
Finland	0.2	–	0.6
Taiwan	0.2	0.5	–
Trinidad	0.2	–	0.6

The first column of data reveals that authors of qualitative scholarship published in this sample of journals primarily (75%) comes from the USA and the UK. The data presented in the second and third columns of Table 4 suggest that qualitative researchers tend to publish their scholarship close to their home base of operations. Specifically, the US authors constitute three-quarters of all authors of qualitative articles in the US journals, and only 13% of authors in the international journals during the study period. Conversely, for the international journals, nearly one-half of authors come from the UK and when adding in Canadian and Australian authors, fully 79.5% of authors in the international journals are from these locations. Authors coming from outside the USA have a larger share of the US publications than the US authors have of international publications. This suggests an international influence on qualitative research in the USA. Though small, it does exist. In summary, only approximately one-quarter of authors of qualitative articles are from nations other than the nation(s) in which a journal is housed.

The institutions in which these authors are employed are also assessed. A total of 161 institutions are represented by the 417 authors. Few institutions account for any sizeable portion of the authors, with only eight institutions (University of Missouri-St. Louis, University of Washington, University of Alabama at Birmingham, Lancaster University, Keele University, Kings College, University of Louisville, and University of Toronto) accounting for more than 1.5% of all authors of qualitative articles in these top journals. Here again, this raises the possibility that the average CCJ graduate student may not have at his/her disposal a cadre of professors who are proficient or impassioned about qualitative methods of inquiry and analysis; if this is the case, one must be wary about whether the next generation of scholars will have well-rounded method-ological understandings and capacities. What is more, the absence of qualitative

Table 5 Rank of authors of qualitative articles[1]

Rank	N	Percent of authors (%)
Professor	79	28.4
Associate Professor	45	16.2
Assistant Professor	70	25.2
Instructor	2	0.7
Student	35	12.6
Non-academic	40	14.4
Other	7	2.5
Total	278	100

[1]Information about rank was missing for 139 authors.

prominence within ranked CCJ doctoral programs (University of Missouri-St. Louis as the lone exception) raises the possibility that these departments may not be recruiting or retaining qualitatively oriented CCJ scholars. We will consider this issue further in the text below.

Examination of the rank of authors of qualitative articles, as presented in Table 5, shows that one-quarter of all authors hold the rank of professor and one-quarter hold the rank of assistant professor. Interestingly, students (primarily graduate students) account for one in eight authors and individuals from outside academic institutions account for one in seven authors. The data in this table suggest that qualitative publication prowess is relatively evenly distributed across the age spectrum of the discipline and that scholars at all rungs of the rank and tenure system pursue qualitative means of inquiry. For the sake of qualitative research this is good as it shows that qualitative researchers are neither in the twilight nor in the dawn of their careers.

Qualitative Dissertations

We now turn to a sample of doctoral dissertations to provide additional insight into the amount of qualitative engagement among novice CCJ scholars. Consideration of these data provides valuable insight into the pipeline of qualitatively inclined scholars. Our analysis reveals that qualitative dissertations account for a small percent of all successfully defended dissertations in the discipline during the five-year period under examination. As shown in Table 6, of the 420 successfully defended doctoral dissertations only 52, or 12.38%, were qualitative studies.

Further examination of representation of qualitative dissertations across schools shows a very distinct pattern of three types of doctoral programs: those where no students do qualitative dissertations, those where qualitative dissertations are done but are a rarity, and those where qualitative dissertations are prominent among the body of dissertations produced. First, it is notable that of

Table 6 Qualitative dissertations by criminal justice and criminology doctoral programs, 2004-2008

Institution	Total completed dissertations	Qualitative dissertations	Qualitative articles published
American University	6	1 (16.7%)	0
Arizona State University	6	3 (50%)	6
Florida State University	20	1 (5%)	1
Indiana University	6	1 (16.7%)	2
Indiana University of Pennsylvania	24	2 (8.3%)	0
John Jay College of Criminal Justice	1	1 (100%)	1
Michigan State University	23	1 (4.3%)	0
North Dakota State University	1	0 (0%)	0
Northeastern University	1	0 (0%)	0
Pennsylvania State University	5	0 (0%)	0
Prairie View A&M University	1	0 (0%)	0
Rutgers University	31	7 (22.6%)	5
Sam Houston State University	67	8 (11.9%)	3
Temple University	13	1 (7.7%)	0
University at Albany	29	6 (20.7%)	1
University of California at Irvine	9	3 (33.3%)	4
University of Central Florida	15	0 (0%)	1
University of Cincinnati	23	1 (4.3%)	5
University of Delaware	7	1 (14.3%)	0
University of Florida	5	0 (0%)	0
University of Illinois at Chicago	11	2 (18.3%)	0
University of Maryland	29	0 (0%)	1
University of Missouri-St. Louis	17	5 (29.4%)	16
University of Nebraska-Omaha	28	2 (7.1%)	0
University of Pennsylvania	6	1 (16.7%)	1
University of South Florida	11	2 (18.3%)	2
University of Southern Mississippi	19	1 (5.3%)	0
University of Texas at Dallas	3	0 (0%)	3
Washington State University	3	1 (33.3%)	0
Total	420	52 (12.38%)	52

the 29 doctoral programs that produced any successfully defended dissertations during the five-year time period, eight programs (27.6%) produced no qualitatively oriented dissertations (North Dakota State University, Northeastern University, Pennsylvania State University, Prairie View A&M University, University of Central Florida, University of Florida, University of Maryland, and University of Texas at Dallas). It is important to note that six of these eight programs are rather small and/or new, producing no more than one graduate per year. Only two of the programs with no qualitative dissertations graduated a significant number of PhDs during the study period: University of Central Florida (15) and University of Maryland (29).

In contrast to the group that produced no qualitative dissertations, the second group of programs is those where some qualitative dissertations were successfully defended, but they are clearly the exception. Here we see that seven programs (Florida State University, Indiana University of Pennsylvania, Michigan State University, Temple University, University of Cincinnati, University of Nebraska-Omaha, and University of Southern Mississippi) had fewer than 10% of their successfully completed dissertations be of a qualitative nature.

A third group comprised of 14 programs (American University, Arizona State University, Indiana University, John Jay College of Criminal Justice, Rutgers University, Sam Houston State University, University at Albany, University of California at Irvine, University of Delaware, University of Illinois at Chicago, University of Missouri-St. Louis, University of Pennsylvania, University of South Florida, and Washington State University) saw more than 10% of their dissertation yield during the study period utilizing qualitative modes of inquiry and analysis. It is notable that these tend to be the programs producing overall larger numbers of doctoral graduates. In raw numbers, the top six institutions that produce qualitative dissertations are Sam Houston State University (eight), Rutgers University (seven), University at Albany (six), University of Missouri-St. Louis (five), Arizona State University (three), and University of California-Irvine (three). Upon close examination, the data reveal that these six programs yielded 62% of the overall number of qualitative dissertations during the 2004-2008 interval.

In a separate examination of the qualitative dissertations and the faculty chairing the dissertation only 10 individuals were identified who chaired multiple qualitative dissertations; nine of these individuals chaired two qualitative dissertations and one chaired three. This suggests that there is not a set of especially highly productive qualitative faculty mentors, and may be one more reason for the low numbers of new qualitatively oriented doctorates being produced and the low concentration of qualitative articles in the discipline's top journals. This is also buttressed by the fact that of the 10 faculties who have chaired multiple qualitative dissertations, only one has published a qualitative article in these journals during this period. Referring to the far right column of Table 6 note that, of the universities where more than 10% of successfully defended dissertations were qualitative, there also tends to be a higher number of qualitative articles published (e.g., 16, or 30.77% of the articles total by the University of Missouri-St. Louis). To extrapolate on this latter point, we note that five institutions, namely the University of Missouri-St. Louis (16), Arizona State University (six), Rutgers University (five), University of Cincinnati (five), and the University of California-Irvine (four) account for more than two-thirds (69.23%) of the 52 qualitative articles that were produced by authors claiming affiliation at the 29 CCJ doctoral programs during the study period.

On the whole, our analysis of dissertations suggests that a small number of programs and a small number of professors within those programs are accounting for a sizable amount of the qualitative expertise and qualitative doctoral research being generated in the US-based CCJ PhD programs. Conversely, there appear to be a sizable number of doctoral-granting programs that are not yielding any qualitatively oriented dissertations or published articles.

Discussion

The present study sets out to update and expand upon our understanding of the prominence of qualitatively derived scholarship appearing in traditional publication venues within the field of CCJ. We began with an assessment of the published work appearing in the top CCJ journals. Upon conducting a content analysis of all articles appearing in the 2004-2008 volumes of what American criminology and criminal justice scholars (i.e., ACJS and ASC members) deemed to be the field's 15 top journals (Sorensen et al. 2006), we found that a total of 120 articles incorporated a qualitative research design and analysis plan. This number comprised 5.74% of the articles appearing in these journals during that time period. This finding approximates what has been reported in previous studies of the same kind. For example, an analysis by Tewksbury et al. (2005) of the articles appearing in the 1998-2002 volumes of five leading CCJ journals revealed that 6.3% employed a qualitative methodology. Similarly, upon reviewing a sample of 375 empirical articles appearing in the 2001 and 2002 volumes of seven leading CCJ journals, Kleck et al. (2006) noted that 4.5% employed qualitative data analysis. It is worth noting that Buckler's journal, by journal analysis of the article content appearing in the 2003-2007 volumes of a sample of top-tier and regional CCJ journals, is found to have slightly higher representations of qualitative work (ranging from 4.9% to 12.1% of the articles in the sample of five top-tier outlets and 13.6% to 14.3% in the flagship journal of three regional CCJ professional associations). However, these larger numbers should be tempered by the fact that Buckler relied on a broader definition of a qualitatively oriented article, one where any article employing any aspect of a qualitative research design (as opposed to a qualitative design and analysis plan) was included in the counts.

We thought it important to expand the assessment of the published CCJ scholarship beyond the borders of the USA. As such, we applied our content analysis strategy to the 2004-2008 volumes of three international CCJ journals. We found a more robust representation of qualitative research in these scholarly outlets. Of the 401 articles appearing in these journals during the study period, 111 or just over 27% were based upon qualitative data collection and analysis efforts. In fact, more than 1/3 (37.44%) of the articles appearing in the *British Journal of Criminology* during this period were qualitative in nature.

A close examination of the US-based journals in our sample reveals that qualitative research articles appear in greater proportions within some peer-reviewed outlets than they do in others. For example, nearly one in three articles published in *Deviant Behavior* during our study period was qualitatively oriented. This trend should not be surprising given the long tradition of qualitatively oriented studies of the broad subject rubric that is deviance. Moving on, we note that one in the five articles appearing in *Theoretical Criminology* and one in seven of those appearing in *Law & Society Review* relied on qualitative data collection and analysis strategies. This too should come as not surprising, as those pursuing theory construction as a goal are often drawn to inductive processes, as are those who engage in socio-legal research.[10]

Our analysis plan also led us to consider the characteristics of authors who produced the qualitative articles appearing in our sample of domestic and internationally based journals. We found evidence of collaboration among qualitative scholars, with co-authorship being the norm across most outlets. We also found that these authors came from diverse backgrounds; while the modal author claimed an academic affiliation in the US department of criminology or criminal justice, solid representation was observed across the social science disciplines, around the globe, and also from individuals working outside of academia. With respect to the US-based productivity, 52 of the 109 (47.7%) qualitatively oriented articles published during the study period included at least one author who claimed affiliation at a PhD-granting CCJ program.

Another motivating factor behind the current analysis was to assess the status of the qualitative research pipeline. Previous research by DiChristina (1997) and Sever (2001) raised the possibility that the field was becoming lax in its efforts to expose aspiring scholars to textbooks and structured training/ instructional opportunities focused on qualitative approaches, and that this might lead to an aging out of qualitatively oriented crime and justice scholarship. We explored this issue in two ways. First we conducted an analysis of all dissertations published during the 2004–2008 time interval. Of the 420 dissertations produced during this period, 52 of them (12.38%) employed qualitative data collection and analysis plans. While our inquiry demonstrated that these qualitative dissertations were concentrated in a few doctoral programs and were supervised by a selected group of major professors, the data suggest that there exists a pipeline of young qualitatively oriented scholars to carry on this style of research.

We used our analysis of published articles in top CCJ journals to shed additional light on the cadre of qualitative scholars. Namely, by considering the rank of the authors of these articles, we gain insight into whether or not qualitative work is being published disproportionately by more senior scholars (i.e., a dying craft) or whether it remains robust among scholars at various steps on the academic career later. Our findings reveal that assistant professors and professors are represented among the qualitative articles in near equal percentages, 25.2% and 28.4% respectively. Similarly, we find that qualitatively oriented dissertations routinely yield peer-reviewed articles and that students obtained

10. Journal-specific representation of qualitative articles does not appear to be the result of author-based selection bias. In other words, we found no evidence that certain scholars repeatedly target a given outlet due to familiarity or perceived friendliness toward qualitative research.

authorship status in robust numbers (comprising 12.6% of the article authors). Here again, our analysis suggests that qualitative scholars are being nurtured at the early career stage. Given the commonly understood reality that research-oriented academic departments tend to recruit and hire individuals with established publication records and that most quantitatively derived articles (especially those derived from existing datasets) can be produced more quickly than qualitative ones, it is encouraging that there is a selected number of the US-based CCJ doctoral programs that remain committed to producing qualitative scholarship. That said, the number of programs and the amount of qualitative scholarship being produced are lower in comparison to the quantitative end of the spectrum.

At this point, we seek to situate our findings within the broader debate about the health and well-being of the academic field of CCJ. In particular, we reflect upon the role of qualitative research and what our findings suggest about the stability of this role as we move forward.

Previous research, while somewhat limited in conceptual scope and suffering empirically from restricted samples and inconsistent operational measures, suggests that crime and justice researchers may be generating limited amounts of qualitative scholarship. Inquiries by Tewksbury et al. (2005), Kleck et al. (2006), and Buckler (2008) imply that this situation exists at the early (graduate school) and later (publish or perish stage) points in the scholarly life course. The present study, based on a more comprehensive sampling strategy and more precise measures, provides qualified support for these assertions. Namely, we find that qualitative articles and dissertations remain in the clear minority, however, there is evidence that the articles are being authored by individuals at various points in their professional careers and that certain CCJ doctoral-granting institutions are committed to producing qualitative articles and dissertations. Given this state of affairs, the next obvious question becomes, so what? Put another way, should we be concerned that criminological and criminal justice knowledge dissemination is short on its qualitatively oriented content?

We turn to recent intellectual exchanges for context on this latter issue. A little over a decade ago, DiChristina (1997) made the case that doctoral programs were emphasizing quantitative training and coursework at the expense of qualitative instruction. He set forth a series of plausible justifications for the quantitative emphasis, including the perceived time demands associated with training individuals in quantitative data collection and analysis techniques, job market demands for quantitative-oriented scholars, and the perception that quantitative research provides better prospects for theory construction and validation. Worrall (2000) responded to DiChristina by noting that the predictive potential of quantitative scholarship is a critical criterion one needs to consider as to why the field has been steadily gravitating toward quantitative training and scholarly production. Worrall went on to place center stage factors such as comparison, manipulation, and control as central tenets of statistical analyses that account for its deserved privilege over its qualitative brethren.

We do not take issue with any of these observations. Each of the DiChristina's justifications carries explanatory power as to why programs and mentors tend toward quantitative training of fledgling CCJ scholars. Similarly, Worrall is correct to note the predictive capacities of statistical modeling as an important selling point for quantitative training in the field. That said, we cannot lose sight of the fact that said prediction and the statistical models that underlie it must be based on solid measures. Qualitative scholars are tasked with doing the local theorizing; they go into the field to watch and interact with offenders, victims, onlookers, and social control agents in hopes of making inductive obser-vations about how these worlds are organized. It is important to remember that many of our field's most important concepts and theoretical frameworks have been generated through systematic field work efforts or exploratory interview-based studies. Such an acknowledgment is not intended to discount that many of the field's theories and concepts have been deductively generated by scholars sitting in their offices pondering the work of their predecessors or struggling with the poor fit or performance of existing measures. Rather, we mean to emphasize that both orientations are critical to the ongoing develop-ment of the field and that we need to remain vigilant to train new scholars and hone the skills of contemporaries as they relate to both qualitative and quanti-tative modes of data collection and analysis.

More recently, Robert Sampson and John Laub engaged Daniel Nagin and Richard Tremblay in a live debate over the appropriate nexus between analyti-cal techniques and theorizing as applied to the developmental course of criminal offending. In a series of exchanges published in *Criminology* (Laub 2006; Nagin and Tremblay 2005a, 2005b; Sampson and Laub 2005), these schol-ars used the body of research specific to life-course criminology to take each other to task over the appropriate balance between statistical sophistication and theoretical development. Nagin and Tremblay (2005a, pp. 898–899) argue

> to understand the complexity of human development over the life-course, we need to accumulate large quantities of data on large representative samples of individuals ... medium scale longitudinal studies have come to maturity, and we are facing the task of making sense of the accumulated data.

They go on to advocate for the statistical technique known as group-based trajectory modeling as one of the "appropriate statistical tools to obtain the best representation of reality possible" in this regard (Nagin and Tremblay 2005a, p. 899). Sampson and Laub (2005, p. 910) counter that "most of the real problems Nagin and Tremblay noted are better addressed with a proper design rather than a post-hoc application of a statistical method." Moreover, they charge that,

> when methods rule we lose focus on the fundamental processes that explain crime and its persistence and cessation over the life course. For us, the bottom line of sound research design and basic scientific inquiry is that methods are inex-tricably linked to, and the servant of, theory. (Sampson and Laub 2005, p. 911)

Later, Laub (2006, p. 241) noted, "Sampson and I have spent nearly twenty years examining the life course of crime. In identifying the principles of life-course criminology I have primarily drawn upon our long-term project examining longitudinal data." The longitudinal data that Laub refers to come from carefully derived classic positivistic datasets formulated by Glueck and Glueck (1950, 1968) as well as several of his own data collection efforts done in tandem with Sampson.

Here again, we see merits in what Nagin and Tremblay are saying about the need to apply the most powerful and appropriate statistical models to the existing datasets that the field has at its disposal. Similarly, Sampson and Laub are correct to note that one cannot let statistical techniques woo us into complacency when it comes to theoretical development and methodological rigor. But we note that both sides of this debate adopt a decidedly deductive and positivistic bent in their arguments. Neither group questions the means through which theoretical connections are initially made or put to the test. It is true that numerous expensive and detailed survey efforts have been undertaken to generate impressive cross-sectional and longitudinal datasets that are readily tapped by capable and motivated scholars. It is also true that these efforts have carefully crafted measures aimed at operationalizing the concepts and theoretical frameworks that populate the field as we know it today. However, we need also to keep in mind that qualitative forays into the field, wherein scholars observe and interact with individuals and environments in real time, often result in conceptual revisions and/or new operational measures of said concepts and frameworks. For sure, much of what qualitative researchers do never rises to the level of prediction or generalizable findings in the traditional sense of these words. Nonetheless, rigorous qualitative research often serves as the catalyst for important conceptual and methodological adjustments that never would be made were we to pursue solely deductive and positivistic approaches to our subject matter. In short, the field needs qualitative inquiry as much as it needs quantitative inquiry and it is in the best interest of all involved parties to nurture and encourage both orientations in our current and future cadre of scholars.

References

Buckler, K. 2008. The quantitative/qualitative divide revisited: A study of published research, doctoral program curricula, and journal editor perceptions. *Journal of Criminal Justice Education* 19: 383–403.

DiChristina, B. 1997. The quantitative emphasis in criminal justice education. *Journal of Criminal Justice Education* 8: 181–199.

Glueck, S., and E. Glueck. 1950. *Unraveling juvenile delinquency.* New York: The Commonwealth Fund.

Glueck, S., and E. Glueck. 1968. *Delinquents and nondelinquents in perspective.* Cambridge: Harvard University Press.

Kleck, G., J. Tark, and J. J. Bellows. 2006. What methods are most frequently used in research in criminology and criminal justice? *Journal of Criminal Justice* 34: 147-152.

Laub, J. H. 2006. Edwin Sutherland and the Michael-Adler report: Searching for the soul of criminology seventy years later. *Criminology* 44: 235-257.

Miller, J. 2005. The status of qualitative research in criminology. *Proceedings from the National Science Foundation's Workshop on Interdisciplinary Standards for Systematic Qualitative Research.* Retrieved May 26, 2010, from http://www.wjh.harvard.edu/nsfqual/Miller%20Paper.pdf

Nagin, D. S., and R. E. Tremblay. 2005a. Developmental trajectory groups: Fact or a useful statistical fiction? *Criminology* 43: 873-899.

Nagin, D. S., and R. E. Tremblay. 2005b. From seduction to passion: A response to Sampson and Laub. *Criminology* 43: 915-918.

Pogrebin, M. 2010. On the way to the field: Reflections of one qualitative criminal justice professor's experiences. *Journal of Criminal Justice Education* 21: 540-561.

Sampson, R. J., and J. H. Laub. 2005. Seductions of method: Rejoinder to Nagin and Tremblay's "Developmental trajectory groups: Fact or fiction?" *Criminology* 43: 905-913.

Sever, B. 2001. Research methods for criminal justice graduate students: Comparing textbook coverage and classroom instruction. *Journal of Criminal Justice Education* 12: 337-353.

Sorensen, J., C. Snell, and J. J. Rodriguez. 2006. An assessment of criminal justice and criminology journal prestige. *Journal of Criminal Justice Education* 17: 297-322.

Tewksbury, R., M. T. DeMichele, and J. M. Miller. 2005. Methodological orientations of articles appearing in criminal justice's top journals: Who publishes what and where. *Journal of Criminal Justice Education* 16: 265-279.

Worrall, J. L. 2000. In defense of the "quantoids": More on the reasons for the quantitative emphasis in criminal justice education and research. *Journal of Criminal Justice Education* 11: 353-360.

Moving Beyond our Methodological Default: A Case for Mixed Methods

John J. Brent and Peter B. Kraska

Within criminal justice/criminology exists a host of available research methods that generally default along qualitative and quantitative lines. Studying crime and justice phenomena, then, generally involves choosing one approach or the other. Although this binary tradition of *qualitative vs. quantitative* has predominated, our field's methodological infrastructure has recently demonstrated a willingness to adopt more inclusive practices. The purpose of this study is to discuss the nascent yet probable transformation of re-orienting our field toward a new paradigm of inclusiveness that acknowledges the use of mixed methods research as being both legitimate and beneficial. This paper examines the role methodological exclusivism has had in delaying an appreciation of both paradigms as credible in their own right and even compatible under certain circumstances. In addition, this effort uncovers the increasingly yet little recognized presence of mixed methods research in our field and illuminates that this approach can be used to conduct rigorous multi-dimensional research.

At their heart, research methods are designed to produce credible and accurate knowledge. They assist researchers in shedding empirical light on complex phenomena by providing avenues to best examine and investigate an object under study—attempting to answer that ever elusive question, "what is really the case?" They also define parameters for the systematic collection of data, provide researchers with ethical boundaries, and guide scholarly activity. Despite these myriad functions, the social sciences, including the discipline of criminology, have struggled with the issue of which method or methodological paradigm is most proper.

Crime and criminal justice studies has embedded under this surface, then, with what Roth (1987) refers to as *methodological exclusivism*: an ideological orientation that presumes a single paradigm for generating credible and legitimate scholarship. These conditions have consequently meant the construction of rigid methodological boundaries that maintain the opposition between qualitative and quantitative paradigms. Instead of utilizing a multi-faceted approach to conducting research, these boundaries eschew any methodological tools that fall beyond their territory. This traditional perspective of "quants versus quals" is, as Kraska and Neuman argue, both greatly "unnecessary and inhibiting" (2008, p. 463).

Situating methodologies in stark opposition, as Wolcott writes, "does a great disservice by detracting from the contribution to be made by each, including what each can contribute to the other" (2002, 99). Fortunately, other scholars have noticed that the exclusionary mindset that situated the quantitative paradigm as dominant over the last 40 years might be changing, allowing for a new outlook that permits greater methodological diversity and compatibility (Creswell 1994; Datta 1994; Denzin 1978, 1989; Greene 2001, 2007; Johnson and Onwuegbuzie 2004; Kraska and Neuman 2008; Tashakkori and Teddlie 2003). The purpose of this study is to examine this nascent yet probable transformation in criminal justice/criminology. The long-range purpose is to begin re-orienting our field toward a paradigm of inclusiveness that acknowledges the use of mixed methods research as being legitimate and beneficial.

To achieve this goal, this study first discusses and critiques the conditions promoting the assumption that criminological research should default along quantitative and qualitative approaches. Second, it deconstructs the circumstances that have maintained separation by keeping at bay "conflicting" methodologies. Third, it outlines the mounting philosophical stance of pragmatism that favors principles of inclusion and compatibility. These principles, in turn, have facilitated favorable conditions that have increased the use of mixed methods research within our discipline. The fourth section addresses the considerations and implications of approaching mixed methods research as being both constructive and advantageous. Finally, it presents a recent scholarship conducted by the authors that used a mixed methods approach. This effort concludes by discussing the benefits of legitimizing mixed methods research within crime and justice studies for our scholarship, disciplinary direction, and redirecting of our pedagogical compass.

Crime and Criminal Justice Studies' Methodological Default

Our discipline has a well-established, albeit contending, set of research methods available for its use. Our relatively young field of study is replete with rigorous research and excellent scholarship that has explored crime and justice phenomena by enlisting these methodological means. The concern here is not the methodological quality of scholarship but, rather, that our field—with some noteworthy exceptions—presumes by default that research should be conducted using either a qualitative or quantitative approach.

Originating in the fundamental assumptions of each paradigm, a divide has arisen that travels beyond philosophical and epistemological debate. Reflecting this divide, our discipline has also experienced a methodological separation that runs throughout and within the research community. Numerous researchers have documented and commented on this divide (Buckler 2008; Kleck, Tark, and Bellows 2006; Pratt 2010; Tewksbury, Dabney, and Copes 2010; Tewksbury, DeMichele, and Miller 2005). Others have noted the near singular focus on quantitative methods in doctoral programs (DiChristina 1997; Ferrell, Young, and Hayward 2008; Sullivan and Maxfield 2003) and the lack of qualitative exposure in criminal justice and criminological curricula (Buckler 2008; DiChristina 1997; Sever 2001). While the issue of methodological *intentional* bias remains controversial, this divide reflects and further reinforces the notion that these approaches are, and remain, mutually exclusive paradigms. Perhaps, Pratt in a recent introduction to a special journal issue on quantitative methods sums up the divide best:

> There has long been a power struggle between quantitative and qualitative approaches to criminal justice and criminological research (DiChristina 1997). While this debate is certainly not limited to our discipline, it has certainly infected it. Indeed, opposing camps have emerged, with fierce loyalties and allegiances to their own peer-reviewed journals, and terms like "quantoids"— a label that is meant to be both pejorative and a badge of honor depending on which side one is on—have even been coined (Worrall 2000). (2010, p. 103)

Overall, it is the quantitative approach that has established clear dominance within criminology's methodological infrastructure over the last 40 years, thus establishing qualitative research as the minority in the field (Tewksbury et al., 2010). Worrall (2000) and others have noted that our field has oftentimes gravitated toward quantitative techniques given its focus on prediction, construction of solid measurements, and generalizability. Although less exclusive attitudes seem to be taking hold, our leading method textbooks still focus predominantly on quantitative methodologies, with qualitative research receiving considerably less attention (generally one cursory chapter; Sever 2001). Moreover, most doctoral programs train future academics to conduct quantitative methods exclusively; although a few are beginning to offer a qualitative methods course in their curricula (Buckler 2008). As a result, criminal justice/criminology students are generally not exposed substantively to the qualitative approach and are socialized into thinking that a researcher must self-identify with either one paradigm or the other—an assumption that often carries over into academic professional identities.

   The quantitative/qualitative divide, then, has become the dominant binary model in our field, which "effectively marginalizes the methodological diversity within them" (Giddens 2006, p. 195). However, there is a third way that "requires our field to change its traditional exclusionary way of thinking about qualitative and quantitative approaches" (Kraska and Neuman 2008, p. 461). It is in this context that discussing a mixed methods approach—a third choice that emphasizes inclusion and compatibility—is quite different from our historical precedent.

Why Not Mixed Methods Research?

Historical Context and Incompatibility

Our field's discussion over methodological standards is neither new nor unique. The qualitative-quantitative divide is far from contemporary, as it has historical roots dating back to the late nineteenth century. Situating itself in the development of early sociological thought, this debate has taken place on epistemological, philosophical, and methodological grounds (Popper 1972). Generally accepted as criminology's forerunner, sociology has long struggled over whether to value alternative approaches to inquiry that fall beyond the boundaries of the natural science model (Kraska 2008; Tewksbury et al. 2005). As a result of this epistemological dispute, two dominant schools of thought developed that have influenced crime and justice studies (see Higgins 2009).

Widely adopted by Columbia during the nineteenth century, the first emulates the work of Comte and Durkheim where the use of experiments, objectivity, exact measures, hypothesis testing, and quantitative methods are paramount. Positivism or the positive social sciences (PSS), thus, became a paradigm for "combining deductive logic with precise empirical observations in order to discover and confirm a set of probabilistic causal laws that can be used to predict general patters of human activity" (Kraska and Neuman 2008; see also Halfpenny 1982). The philosophical force driving PSS is scientific explanation; to discover and document universal causal laws in human behavior. Consequentially, this tradition sees the nature of "reality" as being empirically evident—existing independently from the social world and capable of discovery. Here, scientific knowledge using precise measurements and neutral observations is seen as being superior to all other forms. This paradigm assumes that "truth" and "good evidence" should emanate from deductively testing objective facts and that replication should support any prior findings. In order to remain objective, science, then, must stress the importance of being value free.

However, during that same time, the University of Chicago espoused the interpretive social sciences (ISS) which began making noteworthy contributions to criminology's development. Drawing from Dilthey and Weber, ISS became an inductive paradigm that "emphasizes the systematic analysis and detailed study of people and text in order to arrive at understandings and how interpretations of how people construct and maintain meaning within their social worlds" (Kraska and Neuman 2008, p. 74). Departing from PSS, this approach stresses the importance of an empathetic understanding or *Verstehen*, subjectivity, reflexivity, grounded theory, and qualitative methods (see Glaser and Strauss 1967). The philosophical underpinning of ISS is to acquire an in-depth understanding of other people, appreciate the wider diversity of lived human experience, and better acknowledge shared humanity. In contrast to positivism, this research tradition interprets "reality" as a social or human construct. Accordingly, this paradigm places great significance in understanding social meaning in its context and arrives at Verstehen. "Truth" and "good evidence" do not originate from testing objective facts; instead, they can be discovered and understood only within their specific cultural context. Here, value and value positions become unavoidable in social inquiry.

As a result of the interpretive school's direct challenge and sovereign break from positivism, conflicting philosophical and methodological foundations have hindered the use of mixed methods research. More specifically, many scholars note the *incompatibility thesis* that prevents the mixing of qualitative and quantitative methods. This position holds that "positivist and interpretive paradigms underlie quantitative and qualitative methods, respectively; the two kinds of paradigms are incompatible; therefore, the two kinds of methods are incompatible" (Howe 1988, p. 10). Proponents of this thesis often point to the contrasting notions of reality, truth, and good evidence that formulate each paradigm's methodological toolbox that renders them contradictory. In brief, this position asserts that the fundamental differences between qualitative and quantitative methodologies render them incapable of coexisting with one another in a single study (Howe 1988, 1992; Guba 1987; Guba and Lincoln 1982; Johnson and Onwuegbuzie 2004; Smith 1983a, 1983b; Smith and Heshusius 1986).

Academic Politics

It is important to clarify, however, that the qualitative-quantitative divide is as much a consequence of academic politics as it is the product of philosophical and methodological debate. Exclusive academic ideologies coupled with political territory buttress the seeming inherent incompatibilities between qualitative and quantitative methods. This point however needs further clarification.

The development of an exclusivist position on research in crime and justice studies is a common pattern in organizational dynamics: as a young organization attempts to establish its identity (who it is, what it does, and why it does what it does), differing factions within that organization vie for power, carve out territory, and establish their own identity. Conflicts and power struggles erupt between factions, each attempting to reconstruct the organization's institutional identity in their own image. The factions tend to dismiss, if not outright malign, the views and activities of rival factions in an effort to discredit them. The objective is to dominate, marginalize and, if possible, eliminate the competition—blinding them to the potential worth and benefits of the other factions' views and activities. Sharp lines are drawn around the differing factions' supposedly distinct positions and ideas (Morgan 2006).

Such has certainly been the case in our field. Using the scenario above, we can simply replace "organization" with "crime and justice studies", and "factions" with "qualitative versus quantitative approaches." With each faction—the *quants* and *quals*—adopting a type of binary or exclusionary logic, our methodological choices are limited to either one or the other approach, with both camps viewing each other's as inferior. Tewksbury and colleagues' analogy of "political mud-slinging" is helpful as they state "this debate has fostered a series of extreme criticisms from each side, allowing defense of one position by pointing to the weaknesses of the other (2005, p. 267). Through this lens, a dismissive and exclusive mentality has predominated—more for political reasons than intellectual.

This exclusive position corresponds with sustaining a sort of *purity*—"the need to avoid mixing things that do not go together, and especially mixing the morally doubtful with the virtuous" (Hammersley 2000, p. 125). Maintaining methodological purity may, then, refer to "an emphasis on the need to meet high methodological standards, and a resistance to deviation from those standards" (Hammersley 2000, p. 125). However, purism can serve as an ideological mask that conceals political motivations and reifies a dominant position. Hammersley argues that methodological purism, while seeming concerned with rigorous standards on the surface, ultimately advances the political interests of its promoters or those whom 'purist' principles serve. This is certainly the position of those advancing the area of study known as "cultural criminology" (see Ferrell, Hayward, Morrisan, and Presdee 2004; Ferrell et al. 2008), as well as many feminist scholars (see Harding 1987; Reinharz and Davidman 1992).

Roth (1987) refers to this mindset as *methodological exclusivism*; an ideology that presumes that there is just one proper method of producing credible and worthwhile knowledge. Scholars such as Collins argue that confusion and conflict arise from overly rigid and exclusive definitions of what science is to be. He states that "Modern philosophy of science does not destroy sociological science; it does not say that science is impossible, but gives us a more flexible picture of what science is" (1989, p. 134). In that same vein—although Roth acknowledges and articulates, with precision the inherent philosophical differences between quantitative and qualitative approaches—he ultimately argues that these differences do not render them incompatible, just merely different.

Beyond Conflict and Exclusion

Swinging of the Methodological Pendulum

The resurgence in use and acceptance of qualitative research over the last 15 years has moved the methodological pendulum. Whereas the pendulum has been settled on the quantitative pole for some time, the gaining influence of qualitative work has loosened it from its mooring. Although this is certainly a positive development from our perspective, researchers documenting the presence of qualitative work consistently find that qualitative methods are still only used in 4.5% to 12.1% of our discipline's journal articles (Buckler 2008; Kleck et al. 2006; Tewksbury et al. 2005; Tewksbury et al. 2010). Of course, one might assume that the reaction to the movement of the pendulum would be intensified conflict. However, just as nearly every other social science discipline has already experienced over the last two decades, the third option of mixing quantitative and qualitative methods is quietly emerging.

Criminology has recently demonstrated a willingness to entertain and embrace this third way. This is evident in the recent publications that mix qualitative and quantitative methods, the recent inclusion in many graduate programs of both required and elective qualitative based courses, and the willingness of leading quantitative researchers to employ qualitative methods within their positivist-based studies to bolster their work (see Kraska and Neuman 2008). In fact, according to Creswell and Clarke (2006; see also Creswell, Shope, Clark, and Green 2006)—leading figures in the mixed methods movement—our discipline may be on the cutting edge of producing research that mixes qualitative and quantitative data.

These changes appear to be slowly eroding the ideology of methodological exclusivism, potentially signaling a shift toward methodological tolerance, diversity, and pluralism. Although the process is nowhere near complete, and nor is its trajectory certain, our disciplinary identity may be reconfiguring itself to embrace a paradigm of methodological inclusion and pluralism rather than exclusion.

Pragmatic Underpinnings

As mentioned earlier, mixing qualitative and quantitative methods requires a more inclusive and compatible orientation that abandons traditional dogmas. While sensitive to differences, this approach also assumes that mixing methodologies will, in the end, yield more complete knowledge than any single method—or *monomethod*—might alone. Given this, mixed methods research has often been coupled with the philosophy of pragmatism (Datta 1997a, 1997b; Greene and Caracelli 2003; Johnson and Onwuegbuzie 2004; Reichardt and Cook 1979; Tashakkori and Teddlie 2003). Mixed methods research, thus, views both methodological goals as worth pursuing and that, when combined, each will ultimately advance one another.

Mixed methods research should, as Johnson and Onwuegbuzie argue, "use a method and philosophy that attempt to fit together the insights provided by qualitative and quantitative research into a workable solution" (2004, p. 16). This Kuhnian call for a new paradigm evoked the pragmatic tradition in attempts to move toward methodological pluralism (Johnson and Onwuegbuzie 2004). By arguing that paradigms may be combined effectively to better create informed practice, this call was to increase communication and efforts among researchers from differing camps (Maxcy 2003). While methodological exclusivism has prospered, a key feature of pragmatism is to uncover practical solutions that alleviate traditional paradigmatic dualisms. Creswell argues that the pragmatic philosophy has "argued that a false dichotomy existed between qualitative and quantitative approaches and that researchers should make the most efficient use of both paradigms in understanding social phenomena" (1994,

31

p. 176). Adopting a pragmatic orientation rejects the thesis of methodological incompatibility.

Johnson and Christensen's fundamental principle of mixed methods research is instructive: researchers should collect and analyze "multiple sets of data using different approaches and methods in such a way that the resulting mixture or combination has complementary strengths and non-overlapping weaknesses" (2007, p. 51). In other words, mixing quantitative and qualitative methods draws on the strengths of each while minimizing their weaknesses. Collecting comprehensive data using differing methods and perspectives coincides with the general premise that viewing a phenomenon through more than one theoretical and/or methodological lens yields a more complete picture of our object of study. As Norman K. Denzin said:

> The bias inherent in any particular data source, investigators, and particularly method will be cancelled out when used in conjunction with other data sources, investigators and methods ... The result will be a convergence upon the truth about some social phenomena. (1978, p. 14)

In sum, studying our object from differing angles and attempting to answer differing questions aligned with both interpretive and positivist approaches allows for a more holistic and rigorous answer to that fundamental scientific question that should interest all scholars, "what is really the case?"

Utilizing Mixed Methods

Having discussed the background of mixed methods research and the methodological conditions to which it finds itself, we are better able to address its utility and criticisms.

Weighing in: Advantages and Disadvantages of Mixed Methods

Numerous scholars throughout the social sciences have advocated a mixed methods approach and touted its advantages (Creswell 1994; Greene 2001, 2007; Johnson and Onwuegbuzie 2004; Kraska 2008; Kraska and Neuman 2008; Tashakkori and Teddlie 1998, 2003). As noted above, the most common stated advantage is that it utilizes the strengths of one method to overcome weaknesses in the other. Although seemingly straightforward, this deduction builds from other advantages worthy of discussion.

To begin, qualitative information such as words, pictures, and narratives can add meaning and depth to quantitative data. Likewise, quantitative data have the ability of enhancing clarity and precision to collected words, pictures, and narratives. Second, employing a mixed methods approach unbinds a researcher from a monomethod approach, thus, increasing their ability to accurately answer a wider range of research questions. Third, it can increase the specific-ity and generalizability of results by drawing from both methodological approaches. Mixing qualitative and quantitative techniques also has the poten-tial to enhance validity and reliability, resulting in stronger evidence through convergence of collected data and findings. Lastly, examining an object of study by triangulating research methods allows for more complete knowledge—uncovering significant insights that monomethod research could overlook or miss completely (see Jick 1979).

Whether examining mixed methods research holistically or determining its suitability for a research topic, it is important to also consider its disadvan-tages. The first concerns researcher limitations. While some are uncomfortable with numbers and statistics, others may be ineffectual at achieving an empa-thetic understanding. For that reason, this approach requires a researcher to be adept and competent in properly engaging in and mixing multiple methodolo-gies. Becoming well versed in both paradigms and their respective methods can be more challenging.

In that same thread, carrying out multiple methods, especially if employed concurrently, can be difficult to administer. This approach may necessitate addi-tional researchers, more resources, and further safeguards, making it potentially more expensive and time-consuming. Another disadvantage is that methodolog-ical purists may criticize those who conduct mixed methods research for not operating within either qualitative or quantitative boundaries. Finally, particu-lars of the mixed methods approach remain unclear given that most revolve around the philosophical and methodological difficulties of pragmatism.

Mixing Methods

Another consideration is whether this approach is suitable for a given research topic; and if it is, how should qualitative and quantitative methods be integrated with one another? Mixed methods research is "a class of research where quanti-tative and qualitative data collection and analysis techniques are used in a single study, or series of studies, examining a particular object of study" (Kraska and Neuman 2008, p. 457; for an overview of mixed methods research definitions, see Johnson, Onwuegbuzie, and Turner 2007). The central premise of mixing meth-odologies, according to Creswell and Clark, is "that the use of quantitative and qualitative approaches in combination provides a better understanding of research problems than either approach alone" (2006, p. 5). Kraska and Neuman (2008) demonstrate that these two approaches can be integrated in a number of ways in order to best answer the research question. As seen in Figure 1, we can conceptualize mixed methods research on a three-part continuum.

Briefly, there is pure qualitative research at one end of the continuum, pure quantitative research on the other, and fully integrated mixed methods in the middle. Mixing qualitative and quantitative methods usually involves one of three approaches: (1) a predominantly quantitative study that employs

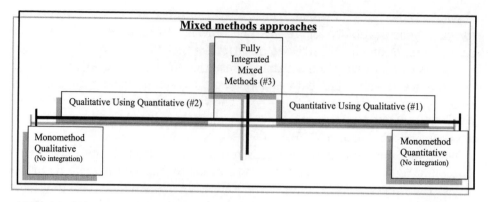

Figure 1 Mixed methods approaches on a continuum[1].
[1]Found in Kraska and Neuman (2008) *Crime and Justice Research Methods*. Allyn and Bacon.

qualitative data and analysis to shed additional light on their quantitative findings, (2) a predominantly qualitative that study employs quantitative data and analysis to bolster their qualitative findings, or (3) both quantitative and qualitative data and analysis are used in a fully integrated fashion. One of the key decisions for the mixed methods researcher, then, becomes whether the research question emphasizes a positivist approach over the interpretive, visa versa, or treats them as equal.

Mixed Methods Research as an Unrecognized Presence

Mixed Methods in Crime and Criminal Justice Studies

If criminological methods refer primarily to the binary positioning of qualitative and quantitative methods, this exclusivist orientation—which polices and regulates academic territory—could hinder the legitimating of mixed methods research. As already established, the label of mixed methods is associated with a "middle-ground" that is methodologically and politically vulnerable to qualitative and quantitative allegiances. Accordingly, mixed methods research is likely to experience resistance not from one side of the methodological pendulum (as do the other paradigms), but from both. Despite a lack of recognition of its presence, there exists a body of scholarship which has utilized this third way in attempts to study and better understand criminal justice phenomena.

Gainey, Steen, and Engen (2005) provide an excellent example of a study that drew primarily from quantitative data while using qualitative techniques to offer much needed context (Approach 1 illustrated above). Their purpose was to examine and describe which drug offenders received alternative sanctions for drug offenses, which did not, and why. This study's model incorporated quantitative data of 25,028 felony drug arrests over a three-year period along with 23 field interviews that included prosecutors, defense attorneys, and judges. By combing secondary data analysis with qualitative field interviews, Gainey and colleagues uncovered some interesting complimentary findings. For example, they found that the high rate of offenders receiving some alternative sanction was likely motivated by legislative penalties that the courtroom workgroup felt to be too harsh. This particular finding would have been difficult to discover using a monomethod approach.

Torre and Fine's (2005) study on the impact that college has on women housed in maximum security facilities provides an excellent example of a predominantly qualitative study employing quantitative methods (Approach 2 illustrated above). While primarily qualitative, the authors also conducted survey research and collected recidivism data on 274 women. The study documents the broad benefits that providing higher educational opportunities to women prisoners has on their family life, the children of inmates, recidivism rates, and society-at-large.

Another notable instance of mixed methods research is Logan, Shannon, and Walker's (2005) study that examined the characteristics of the protective order process for domestic violence situations occurring in both rural and urban areas. In a near fully integrated fashion (Approach 3 illustrated above), they were able to arrive at a comprehensive and multi-perspective view of the phenomenon by utilizing an array of qualitative and quantitative sources including: Emergency Protective Order and Domestic Violence Order data, daily court dockets, semi-structured interview, focus groups, and in-depth interviews. The authors found that rural women experience unique and in some ways significantly worse domestic violence problems than do women living in urban areas. They also discovered that criminal justice measures such as protective orders are imple-mented more poorly in rural areas—a finding the authors saw stemming from the culture and legal system existing in rural communities.

Indeed, there are a host of additional studies, even classics in our discipline, that have utilized a mixed methods approach. Indeed, some of our field's most well-known projects have combined methodologies; cornerstone works such as Shaw and McKay (1942, 1969), Short and Strodtbeck (1965), and Sampson and Groves (1989). These examples highlight the utility of mixing qualitative and quantitative data and analysis within criminology/criminal justice studies. Although mixed methods research is not new to the field, Tewksbury and colleagues (2005, p. 274) found that only 1.4% of all articles in criminal justice's top five journals between 1998 and 2002 incorporate some form of mixed methods research.

Uncovering the Late-Modern Steroid Marketplace

We (the authors) recently completed our own mixed methods study (Kraska, Bussard, and Brent 2010). The purpose in discussing this piece is to provide another tangible and a little more detailed example of mixed methods research in practice. However, this presentation does not suffice as any sort of guide on how to conduct mixed methods work; fortunately there are comprehensive books that lay the thinking and process out in great detail (Creswell 1994; Greene 2007; Tashakkori and Teddlie 2003).

Aside from producing new knowledge about an intriguing criminological phenomenon, one of our objectives in this piece was to demonstrate the utility and promise of the third way. This study provides the social sciences with the first real research on steroid trafficking and uncovers a theoretically fascinating trafficking scheme. We employed a sequential mixed model design which included both ethnographic field research and quantitative content analysis. We attempted to link the micro-interactive qualitative findings with broader-based findings produced by the quantitative component.

Figure 2 illustrates the thinking and process involved in conducting both ethnography and a content analysis within a single study. As noted in the box labeled "Purpose/Question," each method attempts to answer a different research question. The qualitative component provides an in-depth and theoret- ically informed description of the grounded reality of Internet-based steroid trafficking. The content analysis by contrast attempts to determine the extent to which our micro-interactional findings might be indicative of a larger phenomenon (hence using positivist social science to bolster "generalizability"). By linking the micro-phenomenon with macro-trends, we can then credibly

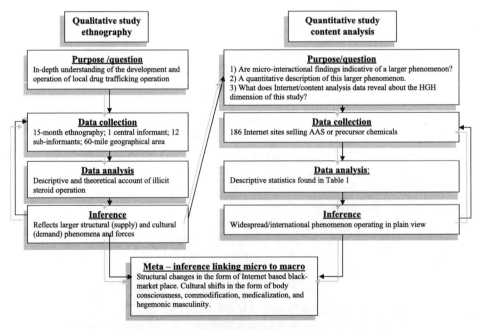

Figure 2 Visual representation of sequential mixed methods approach[1].
[1]Modified from work found in: Tashakkori and Teddlie (2003). The past and future of mixed methods research: From data triangulation to mixed model designs. In Tashakkori and Teddlie (2003). *Handbook of Mixed Methods in Social and Behavioral Research.* London: Sage.

explore the likely macro-theoretical and structural forces that would help explain the popularity of body and performance enhancing drugs.

The first method presented in this piece, therefore, was 15 months of ethnographic field research lasting from 2005 through the first four months of 2006. Fieldwork initiated at a commercial gym where several nationally recognized bodybuilders trained, including "Mike," the study's primary informant. Research sites quickly expanded to include the central informant's home, local bars, and several strength and bodybuilding competitions. Additional contacts were made through snowball sampling—resulting in a study group of 12 participants, consisting of 2 women and 10 men; and another fifty-three additional individuals were also included in lesser roles. Research was conducted through direct observations and numerous informal interviews that were initially pre-arranged and face-to-face, but developed into more informal and semi-structured settings.

This ethnography pointed to a society gripped by a culture preoccupied with health and body aesthetics, which certainly fueled a demand for this growing illicit steroid market. Numerous informants frequently discussed their goals of "being ripped/shredded/massive," "looking scary," "being crazy strong," and "wanting the ultimate body." Unexpectedly, these ethnographic data also revealed an interesting trafficking scheme where the primary informant established an apartment-based manufacturing operation by converting raw steroid compounds ordered off the Internet (from China) into more potent injectable solutions. Armed with an in-depth understanding of the infrastructure, nomenclature, and operations of the underground steroid marketplace, the authors then attempted to collect quantitative data that would indicate whether these micro-level data were reflective of a larger macro-level phenomenon.

As described above, a key element exposed by the ethnography was the central role the Internet plays in obtaining, manufacturing, and distributing steroids. Given this, the second method within this mixed methods study was a quantitative content analysis of websites that supplied anabolic androgenic steroids (AAS). A total of 230 illicit Internet sites were located that purported to have and sell AAS or human growth hormone—186 of these sites were both appropriate and functional for coding. While this of course is not an exhaustive sample of illicit Internet sites, the authors quickly discovered how deeply underground one can go into this maze of encrypted communications, sites preserved for only trusted clients, and sites that sell AAS materials without any indication. Of course, infiltrating this underground network would not have been possible without the knowledge gained from our field research.

Differing levels of contact were established with each of the 186 Internet sites to ensure they were active and willing to sell AAS-related products. Due to ethical constraints, this never involved actually purchasing these illicit materials, but did include email correspondence about costs, products, methods of payment, etc. The coded variables included: site name, IP address, usable contact information, products sold, ease of access to site, how the business was

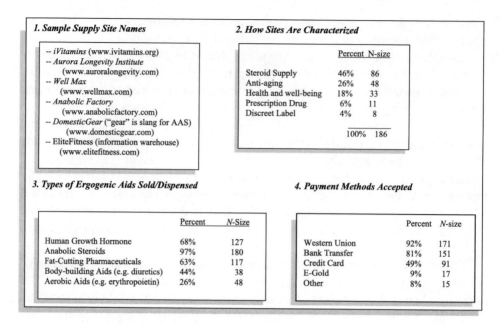

Figure 3   Content analysis finding overview[1].
[1]Found in Kraska, Bussard, and Brent (2010). Trafficking in bodily perfection: Examining the late-modern steroid marketplace and its criminalization. *Justice Quarterly*.

characterized, number of pages included within website, accepted payment methods, and shipping methods. Figure 3 provides some of the more important descriptive findings. These data were a clear indicator of an expansive on-line steroid marketplace—thereby providing a measure of reliability to our ethnographic findings.

As noted earlier, combining methodologies provides us with the legitimate means to situate our micro-level data within the larger structural-cultural forces driving this phenomenon. Consequently, we were able to illustrate the massive market and growth potential of the illicit AAS industry. The structural dimension illuminated a rapidly developing late-modern supply apparatus: a globalized yet decentralized marketplace allowing a lone individual to learn the tactical knowledge and obtain necessary materials to establish a functioning pharmaceutical lab. On the other hand, the cultural milieu fueled this illicit marketplace by cultivating micro-motivations geared toward enhancing one's bodily appearance and/or performance; certainly occurring within conditions that place a premium on body aesthetics.

Utilizing a mixed model approach allowed the authors to contextualize this emerging phenomenon as well as unpack its situated meaning and social significance. The importance in mixing methods for this study is that it helped shed additional quantitative light on initial ethnographic findings so as to add to their larger significance. Also, the ethnographic fieldwork helped develop a substantive understanding by presenting the "context" essential for uncovering the meaning of quantitative data. By mixing qualitative and quantitative research, this model was effective in exploring in more depth and from different angles the late-modern steroid marketplace—an end that monomethod research could not accomplish.

Conclusion: Beyond Exclusivism and Toward Inclusivity

Reorienting our field toward approaching mixed methods research as being legitimate and beneficial should be fairly simple given its utility for studying crime and justice phenomena. It is likely, however, that tradition and political interests will construct additional barriers that hinder this process. As stated earlier, for both intellectual and political reasons, our field of study has established a methodological infrastructure that defaults among qualitative and quantitative lines.

As discussed in aforementioned sections, mixed methods research has become for most other social science disciplines a solution to this paradigm conflict that has existed since the 1960s (Gage 1989; Giddens 2006, 2007; Hammersley 1992). However, mixed methods research does have its critics, and some have argued that this "third methodological movement" is fraught with serious implications and unintended consequences (Denzin and Lincoln 2005; Freshwater 2007; Giddens 2006, 2007; Howe 2004). These potential consequences, as Freshwater states, "may undermine and contradict the very foundations upon which the method is based" (2007, p. 145).

Giddens (2007) posits that this epistemological middle—despite its seeming utility—is loaded with theoretical, methodological, and political issues. Alongside these complexities, mixed methods research still operates on the qualitative-quantitative divide that further reifies traditional methodological labels. These labels signify a dichotomous relationship that "makes clear who has the power and who is benefiting within certain relationships and situations" (Giddens 2006, p. 198). Trenched in the guise of inclusiveness and compatibility, mixed methods may "serve as a cover for the continuing hegemony of positivism," which would further marginalize non-positivistic research (Giddens 2006, 2007). The primary concern is that mixed methods research has become a "Trojan Horse" for a "pragmatic post-positivism" that would systematically subsume qualitative research in the service of quantitative studies (Denzin and Lincoln 2005; Freshwater 2007; Giddens 2006, 2007; Howe 2004).

According to Howe (2004), the uncritical adoption of mixed methods has shut down an important methodological conversation. The tendency for researchers to adopt this approach uncritically has contributed to a sort of *methodological imperialism*; a condition in which one "paradigm" takes a superior position able to overcome the other (Freshwater 2007; Howe 1992). Here, this "third approach" may provide positivism with another opportunity to push qualitative research to a secondary, more auxiliary status—thereby sustaining conditions that place quantitative methodologies at the "top of the methodological hierarchy" (Howe 2004, p. 53). Put briefly, the concern is that the epistemological foundations of mixed methods research create prolific grounds for positivism and quantitative methods which, in turn, sideline interpretive and qualitative research.

Creswell et al. (2006) disagree. By drawing from an extensive literature, they reject the notion that mixed methods privileges more positivistic research and pushes qualitative research to an auxiliary or secondary position. They also contest those who argue that mixed methods research does not employ critical interpretive approaches to qualitative research. The research reviewed above on steroid trafficking corroborates Creswell's view in that this study uses quantitative methods to bolster a critical ethnographic approach.

Aside from entering the mixed methods debate, Creswell and others effectively demonstrate that the rigorous production of scholarship using mixed methods research has become, more recently, a part of criminology and criminal justice. It is well documented that mixed methods research is becoming a key component within this once traditionally exclusive infrastructure (Creswell 1994; Greene 2001, 2007; Johnson and Onwuegbuzie 2004; Kraska 2008; Kraska and Neuman 2008; Tashakkori and Teddlie 1998, 2003). However, the conditions that have initiated inclusivity must also bring to attention that our field is rich with opportunities that can utilize this third methodological approach.

The argument for mixed methods as being methodologically legitimate has been made repeatedly as scholars attempt to shift exclusive ideologies toward inclusive principles (Creswell 1994; Greene 2001, 2007; Johnson and Onwuegbuzie 2004; Kraska 2008; Kraska and Neuman 2008; Tashakkori and Teddlie 1998, 2003). This approach requires that our field abandon the incompatibility thesis and dismissive thinking. Our research objectives, and not methodological preference, should guide method selection—whether qualitative, quantitative, or both. This pragmatic movement not only upends the deep tradition of exclusionary and dismissive thinking, it can also yield practical advantages. Mixing methodologies harbors potential to produce a broad and diverse body of credible scholarship.

The ultimate goal of examining the mixed methods approach is to change the status quo. In our view this movement is essential for redirecting our field's pedagogical compass toward inclusion and compatibility. Debating quantitative versus qualitative ultimately implies that one is superior while the other is misguided. A more conducive avenue would be to examine differences for purpose of comparison and to illuminate their compatible and mutually reinforcing qualities. This approach harbors better potential to legitimize and clarify both valued traditions. Criminology and criminal justice students, especially those in graduate programs, should have a firm command over our field's entire methodological offerings in order to more competently and completely produce knowledge about our field's most pressing questions.

Fortunately, there are clear signs that crime and justice studies appear to be maturing beyond the tradition of methodological exclusivism, and are seeking out the third way. This growing inclination signals the extent to which more inclusive and pragmatic attitudes are beginning to become institutionalized within criminological scholarship. Perhaps someday the crime and justice research community won't question why someone mixed quantitative and qualitative methods but, rather, why they did not.

References

Buckler, K. 2008. The quantitative/qualitative divide revisited: A study of published research, doctoral program curricula, and journal editor perceptions. *Journal of Criminal Justice Education* 19: 383-403.

Collins, R. 1989. Sociology pro-science or anti-science? *American Sociological Review* 54: 124-139.

Creswell, J. 1994. *Research design: Qualitative and quantitative approaches.* London: Sage.

Creswell, J., and V. Clark. 2006. *Designing and conducting mixed methods research.* Thousand Oaks, CA: Sage.

Creswell, J., R. Shope, P. Clark, and D. Green. 2006. How interpretive qualitative research extends mixed methods research. *Research in the Schools* 13, 1-11.

Datta, L. E. 1994. Paradigm wars: A basis for peaceful coexistence and beyond. In C. S. Reichardt and S. F. Rallis (Eds.), *The qualitative quantitative debate: New perspectives, new directions for program evaluation* (No. 61, pp. 53-70). San Francisco: Jossey-Bass.

Datta, L. E. 1997a. Multimethod evaluations: Using case studies together with other methods. In E. Chelimsky and W. R. Shadish (Eds.), *Evaluation for the 21st century* (pp. 344-359). Thousand Oaks, CA: Sage.

Datta, L. E. 1997b. A pragmatic basis for mixed-methods designs. In J. C. Greene and V. J. Caracelli (Eds.), *Advances in mixed-method evaluation: The challenges and benefits of integrating diverse paradigms. New Directions for evaluation,* 74 (pp. 33-46). San Francisco: Jossey-Bass.

Denzin, N. K. 1978. The *research act: A theoretical introduction to sociological methods.* New York: McGraw-Hill.

Denzin, N. K. 1989. *The research act: A theoretical introduction to sociological methods* (3rd ed.). Englewood Cliffs, NJ: Prentice-Hall.

Denzin, N. K., and Y. S. Lincoln. 2005. Introduction: The discipline and practice of qualitative research. In N. K. Denzin and Y. S. Lincoln (Eds.), *The Sage handbook of qualitative research* (pp. 1-28). Thousand Oaks, CA: Sage.

DiChristina, B. 1997. The quantitative emphasis in criminal justice education. *Journal of Criminal Justice Education* 8: 181-199.

Ferrell, J., K. Hayward, W. Morrisan, and M. Presdee. 2004. *Cultural criminology unleashed.* London: Glass House.

Ferrell, J., J. Young, and K. Hayward. 2008. *Cultural criminology.* London: Sage.

Freshwater, D. 2007. Reading mixed methods research: Contexts for Criticism. *Journal of Mixed Methods Research* 1: 134-146.

Gage, N. 1989. The paradigm wars and their aftermath: A "historical" sketch of research and teaching since 1989. *Educational Researcher* 18 (7): 10-16.

Gainey, R. R., S. Steen, and R. L. Engen. 2005. Exercising options: An assessment of the use of alternative sanctions for drug offenders. *Justice Quarterly* 22: 488-520.

Giddens, L. 2006. Mixed-methods research: Positivism dressed in drag? *Journal of Research in Nursing* 11 (3): 195-203.

Giddens, L. 2007. A Trojan horse for positivism?: A critique of mixed methods research. *Advances in Nursing Science* 30: 52-60.

Glaser, B., and A. Strauss. 1967. *The discovery of grounded theory.* Chicago: Aldine.

Greene, J. C. 2001. Mixing social inquiry methodologies. In V. Richardson (Ed.), *Handbook of research on teaching* (4th ed., pp. 251-258). Washington, DC: American Educational Research Association.

Greene, J. C. 2007. *Mixed methods in social inquiry.* San Francisco, CA: Wiley.

Greene, J. C., and V. J. Caracelli. 2003. Making pragmatic sense of mixed methods practice. In A. Tashakkori and C. Teddlie (Eds.), *Handbook of mixed methods in social and behavioral research* (pp. 91-110). Thousand Oaks, CA: Sage.

Guba, E. 1987. What have we learned about naturalistic evaluation? *Evaluation Practice* 8: 23-43.

Guba, E., and Y. Lincoln. 1982. Epistemological and methodological bases of naturalistic inquiry. *Educational Communication and Technology Journal* 30: 233-252.

Halfpenny, P. 1982. *Positivism and sociology: Explaining social life.* London: Allen and Unwin.

Hammersley, M. 1992. The paradigm wars: Reports from the front. *British Journal of Sociology of Education* 13: 131-143.

Hammersley, M. 2000. *Taking sides in social research.* New York: Routledge.

Harding, S. G. (1987). *Feminism and methodology.* Bloomington, IN: Indiana University Press.

Higgins, G. 2009. Quantitative versus qualitative methods: Understanding why quantitative methods are predominant in criminology and criminal justice. *Journal of Theoretical and Philosophical Criminology* 1: 23-37.

Howe, K. 1988. Against the quantitative-qualitative incompatibility thesis or dogmas die hard. *Educational Research* 17: 10-16.

Howe, K. 1992. Getting over the quantitative-qualitative debate. *American Journal of Education* 100: 236-256.

Howe, K. 2004. A critique of experimentalism. *Qualitative Inquiry* 10: 42-61.

Jick, T. 1979. Mixing qualitative and quantitative methods: Triangulation in action. *Administrative Science Quarterly* 24: 602-611.

Johnson, B., and L. Christensen. 2007. *Educational research: Quantitative, qualitative, and mixed approaches.* Boston: Allyn and Bacon.

Johnson, R. B., and A. Onwuegbuzie. 2004. Mixed methods research: A research paradigm whose time has come. *Educational Researcher* 33: 14-26.

Johnson, R. B., A. Onwuegbuzie, and L. Turner. 2007. Toward a definition of mixed methods research. *Journal of Mixed Methods Research* 1: 112-133.

Kleck, G., J. Tark, and J. J. Bellows. 2006. What methods are most frequently used in research in criminology and criminal justice? *Journal of Criminal Justice Education* 34: 147-152.

Kraska, P. 2008. The third way: Teaching mixed methods research. *ACJS Today* 23: 1-8.

Kraska, P., C. Bussard, and J. Brent. 2010. Trafficking in bodily perfection: Examining the late-modern steroid marketplace and its criminalization. *Justice Quarterly* 27: 159-185.

Kraska, P., and L. Neuman. 2008. *Criminal justice and criminology research methods.* New Work: Pearson.

Logan, T. K., L. Shannon, and R. Walker. 2005. Protective order in rural and urban areas: A multiple perspective study. *Violence Against Women* 11: 876-911.

Maxcy, S. J. 2003. Pragmatic threads in mixed methods research in the social sciences: The search for multiple modes of inquiry and the end of philosophy or formalism. In A. Tashakkori and C. Teddlie (Eds.), *Handbook of mixed methods in social and behavioral research* (pp. 51-90). Thousand Oaks: Sage.

Morgan, G. 2006. *Images of organization.* London: Sage.

Popper, K. 1972. *Objective knowledge: An evolutionary approach.* Oxford: Clarendon Press.

Pratt, T. 2010. Introduction: Special issue on quantitative methods for criminal justice and criminology. *Journal of Criminal Justice Education* 21: 103-104.

Reichardt, C. S., and T. D. Cook. 1979. Beyond qualitative versus quantitative methods. In T. D. Cook and C. S. Reichardt (Eds.), *Qualitative and quantitative methods in evaluation research* (pp. 7-32). Thousand Oaks: CA: Sage.

Reichardt, C. S., and S. F. Rallis. 1994. Qualitative and quantitative inquiries are not incompatible: A call for a new partnership. *New Directions for Program Evaluation* 61: 85-91.

Reinharz, S., and L. Davidman. 1992. *Feminist methods in social research*. Oxford: Oxford University Press.

Roth, P. A. 1987. *Meaning and method in social science: A case for methodological pluralism*. New York: Cornell University Press.

Sampson, R. J., and W. B. Groves. 1989. Community structure and crime: Testing social disorganization theory. *American Journal of Sociology* 94: 774-802.

Sever, B. 2001. Research methods for criminal justice graduate students: Comparing textbook coverage and classroom instruction. *Journal of Criminal Justice Education* 21: 337-353.

Shaw, C., and H. D. Mckay. 1942. *Juvenile delinquency and urban areas*. Chicago: University of Chicago Press.

Shaw, C., and H. D. Mckay. 1969. *Juvenile delinquency and urban areas*. Rev. ed. Chicago: University of Chicago Press.

Short, J. F., and F. L. Strodtbeck. 1965. *Group process and gang delinquency.* Chicago: University of Chicago Press.

Smith, J. K. 1983a. Quantitative versus qualitative research: An attempt to clarify the issue. *Educational Researcher* 12: 6-13.

Smith, J. K. 1983b. *Quantitative versus interpretive: The problem of conducting social inquiry.* In E. House (Ed.), *Philosophy of evaluation* (pp. 27-52). San Francisco: Jossey-Bass.

Smith, J. K., and L. Heshusius. 1986. Closing down the conversation: The end of the quantitative-qualitative debate among educational inquirers. *Educational Researcher* 15: 4-12.

Sullivan, C. J., and M. G. Maxfield. 2003. Examining paradigmatic development in criminology and criminal justice: A content analysis of research methods syllabi in doctoral programs. *Journal of Criminal Justice Education* 14: 269-285.

Tashakkori, A., and C. Teddlie. 1998. *Mixed methodology: Combining qualitative and quantitative approaches*. Thousand Oaks, CA: Sage.

Tashakkori, A., and C. Teddlie. 2003. *Handbook of mixed methods in social and behavioral research*. London: Sage.

Tewksbury, R., D. A. Dabney, and H. Copes. 2010. The prominence of qualitative research in criminology and criminal justice scholarship. *Journal of Criminal Justice Education* 21: 391-411.

Tewksbury, R., M. T. DeMichele, and M. Miller. 2005. Methodological orientations of articles appearing in criminal Justice's top journals: Who publishes what and where. *Journal of Criminal Justice Education* 16: 265-279.

Torre, M., and M. Fine. 2005. Bar none: Extending affirmative action to higher education in prison. *Journal of Social Issues* 61: 569-594.

Wolcott, H. F. 2002. Writing up qualitative research ... better. *Qualitative Health Research* 12: 91-103.

Worrall, J. L. 2000. In defense of "quantoids": More on the reasons for the quantitative emphasis in criminal justice education and research. *Journal of Criminal Justice Education* 11: 353-360.

Collecting and Analyzing the Stories of Offenders

Lois Presser

The stories of offenders are invaluable for detailing the meanings that people give to their own violations. One would expect a broad knowledge base of methods for collecting and analyzing such stories, but no such thing currently exists. This article attempts to fill that gap, drawing on my own and others' research experiences. Research practice depends on the way that a researcher conceptualizes both narrative and offender, so I pay careful attention to these conceptualizations. I then offer practical advice on best practices of narrative research in criminology.

Criminologists generally acknowledge that subjective evaluations go into the processes whereby something comes to be called a crime and someone comes to be called an offender or a victim. And yet, most of our information on crime and its proposed causes are shorn of subjective evaluations of crime. The objectified version of what people say about their own actions or those of others—arrest statistics and survey data—permits large numbers of observations. However, in-depth qualitative accounts about one's actions—stories—remain the very best data with which researchers might retrieve the meanings that people give to their own violations, including violations that state officials do not know or care about. Simply, our stories draw on the events, symbols, and phenomenological tensions that matter to us.

Little attention has been paid to methods for collecting and analyzing such stories. When we teach students how to do narrative research in criminology, what do we tell them? What *should* we tell them? Narrative research methods *in general* have been amply explored (e.g., Atkinson 1998; Lawthom, Clough, and Moore 2004; Reissman 1993). However, the methodological issues surrounding the narratives of persons involved in crime are unique. The issue of the truth of offenders'[1] stories is particularly thorny, complicated by the social rewards of

---

1. I use the term "offender" to refer to a person who did and/or does harm. The more conventional meaning of "offender" is a person who has been formally designated as such, especially by formal authorities. Presently, I dissect the use of this term.

explaining one's behavior and/or resisting identification as a "public enemy," and the scholarly and popular view that "offenders lie."

With this article, I hope to begin a discussion about best practices of narrative research in criminology. The article is based on my own interview data and the interview data of other narrative researchers. My focus on the aspects in the article is as follows. I consider only the stories that *offenders* tell, as opposed to the stories of others affected by crime. Victims' stories are crucial—I would say central—to criminological understanding. But offenders' stories raise particular questions of truth and perspective with which I wish to grapple here. Also, my concern in this article is with the stories themselves, and not with questions of access and safety. Finally, I am writing for a researcher who would embark on a primary data collection effort, as opposed to those who would use already-collected stories. How should we obtain offenders' stories and how should we analyze them? Before addressing these questions, I will discuss how social scientists including criminologists have conceived of narratives and offenders.

Defining Narrative

What is a story? What is a narrative? Is it the same thing as a story? The term narrative is rather trendy right now in both the social sciences and in popular culture, resulting in some misuse. For example, I have reviewed manuscripts in which narrative stands in for anything an informant says during an open-ended interview. A setting out of terms is in order.

The words narrative and story are used interchangeably, though scholars often reserve "narrative" for a lengthy treatise in which the individual recounts a considerable portion of her/his life, and "story" for a shorter rendering of a single life episode.[2] In this article and in my work, I generally treat the terms narrative, story, self-narrative, and self-story interchangeably. And yet, there are certainly narratives/stories (e.g., biographies, novels) in which the protagonist is someone besides the narrator.

A useful definition of self-narrative is offered by social psychologists Kenneth and Mary Gergen: "the individual's account of the relationship among self-relevant events across time" (Gergen and Gergen 1988, p. 19). In a classic article, sociolinguists Labov and Waletzky (1967) emphasized the sequencing of events, specifying that "the *a*-then-*b* is in some sense the most essential and characteristic of narrative. Some narratives may use it exclusively, and every narrative must, by definition, use it at least once" (p. 30). As such, Nelson, a Guyanese man convicted of armed robbery whom I interviewed in New Jersey in 1999, offered a short narrative when he related: "I used to go to Sunday schools and churches before I came to the USA. But then after—you know—after a while,

---

2. For historian White (1987), who has written extensively on narrative within his discipline, a narrative has a plot, whereas a story need not (see p. 172). I consider both narrative and story as having plots.

the devil overcame me and I got lost on the outer world." The self-relevant events of the narrative are his immigration to the USA and his subsequent capture by the devil. Besides ordering events, a narrative makes a point, hence Barthes (1977) states that narrative "ceaselessly substitutes meaning for the straightforward copy of the events recounted" (p. 119). The meaning of the aforementioned narrative from Nelson is moral fall.[3]

Narratives depict a change from one condition to another. Indeed, Brock-meier (2004) observes that narrative makes its point *because* "the second event does not logically follow from the first event" (p. 298). For Bruner (1990), the narrative would make sense of a "cultural aberration" (p. 82). As such, the point of a narrative is always a moral stance (Bruner 1990; White 1980). No wonder, then, that narratives have special utility for those who have violated norms and laws: narratives are explanatory devices and bids for moral reappraisal.

Coupled with the observation that narratives explain one's actions to others, psychologists observe that narratives explain one's actions—and thus one's self— *to oneself*. That is, we know ourselves through an evolving self-story (Bruner 1990; Holstein and Gubrium 2000; Polkinghorne 1988; Sarbin 1986; Somers 1994). From the idea that identity is an evolving story—that it is narrated—label-ing theory gets a new lease on intellectual life. Criminology's labeling theory posits that being labeled and treated as an offender could, by various means, including through the adoption of a criminal identity, lead to re-offending. If identity is storied, then self-stories may influence offending actions and a "narrative criminology" has great promise.

Conceptualizing Narrative

The philosopher Ricoeur (1984) identified three basic conceptualizations of the relationship between narrative and experience, which help me to categorize criminologists' work with stories (Presser 2009). Polkinghorne (1988) usefully paraphrases these three conceptualizations:

> The first two ... assume that life, as lived, is independent of narrative descrip-tion. If this separation is accepted, then one can hold either that narrative gives an accurate description of the way the world really is or that it is descriptively discontinuous with the real world it depicts. The third position ... is that aspects of experience itself are presented originally as they appear in the narration and that narrative form is not simply imposed on preexistent real experiences but helps to give them form. (pp. 67-68)

---

3. Actually, the larger life story in which this story is "nested" (Gergen and Gergen 1988) is about moral redemption following a fall. Hence, the importance of getting a person's whole life story, recognizing, however, that one's life story changes with time and place of telling.

I call these three conceptualizations, (1) narrative as record, (2) narrative as interpretation, and (3) narrative as a shaper of experience—in other words, as constitutive of experience.

The first two of Ricoeur's conceptualizations are similar in that both value narrative for its ability to tell us about the past. What differs is that, in conceptualizing narrative as interpretation, the analyst engages more with individual *perceptions* of the past, often appreciatively. In conceptualizing narrative as record, the analyst confronts the subjective cast of the narrative, if s/he even acknowledges it, as a source of bias to be managed.

In contrast to both of these, the third view values narrative for its ability to tell us about past, present, *and* future according to the narrator. The emphasis in this view is on the reciprocal influence of discourse and action. Therefore, those who take the third view also tend to consider how broader (e.g., national) discourses shape the narrative. The veracity of the events recounted in the story is not central.

It should be clear that the view of narrative as a shaper of experience runs on the same philosophical track as post-structuralist thought. The inclinations of the post-structuralist scholar—to tell local stories and avoid supposedly global and universal ones, to recognize different levels of truth, to privilege meaning-making, to understand meaning-making as inevitably social, dynamic, and open-ended, and thus to doubt the possibilities of predicting human action (cf. Presser 2009)—all apply. As Holstein and Gubrium (2000) state:

> Narrative analysts no longer view storytellers and their accomplices as having unmediated access to experience, nor do they hold that experience can be conveyed in some pristine or authentic form separate from the institutions and events of the day. (p. 103)

Just as most criminologists are inclined toward positivism, most criminologists treat narrative either as record or as interpretation (Presser 2009). That is to say, we generally treat narrative as a source of information on "what happened."

Mainstream criminologists look to stories for the facts they contain—the narrative as record. Recently, for example, Agnew (2006) has encouraged scholarly use of the "storylines" generated by offenders, for these describe "those particular combinations of events and conditions that are especially likely to result in a crime or series of related crimes" (p. 122). Notably, he distinguishes storylines, identified by the analyst, from accounts and neutralizations, which "present a selective and often distorted portrayal of the events and conditions leading up to a crime" (p. 122). Agnew would recommend harvesting the events and conditions from the story, leaving the story's "connective tissue."

Ethnographers of crime and victimization appreciate speakers' interpretations, but are mainly interested in the substance of the stories (e.g., Bourgois 2003; Duneier 1999; Messerschmidt 2000; Miller 2008). For example, whereas Messerschmidt (2000) recognizes "each life history as a *situational truth*" (p. 20; emphasis in original), he collected a small sample of boys' life histories in order to "signal contributing factors to violence and nonviolence" (p. 17).

Likewise, feminist and other critical criminologists tend to adopt the view of narrative as interpretation because they recognize the subjectivity and partiality of all discourses. With the understanding that certain groups have been dominated by hegemonic discourses, they urge us to let those members of disenfranchised groups who are involved in crime as offenders, victims, and workers tell their as-yet-unheard stories. These stories are considered as meaningful and uniquely valid interpretations of reality. Chesney-Lind and Pasko (2004), for example, reject erroneous "girlz in the hood" stories disseminated by the media and urge us instead to both heed the social contexts within which offending takes place and listen to the actual stories of female offenders (p. 176).

The view of narrative as a shaper of experience is least common in our discipline but discernible in the work of psychologically oriented criminologists Toch (1993), Katz (1988), and Maruna (2001). Each has probed the meanings that speakers give to their lives in the form of stories and have shown how stories promote criminal action or (in Maruna's study) desistance from crime.[4]

Does it matter *methodologically* how researchers conceptualize narrative? It does. My advice for research methods depends on a researcher's approach to narrative.

Collecting the Narratives of "Offenders"

In this section, I offer suggestions on how to elicit stories from offenders. On the way to doing so, I also deliberate about who an "offender" is.

Getting the Story

It is not hard to get people to tell stories, assuming the topic has some relevance to their lives, and sometimes even when it does not. Human beings are storytelling creatures. Yet, humans are also, generally speaking, inclined to avoid pain, and, again generally speaking, they try to avoid talking about painful moments in their lives. I have found that the inclination to tell stories, including painful stories or ones that cast the speaker in a negative light, varies greatly across individuals.

In my experience, it is relatively easy to elicit stories of a participant's own harm-doing *when that participant is a labeled offender*. When a participant's offending history has been given some official imprint, as when s/he is currently incarcerated or on probation or parole, the researcher can ask directly about that history. Usually, participants in such contexts themselves initiate a story

4. Maruna and Copes (2005) have located neutralizations (i.e., discourses that legitimize criminal actions) within self-stories and have theorized that self-stories shape action through neutralizations. Both labeling theory and neutralization theory (Sykes and Matza 1957) may be revisited from the perspective of the story-action relationship.

about the instant offense, if not about their entire offense histories. In case, they do not, a useful interview question is: "How did you get here (in prison, on probation, etc.)?" One reason that such participants are likely to tell stories about their offending is that stories are excellent vehicles for explaining oneself (Stone 1982), *and* we are especially inclined to explain ourselves when we have been sanctioned (Scott and Lyman 1968). Authorities have labeled the participant as "bad" and "wrong," and s/he has an interest in refuting those attributions, even to a stranger. The foregoing does not mean that such persons will freely share all aspects of "the story" with an eye toward fidelity to facts. On the contrary: their (and all) stories are shaped by their interests in telling them, including that of being seen as a good person (Presser 2008). Also, the story will follow some cultural template (discussed in some depth presently). Nonetheless, such persons are likely to recount *a* story about their crime or crimes.

I have found it *more* difficult to obtain stories of having offended from "regular people"—those whom the interviewer has given no sign of viewing as "an offender." The experience of causing harm is painful, perhaps as or more painful than that of having *been* harmed. Outside of the interview, there may never have been any call to talk about the harm with another person. In a current project that has me asking regular people about their own acts of harm, one research participant told me about having rejected a girl at her middle school as a 10-year-old. Now in her late 20s, this participant had never been encouraged to talk about that harming action and to do so was clearly heartbreaking for her. Another research participant rejected my research assistant's query about his having perpetrated harm. He firmly replied: "You can move to another subject."

With "known" offenders, who are usually referred by a criminal justice agency and interviewed within a criminal justice facility (cf. Wright, Decker, Redfern, and Smith 1992), offending history is the undeniable "elephant in the room." In contrast, regular people have not been "outed" for doing harm. I ask regular people "Have you ever done harm to anyone or anything?", but I need not ask that question with known offenders. In fact, I pose that question to "regular people" only after discussing their views of and experiences of harm as a victim—thus negating the suggestion that the interview is "about" their offending, and that they are "an offender." I admit in this regard to effectively preserving the status quo which would type people as either "offender" or "non-offender."

In trying to get people to tell stories, interviewers benefit from standard prompts (see Table 1). My personal cache of generic prompts includes: "Would you tell me more about that?" "Is there a story behind that?" "That's interesting" and "Huh." Also, to my mind nothing compares to simply reflecting back what the participant has said or remaining silent for some moments after the participant has spoken. My list of go-to prompts is short because I want to first allow for spontaneous storytelling before I actively solicit stories. I want to include in my assessment whether participants *elect* to tell a story on a certain topic and, if so, *which* stories participants themselves elect to tell. These are the inclinations of one who holds a perspective on narrative as a shaper of

Table 1   Generic prompts for narrative research

Would you tell me more about that?
Is there a story behind that?
That's interesting.
Huh.
Mm-hmm.
(Simply reflecting back what the participant has said)
(Silence)

---

experience—that narratives are productive of identities and that the story one would tell about oneself matters to action. From other perspectives, there is no need for data on how the self is constructed, and so the researcher can just ask for a story on a particular theme.

The prompts are concise because I want to talk as little as possible during the interviews. Along these same lines, the story-seeking interviewer does best by listening much more than talking, by tolerating silence, and by asking open-ended questions (Seidman 1991). As in any research encounter, it is crucial that the interviewer make the participant feel comfortable if s/he is to elicit data. The interviewer should aim for a non-evaluative, friendly and yet professional manner. The interview should seem very interested in *who* the participant *is*. If the research is to uncover the bases of self-awareness, she/he should furthermore not say too much either about her/himself or about the research. The researcher who takes the view of narrative as record or interpretation can be more directive.

The researcher who conceptualizes narrative as a shaper of reality should be disinclined to influence the speaker's articulation of the narrative. As much as is possible, this researcher should avoid giving participants the language with which they construct narratives, for this language will be data for understanding constructions of self and the world. Consider the following example, which captures part of "Caitlin's" response to a question about the meaning of violence:

> But if it was just—you know—you kick some- you happen to kick someone because you're angry at that one second, and then hurt them, I wouldn't consider that violence.

Of interest, among other things, is the passivizing device Caitlin uses: "happen to" in regard to kicking another person. If the interviewer had stipulated parameters for speaking—say, if she had asked for a one-sentence definition—she might not have elicited that construction.

I am not suggesting that the interviewer never challenge what research participants say; I am suggesting that the interviewer avoid structuring their responses linguistically. I offer this recommendation of minimal intervention with some hesitation, simply because I am convinced that we can only limit our influence on the participants' words and never eliminate it entirely (Presser 2005, 2008). Thus, I also recommend that the researcher take account of that influence in analyzing the data; I will explain it in the next section.

Criminologists may wish to hear stories of either committing crimes *or* they may want "whole" life stories. To stimulate stories of offending, the interviewer might ask something like "Would you tell me about the offense that led to this conviction?" In stimulating life stories, a question along the lines of "Would you tell me about your life?" is useful. Or, the interviewer may simply ask the participant: "Would you share your life story with me?" People seem to enjoy telling their life stories. However, they are rarely asked to do so; an explicit invitation is usually necessary. In fact, researchers have traditionally cut participants off when they begin to tell stories (Bruner 1990; Seidman 1991). I think that we do so because we cannot be sure what the point of the story is until its conclusion, and we do not want to waste time. But we should!

If the participant sticks with current or fairly recent events, the interviewer may need to ask, specifically, about earlier life experiences. As Maynes, Pierce, and Laslett (2008) write, "the probing of life history research needs to extend back far enough in time to capture the social-historical and individual dynamics relevant to the questions under investigation" (p. 35). Of course, the scope of questioning follows from one's research objectives and theoretical orientation. For instance, within criminology, whereas the life-course criminologist will probe back to early childhood, the routine activities theorist will ask only about the crime situation.

Analyzing Narratives and Narration

In a recent report, criminologist Miller (2005) referred to strategies of analysis as "the black box of qualitative research in criminology" (p. 71). I agree: qualitative researchers are not in the habit of telling their own stories of doing research after gaining access. We rarely see detailed discussions of how the researchers went from raw discursive data to the colorful findings they share: it is simply not conventional. What did they include and what did they leave out? Did they worry over some remarks or stories that did not fit their developing theoretical perspective? If so, what did they do with such remarks or stories?

It is likely that the positivist past and present of criminology keeps us from telling detailed stories of our qualitative research practice. To a large extent, intuition—a deep sense of what is remarkable—guides qualitative analyses. The researcher herself, and no survey or experimental protocol, is the instrument. Notwithstanding the prominent role of intuition, the qualitative interviewer brings replicable procedures to the analysis, and these can be shared and taught.

Basic Analytical Tasks

In my own work with narratives, I perform three main analytical tasks: (1) I code for themes of interest; (2) I create a running summary of each participant's narrative as events across time; and (3) I create a memo of the interpersonal interaction between an interviewer and a participant.

I generate themes of interest based on intuition as well as past research on the topics with which I am concerned. Actually, I view intuition as a product of all that I have read and heard, and my personal experiences besides. In this way, I do not follow Glaser and Strauss' (1967) grounded theory method for doing inductive qualitative research, which warns against receiving guidance from prior theory. They write: "An effective strategy is, at first, literally to ignore the literature of theory and fact on the area under study, in order to assure that the emergence of categories will not be contaminated by concepts more suited to different areas" (Glaser and Strauss 1967, p. 37). I do not take issue with "contamination" by other concepts. On the other hand, I am influenced by Glaser and Strauss' advice in that I avoid theorizing until I have studied all of the data, and I privilege the data over any other inputs into the research.

My running summary includes answers to the questions: what is the logic or plot that is being developed? What has propelled the various actions being described? Who is the protagonist in relation to people and institutions? I try to write freely, and not to censor any emergent ideas.

Finally, the memo of interpersonal interaction records overt statements of who "the other" is as well as power-relevant actions. An example of the latter is repeated interruption of the other's speech by either interviewer or partici-pant. I code these because I am interested in how the micro-political context of research—not least research with "captured" (e.g., incarcerated) persons—shapes communication (Presser 2005).

I use text analysis software to help me organize and retrieve, and then compare, the various codes (sometimes known as nodes, i.e., themes) I create and memos I develop. It makes at least two contributions to my work. It facili-tates the organization of large amounts of data. And, the search/compare function of the software helps me to study how different themes relate to one another. However, software is not necessary for narrative analysis. It does not substitute for the hard work of discerning meanings. The researcher, and not the software, identifies the remarkable in the data.

Studying Language

For the researcher who collects narratives in order to gauge realities they are seen as representing—viewing narrative as either record or interpretation—the linguistic and poetic characteristics of the narratives (e.g., active versus passive construction; repetition of certain phrases; use of certain tropes) are of little interest. But for the researchers who posit narrative as constitutive of reality, these sorts of characteristics are as informative as the story "itself." The view of narrative as a shaper of experience has it that the plot or meaning of the story is conveyed not only through its content but also through its form (White

1987). Therefore, those who take this view must attend to how the story gets told and therefore should take pains with transcription, including as much of the exchange and articulation as possible and being exact with all that was uttered.

Then, during analysis, those linguistic characteristics are fodder for analysis. For example, from her interviews with 19 African-American men in a maximum security prison in the District of Columbia, resulting in 101 narratives of criminal acts, sociolinguist O'Connor (2000) reports on various linguistic patterns, including the following patterns of recalling criminal action (p. 40):

(1) deflecting or passivizing structures, or "arrangements of words that shift the focus from the speaker's agentive act (robbing, shooting, etc.) to his position as acted upon by the criminal justice system"
(2) justifying devices—"phrases that interject, before the action, a structure that makes the criminal act seem appropriate or necessary" and
(3) delaying tactics, or postponing the words that tell of the criminal act.

In addition, analysis of the following patterns can pay off as insights into the deep meaning of a story:

(4) Repetitions. Some participants keep using a particular expression or idiom. Tim, whom I interviewed on three occasions in the spring of 1999, explained his violence, which included rape, assault, and attempted murder, in terms of internal or external forces. He regularly began stories about his violent actions with the words "I just" (or "I jest," in his Appalachian accent). Whereas he and other participants used "just" with great frequency, Tim used this adjective most often when framing his violence. The following are exemplary excerpts:

> I just moved to this neighborhood and it was a whole different scene and I just. I—I look at it now, I think it was just—just peer pressure—most of it—was just— you know—I moved to the neighborhood, the first things that started happening to me was fights. People wanted to fight me. I didn't want to fight (*aggressive behavior as a teenager*).

> I just—my instincts just took over me. I just went crazy. And I grabbed this guy and I punched him (*assault in bar*).

> I was just—I was a little bit pressed for some sex. You know, I just had those urges. (*acquaintance rape*)

> And I just got mad. Said, well you'll finish it. I just told her you'll finish it ... I was just hearing myself say these things. (*acquaintance rape*)

> I just felt trapped. Ah, it was like I was trapped. I give you a—you know—this is— this is what I am as a man, this is what I'm supposed to do (*repeated domestic violence*).

For Tim, the expression "I just" was more often associated with a comment on lost agency than it was any other self-claim. The frequency of that expression alerted me to the passive role Tim assigned for himself in his violent encounters.

(5) Inconsistencies and missing parts. Does something in the story seem missing? What is *not* said? Is the story lacking in coherence? Every narrator picks and chooses among possible events and details that could have been included, but were not. The fact that the narrator leaves some things out should not surprise us. The analyst's job is to study the choices of inclusion and omission and to consider how they serve the construction of a desired point or identity.

(6) Awkward or unusual phrasing. O'Connor's (2000) passivizing structures are one kind of awkward phrasing. But anything that simply sounds weird may cue the analyst to some avoidance effort on the part of the narrator. For example, I interviewed Cyrus on two occasions, in 1999 and 2000, and over the course of the interviews I asked him about each of three murders he had committed. Cyrus had this to say during our second interview, "The one in '70, that was just a straight-up robbery, and the guy pulled a gun and we got him to shoot me and—you know—he got shot." "We got him to shoot me" is clumsy, to say the least: the victim was a convenience store clerk without any suicidal intent, so his agency in this sentence is false. The more obvious and true version would be "I shot him." Cyrus' phrasing provides a clue to a desire to minimize his responsibility for violence.

Analyzing Context

Researchers using narrative data must take the contexts of story telling into account. If they do not—and usually they do not—they risk making mistakes about what the story and its delivery *mean*. Several contexts are relevant.

Structural contexts

Criminologists frequently state—especially in concluding sections of journal articles—that social context matters, yet we rarely include social context specifics, even in qualitative work. As Maynes et al. (2008) write:

> The insistence that historical contexts and the institutions embedded within them matter is right on the mark, but the analysis must make these connections in concrete ways, in ways that sometimes push the analyst beyond the life story. Only then can we understand why and how context matters. (p. 53)

Bourgois (2003) is exceptional. A cultural anthropologist in the tradition of Pierre Bourdieu, he devotes an early chapter of his book on Nuyorican cocaine dealers, *In Search of Respect*, to the history of Puerto Rico on the island and in the USA. He subsequently draws upon that history to frame the stories told to him by drug dealers in the 1990s. Presser (2005) considers state (e.g., prison) control as a factor shaping the stories and storytelling of men convicted of violent crimes. The circumstance of incarceration, for example, clarifies the efforts by many of the men to be in control in the interview. These researchers conceptualize narrative differently: Bourgois treats narrative as interpretation exclusively, whereas Presser treats narrative as a shaper, particularly a shaper of identity. But both benefit immensely by including these historical and institutional contexts in the analysis.

Experience of storytelling

Beyond individual (e.g., childhood), institutional (e.g., imprisonment), and societal/cultural contexts, individuals have histories of self-disclosure. Stories *tell* a history, but they also *have* a history—a social location of production. We all have told some version of "our story" before, and those experiences linger. Likewise, "offenders" who are interviewed about their crime(s) have told stories of the crime(s) before. In legal hearings and then in correctional settings, their stories have been interrogated, even cast as criminogenic (see, e.g., Fox 1999). Storytelling is a loaded activity for people cast as offenders.

Genres and standard plots

All stories are shaped by genres and plots that have currency in the culture (Gergen 1992; Maynes et al. 2008; Polanyi 1985). Whether narrators deploy or reject these cultural templates, they always engage with them. For instance, one of my research participants, Lyle, age 17, was incarcerated in an adult correctional facility for armed robbery. During our interview conducted when Lyle was 17, he spoke of his desire to share his life story in the form of a book:

Lo[5]	What's the book gonna be about?
Lyle	About my *life*! Autobiography. You know, I mean I'm gonna put in details. How I came out the hood. You know. And just *made* it.
Lo	Mmm.
Lyle	Got locked up. Still having the chance. And just *made* it.

Lyle is clearly influenced by a tale of triumph against the odds popularized in popular culture, especially in films. In Maruna's (2001) study, redemption scripts, comparable to the standard Alcoholics Anonymous story, were common. Some scholars are dismayed by uniform-sounding or "clichéd" accounts, especially when these seem to shed too positive a light on the past (e.g., Wiersma 1988). In my view, a cliché is simply a cultural construction that *sounds like* a

---

5. The author goes by the name "Lo."

cultural construction to the listener. Often the element of *reaching toward* a new-life circumstance or self—laid out in genres and standard plots—is more apparent in clichéd remarks or tales than in others. Clichés remind us that narratives inevitably include what we wish for, *and* that narrative research is necessarily an exploration in the culture of the storyteller, and never just her/his life or even how s/he views that life.

The research encounter

You and I have no all-purpose, once-and-for-all story. Rather, stories are always *made for* (and on) occasions of use, and they are subsequently *remade* for occasions of presentation. Therefore, to understand "the" story that is told on any one occasion, it is important that researchers reveal the contexts within which they obtained stories. Those who view narrative as record or as interpretation of experience are not typically students of the conditioning influence of the narratives of the researcher and the research setting. Nor do they generally attend to historical and cultural contexts that shape "one's" narrative. When what matters are simply the events recalled, social influence—construed broadly—is only of interest if it biases the recall, perhaps by discouraging revelation or encouraging embellishment. In contrast, those who view narrative as a shaper of reality wonder exactly how the researcher lends a hand in achieving coherence. Oftentimes instead of deeming this bias, the analyst takes it to offer valuable insight into how narratives get shaped in social settings, of which the research encounter is one.

The coding and editing of stories to create knowledge (i.e., prepare reports, books, and articles) further shapes "what was said." Ethnographer Behar (1993) makes this point very eloquently: "As I undid the necklaces of elegant sentences and paragraphs of prose, as I snipped at the flow of talk, stopping it sometimes for dramatic emphasis long before it had really stopped, I no longer knew where I stood on the border between fiction and nonfiction" (pp. 12-13). I understand Behar's point well when I recall the stories told to me by men who committed violent crimes, and how I presented the stories for publication—in snippets designed for optimal delivery of a larger point. For example, Harry told a story of trying to push his wife, whom he believed had cheated on him, from a fast-moving car. He did not succeed in killing her because she quickly found his gun in the car's glove compartment and shot him, non-fatally. In reporting this story (Presser 2008), I closed with Harry's words, "So, um, and—and we tried to make it work from there but it just—you know—sometimes you just—the magic's gone." Whereas Harry continued talking, I ended the excerpt where I did to stress his casualness (hence the everyday rhetoric of marital fulfillment) concerning extreme violence. I wonder now if my choice to end the presentation of Harry's story with that rhetoric makes him seem *especially* hardened to the use of violence. The words with which an author closes a story have particular punch, and are therefore supposed to have special meaning. Am I faithful to

Harry's story? Perhaps, and yet I am very definitely honing the rendering of this story to make my own meaning.

That example suggests that the analyst and not the narrator ultimately determines the meaning of the story—an observation that sits rather uneasily alongside critical scholars' views of the incisive, albeit ignored knowledge that oppressed people possess. For example, feminists have protested researchers' tendency to *re*-interpret what women say. It is therefore common for feminist researchers to share their reports with the participants for validation (e.g., Messerschmidt 2000). I do not. My projects follow from a view of narrative as a shaper of experience, and so I am minimally concerned with facts in the lives of those I interview. Further, I believe that storytellers have only partial understandings of the meanings of the stories they are telling. I share Hearn's (1998, p. 146) insight:

> When men talk about violence, many things are not said. This is even so when men appear to be fully co-operative in disclosing violence. Those contexts that are not explicitly referred to—gender, sexuality, age, race, family life, and so on— do not disappear; they remain within the text but as subtexts, scarcely spoken.

All our stories are framed by social relations of which we have minimal consciousness; it must be so, since those relations are ever in flux. The researcher makes a contribution not because s/he stands outside of these relations, but rather because s/he takes it upon her/himself to understand them as frame for "what is said."

Conclusions

Criminologists have long embraced the use of narratives (Bennett 1981), but we have not much discussed methods of collecting and analyzing them. Stories pose unique challenges to researchers. I have shared my own ideas about best methods for collecting and analyzing the stories of offenders, first stopping to problematize both what we mean by stories and what we mean by offenders.

Offenders' stories are complex, and so are our attitudes about them. Laypersons and scholars alike harbor a suspicion that offenders' stories are inauthentic. What I like about this suspicion is that it recognizes that stories *do* things (Austin 1962)—things like getting one out of a lengthy prison sentence. Storytelling is "motivated" activity (Maynes et al. 2008, p. 120). But, if stories influence others and are meant to do so, they also influence the storyteller her/himself. Hence, a constitutive view of offenders' stories—as a shaper of reality, which is concerned with how stories are put together and how they affect action, and not primarily or at all with the truth of those stories.

The ways that we conceptualize narrative—as record, interpretation or a shaper of reality—have implications for methods of doing research on narrative. And so, the researcher should get very clear about what the role of the story in her/his research, even before designing the study. I have delineated ways in which methods of collection and analysis depend on one's conceptualization of narrative.

No matter the orientation to narrative, the analyst using narrative data should reveal as much as possible about the stories and the circumstances of their telling. However, much or little one says, the research and the researcher influence the stories that get told, often in unexpected ways (Presser 2004). There is no interview setting that is not also a social setting, and, as such, a setting for the social processes that potentially promote or inhibit harmful action.

References

Agnew, R. 2006. Storylines as a neglected cause of crime. *Journal of Research in Crime and Delinquency* 43: 119-147.

Atkinson, R. 1998. *The life story interview.* Thousand Oaks, CA: Sage.

Austin, J. L. 1962. *How to do things with words.* Cambridge, MA: Harvard University Press.

Barthes, R. 1977. *Image, music, text* (S. Heath, Trans). New York: Hill and Wang.

Behar, R. 1993. *Translated woman: Crossing the border with Esperanza's story.* Boston: Beacon Press.

Bennett, J. 1981. *Oral history and delinquency.* Chicago: University of Chicago Press.

Bourgois, P. 2003. *In search of respect* (2nd ed.). Cambridge, UK: Cambridge University Press.

Brockmeier, J. 2004. What makes a story coherent? In A. U. Branco and J. Valsiner (Eds.), *Communication and metacommunication in human development* (pp. 285-306). Charlotte, NC: Information Age.

Bruner, J. 1990. *Acts of meaning.* Cambridge, MA: Harvard University Press.

Chesney-Lind, M., and L. Pasko. 2004. *The female offender: Girls, women, and crime* (2nd ed.). Thousand Oaks, CA: Sage.

Duneier, M. 1999. *Sidewalk.* New York: Farrar, Straus and Giroux.

Fox, K. J. 1999. Changing violent minds: Discursive correction and resistance in the cognitive treatment of violent offenders in prison. *Social Problems* 46: 88-103.

Gergen, M. 1992. Life stories: Pieces of a dream. In G. C. Rosenwald and R. L. Ochberg (Eds.), *Storied lives: The cultural politics of self-understanding* (pp. 127-144). New Haven, CT: Yale University Press.

Gergen, K. J., and M. M. Gergen. 1988. Narrative and the self as relationship. In L. Berkowitz (Ed.), *Advances in experimental social psychology* (Vol. 21, pp. 17-56). San Diego, CA: Academic Press.

Glaser, B. G., and A. L. Strauss. 1967. *The discovery of grounded theory: Strategies for qualitative research.* Hawthorne, NY: Aldine de Gruyter.

Hearn, J. 1998. *The violences of men: How men talk about and how agencies respond to men's violence to women.* London: Sage.

Holstein, J. A., and J. F. Gubrium. 2000. *The self we live by: Narrative identity in a postmodern world.* New York: Oxford University Press.

Katz, J. 1988. *Seductions of crime: Moral and sensual attractions in doing evil.* New York: Basic Books.

Labov, W., and J. Waletzky. 1967. Narrative analysis: Oral versions of personal experience. In J. Helms (Ed.), *Essays on the verbal and visual arts* (pp. 12-44). Seattle, WA: University of Washington Press.

Lawthom, R., P. Clough, and M. Moore (Eds.). 2004. *Researching life stories: Method, theory and analyses in a biographical age.* London: RoutledgeFalmer.

Maruna, S. 2001. *Making good: How ex-convicts reform and rebuild their lives.* Washington, DC: American Psychological Association.

Maruna, S., and H. Copes. 2005. What have we learned from five decades of neutralization research? *Crime and Justice: A Review of Research* 32: 221-320.

Maynes, M. J., J. L. Pierce, and B. Laslett. 2008. *Telling stories: The use of personal
narratives in the social sciences and history.* Ithaca, NY: Cornell University Press.

Messerschmidt, J. W. 2000. *Nine lives: Adolescent masculinities, the body, and violence.*
Boulder, CO: Westview.

Miller, J. 2005. *The status of qualitative research in criminology* (Workshop on
Interdisciplinary Standards for Systematic Qualitative Research). Arlington, VA:
National Science Foundation.

Miller, J. 2008. *Getting played: African-American girls, urban inequality, and gendered
violence.* New York: NYU Press.

O'Connor, P. E. 2000. *Speaking of crime: Narratives of prisoners.* Lincoln, NE: University
of Nebraska Press.

Polanyi, L. 1985. *Telling the American story: A structural and cultural analysis of
conversational storytelling.* Norwood, NJ: Ablex.

Polkinghorne, D. E. 1988. *Narrative knowing and the human sciences.* Albany, NY: State
University of New York Press.

Presser, L. 2004. Violent offenders, moral selves: Constructing identities and accounts in
the research interview. *Social Problems* 51: 82-101.

Presser, L. 2005. Negotiating power and narrative in research: Implications for feminist
methodology. *Signs: Journal of Women in Culture and Society* 30: 2067-2090.

Presser, L. 2008. *Been a heavy life: Stories of violent men.* Urbana, IL: University of
Illinois Press.

Presser, L. 2009. The narratives of offenders. *Theoretical Criminology* 13: 177-200.

Reissman, C. K. 1993. *Narrative analysis.* Newbury Park, CA: Sage.

Ricoeur, P. 1984. *Time and narrative* (K. McLaughlin and D. Pellauer, Trans.). Chicago:
University of Chicago Press.

Sarbin, T. R. 1986. The narrative as a root metaphor for psychology. In T. R. Sarbin (Ed.),
Narrative psychology: The storied nature of human conduct (pp. 3-21). New York:
Praeger.

Scott, M. B., and S. M. Lyman. 1968. Accounts. *American Sociological Review* 33: 46-62.

Seidman, I. E. 1991. *Interviewing as qualitative research: A guide for researchers in
education and the social sciences.* New York: Teachers College Press.

Somers, M. R. 1994. The narrative constitution of identity: A relational and network
approach. *Theory and Society* 23: 605-649.

Stone, A. 1982. *Autobiographical occasions and original acts.* Philadelphia, PA: University
of Pennsylvania Press.

Sykes, G. M., and D. Matza. 1957. Techniques of neutralization: A theory of delinquency.
American Sociological Review 22: 664-670.

Toch, H. 1993. Good violence and bad violence: Self-presentations of aggressors through
accounts and war stories. In R. B. Felson and J. T. Tedeschi (Eds.), *Aggression and
violence: Social interactionist perspectives* (pp. 193-206). Washington, DC: American
Psychological Association.

White, H. 1980. The value of narrativity in the representation of reality. *Critical Inquiry*
7: 5-27.

White, H. 1987. The metaphysics of narrativity: Time and symbol in Ricoeur's philosophy
of history. In *The content of the form: Narrative discourse and historical representation* (pp. 169-184). Baltimore, MD: The Johns Hopkins University Press.

Wiersma, J. 1988. The press release: Symbolic communication in life history interviewing. *Journal of Personality* 56: 205-238.

Wright, R., S. Decker, A. K. Redfern, and D. L. Smith. 1992. A snowball's chance in hell:
Doing fieldwork with active residential burglars. *Journal of Research in Crime and
Delinquency* 29: 148-161.

What can "Lies" Tell Us about Life? Notes towards a Framework of Narrative Criminology

Sveinung Sandberg

In criminology even studies that involve extensive fieldworks rely a great deal on research participants own accounts. The main question raised in the paper is: how do we know if research participants are telling the truth, and does it matter? It argues that criminological ethnographers have been too preoccupied with a positivist notion of truth, and the related question of whether research participants are telling the truth. For narrative analyses, this is not really important. The paper will present interview data from offenders to illustrate the fruitfulness of a narrative approach in criminology. Whether true or false, the multitude of stories people tell reflect, and help us understand, the complex nature of values, identities, cultures, and communities. The emphasis will be on offenders' shifts between subcultural and more conventional narratives. The argument expands upon Presser's notion of narrative criminology. The result is a framework that further challenges positivism and individualism in contemporary criminology.

It was a bitterly cold winter's night at the street drug market. Not many people where around and I was tired and looking forward to a dry room and something hot to drink. I was together with a social worker and we had been walking around for hours. She was used to it, I was not. Suddenly we spotted the light of a fire under a bridge. The street drug dealers often sought sanctuary there in bad weather. They were burning planks found in the vicinity. Three young men stood around the fire, talking and keeping the fire going. I knew one of them— the others were new to me. I tried to convince them to do an interview with me, now or later. Ali, whom I was on speaking terms with, told me "I don't sell drugs anymore." I doubted it, but said nothing. They soon lost interest. Their attention was caught by a quarrel about how the fire should be tended. (From the author's fieldwork in Oslo; Sandberg and Pedersen 2009)

Doing research on offenders is not essentially different from doing any other kind of ethnographic research. The researcher has to address the same issues of getting access to the field, establishing rapport with research participants, learning and understanding hidden codes, and balancing the roles of insider and outsider to get interesting, theoretically relevant data. That being said, these issues are more difficult to reconcile when the subjects of study are engaged in illegal activity. The social distance between the researcher and the participants is often greater than in other kinds of social research, which has the potential to cause participants to be especially skeptical of the researcher's intentions and motivations. Thus, establishing a bond with participants becomes even harder and the codes of conduct even more hidden when studying deviant groups. This distance also fortifies the question all qualitative researchers at some point ask themselves: how do we know if research participants are telling the truth? For many researchers, eliciting the truth from participants is the hallmark of sound research. But not all share this stance on validating the accuracy of partici-pants' claims. In this paper I argue that discerning the "truth" is not always important. Whether true or false, the multitude of stories people tell reflect, and help us understand, the complex nature of values, identities, cultures, and communities. Thus, "truth" may not be the best measure of interesting and theoretically relevant data.

As early as in the 1950s, John P. Dean and William Foote Whyte argued that statements represent only the *perception* of research participants. We must recognize that such statements are "filtered and modified" by their "cognitive and emotional reactions" and reported through their "personal verbal usages" (Dean and Whyte 1958, p. 34). The implication is that researchers should not be as concerned with determining whether or not research participants are lying. Rather, they should seek to answer the question, "What does the informant's statements reveal about his feelings and perceptions and what inferences can be made from them about the actual environment or events he has experi-enced?" (Dean and Whyte 1958, p. 38). This is still an insight of which criminol-ogists need to be reminded.

In this paper I also challenge the ethnographic rationale that "having been there" is always better than "having heard someone talk about it," and discuss the widespread opposition between data quality and efficiency. I then present a discussion of narrative criminology (Presser 2008, 2009), discuss the concept of validity, and present insights from ethnomethodology and discourse analysis to illustrate the point. Interview data from my own research will be presented to show the fruitfulness of a narrative approach for studies of offenders. The examples include data from an ethnographic fieldwork with street drug dealers and in-depth interviews with drug smugglers in prison.[1] The emphasis will be on offenders' constant shifts between subcultural and more conventional narra-tives (see also Sandberg 2009a, 2009b). It is my hope that the issues raised here will be of interest to qualitative researchers in general, and, more importantly, to criminologists, regardless of their methodological orientation.

---

1. Because they all involve leaving the office, interacting with people, and seeing them in their social surroundings, they will be considered ethnographic.

Challenging the Ethnographic Rationale

There are many methodological challenges in ethnographic research, but knowing if research participants can be trusted is often described as one of the most important. The concern is particularly often raised in criminology since offenders apparently have many reasons to lie about their activity—the most obvious is that the truth may put their status as free citizens in jeopardy. Ethnographers usually recommend interacting with offenders in their "natural" social context and "getting to know them" as the best way to get valid data. Extensive ethnographic fieldworks and observation is thus often portrayed as the ideal methodological design.

According to the ethnographic rationale, the further away the researcher is from the actual places, settings and networks of people, the greater the reason to be skeptical about the information received. That is, when evaluating ethnographic research, "having been there" is thought better than "having heard someone talk about it."[2] The ethnographic rationale emphasizes that observations provide better quality data than interviews, and that interviews in a "natural" setting give better data than interviews in institutions. Many are also skeptical about the involvement of outsiders when recruiting participants, because these may influence participants. For example, they question the validity of data that come from participants recruited by correctional officers because they assume that inmates will disguise the truth to frame their actions in the best possible light. They argue that ethnographers who engage in extensive fieldwork and observation are better able to see through these deceptions and to provide the most trustworthy data and analysis. This is because doing so provides a stronger bond between the researcher and the participants due to more direct contact between the parties. For efficiency reasons, interviewing, getting help in recruiting, and doing interviews in institutions can be an option, but the ethnographic rationale considers this to be data of poorer quality.

The ethnographic rationale is the driving force behind most fieldwork studies in criminology—including my own (e.g., Sandberg and Pedersen 2008, 2009). However, while the opposition between data quality and efficiency is intuitive, it is also too simple. The differences between the varying approaches may not be as great as they seem. The underlying assumption about offenders can, for example, be questioned. For example, Jacobs (2000) argues convincingly that there is no reason to believe that offenders lie more than non-criminal participants (see also Wright and Decker 1994). Rather, the secrecy of the business turns the research interview into one of the few safe contexts where, for example, dealers can demonstrate their extensive and complex knowledge

---

2. Ethnographic research can be categorized in different ways. Categorizations often include the questions: (1) were extensive fieldwork or interviews the primary source of data; (2) has fieldwork been conducted, but secondary to interviews; (3) have research participants been recruited by the researcher or by others; and (4) have institutionalized populations been interviewed. Following the ethnographic rationale, methodological approaches can best be seen on a continuum from extensive fieldworks to interviews in institutions.

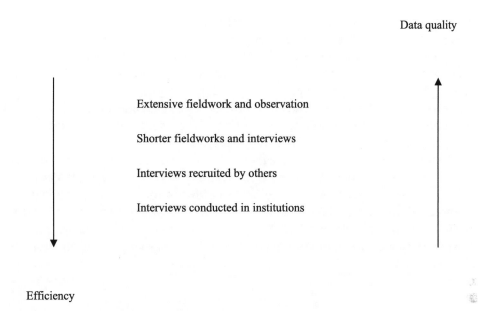

Figure 1 The ethnographic rationale.

to outsiders. Moreover, the risk of getting caught by police or accused of snitching is probably perceived as small, especially when talking about the past.

There are also those who argue against the assumption that fieldwork or interviews with active offenders inherently produce better data. Pearson and Hobbs (2004) argue that ethnographic fieldwork may not be particularly helpful for studying illegal drug markets. The rule of the drug game for most participants is that they do not ask too many questions. They often think that the less they know about the dealing of others, the safer all parties will be. Thus, ethnographic field observation might do little more than reproduce fragmented perceptions. In a similar way, Copes and Hochstetler (2010) argue that it is easier to meet motivated and interested participants in prison; here they are less likely to be under the influence of drugs, have more time to think about their past, and present more cohesive and meaningful interpretations of their lives. The prison context also makes it easier to recruit a more representative group of participants because researchers do not have to recruit through social networks.

In studies of crime, the ironic ethnographic contrast between "what people do" and "what people say they do" (Atkinson and Coffey 2003), and between quality and efficiency of data, is particularly problematic. Most ethnographic analyses of offenders are based on self-reported data. Observing criminal activity is difficult because it is infrequent, hidden, and people will be uncomfortable with doing it in front of researchers.[3] Illustratively, even in studies that

3. As Ward (2008) points out, "standardized codes of ethical conduct cannot easily be translated to ethnographic research on criminal activity." Observing crime in progress can be ethically problematic. While observing petty crime may be acceptable, observing large-scale drug dealing, violence, or sexual offences should probably not be the goal of any researcher.

involve extensive fieldworks, analysis of criminal activity is usually (if not always) based upon the offenders' own accords. Venkatesh (2006, 2008) spent many years with a Chicago gang, but observed violence just a few times and was privy to no large-scale drug dealing. Bourgois (1996) also relied mainly on self-reported stories when it came to violence, rape, large-scale drug dealing, and other more sensitive issues. Thus, even the best ethnographers must rely on the retrospective descriptions of crime. This rather obvious detail is often down-played in ethnographic debates in criminology.

When studying the use of language we also experience another paradox; one that is completely opposite to the ethnographic rationale. The more data you have, either from year-long ethnographic fieldworks or from large samples of qualitative interviews, the harder it will be to discover the nuances of narratives. If analyses are detailed, and emphasize semiotics or sociolinguistics, one interview, conversation, or fragment of text can be enough to make an interesting observation.

Narrative Criminology

Ethnography is absolutely crucial to understand both mainstream society and subcultures. The ethnographic rationale is also important, but it is often embedded in a problematic positivist notion of truth. Firstly, while self-reported data from extensive fieldwork may be taken from a more "natural" setting than formal interviews, and the extensive fieldwork provides important background information, they are still narrative data shaped by the research participants—and must be analyzed accordingly. Secondly, which the paper returns to later, even *events* are narrative in structure and the observer's capacities to recognize them are also narrative in form (Atkinson and Coffey 2003).

Presser's (2008, 2009) methodological and theoretical framework of *narrative criminology* is of great help when analyzing the self-reported data of offenders. Presser defines narrative as a "temporally ordered statement concerning events experienced by and/or actions of one or more protagonists" that "draws selectively on lived experience" (Presser 2009, pp. 178-179). She describes three ways in which "narrative" has been conceptualized in criminology: narrative as record, narrative as interpretation, and a constitutive view of narrative. The first treats narratives as indicators of criminal behavior, and Presser argues that this perspective still dominates criminology. Most criminologists utilize narratives as stores of data on criminal behavior and its causes. Methodologically, this has meant an emphasis on whether or not research participants are telling the truth and skepticism towards, or exaggerated belief in, offenders' narratives. Narrative as interpretation means studying how people see their world, but the social world still exists as an objectively given entity. The emphasis shifts from narrative as representing what really happens to narrative being socially constructed versions of what happened. This is the perspective of Dean and Whyte (1958), and numerous other ethnographic researchers.

Presser's own position is the constitutive view of narrative. This is a more radical constructivist approach on a social level that privileges language and stresses that narratives are made available by social order and culture (Presser 2009, p. 185). Her most important argument, however, is that studying narratives are still useful for realist criminology, because stories are *antecedents* to crime. In this way, the concept narrative "circumvents the realism to which other theories of criminal behavior are bound" (Presser 2009, p. 177). Narratives are important not because they are true records of what happened, but because they influence behavior in the future.

Presser's (2009) theoretical work marks a watershed for narrative analysis in studies of offenders. She introduces insights from other social sciences and humanities to criminology, where simple descriptions of neutralization techniques (Sykes and Matza 1957) and excuses and justifications (Scott and Lyman 1968) have dominated (Maruna and Copes 2005). Her empirical work (Presser 2008) includes a study of the oral self-narratives of violent men in prison. She finds reform narratives, stability narratives, and elastic narratives. The latter are the most widespread. One issue still needs to be raised. Presser analyzes self-narratives as unified, and sometimes they are. However, I think that narrative criminology also needs to include a less "rational" and individualistic understanding of the way language works.

Can Observations Validate Interviews?

The question about whether or not research participants are telling the truth is closely linked to concerns about the *validity* of data. When narratives are conceptualized as record, an account has been understood as valid "if it represents accurately those features of the phenomena, that it is intended to describe, explain or theorise" (Hammersley 1987, p. 69). This is also consistent with a positivist notion of truth, which narrative criminology challenges.

Validity is for example at the core when Jacobs states that he "attempted to minimize lying and distortion in every way possible" and monitored the truthfulness of responses by checking for and questioning inconsistent answers (Jacobs 2000, p. 18). In the same way as Wright and Decker (1994, 1997), he also recommends interviewing active criminals rather than incarcerated ones, because in prison criminals are claimed to rationalize their behavior. Other related validity concern about prison interviews are offenders' ulterior motives, impression management, and difficulties in establishing rapport (Copes and Hochstetler 2010). However, as Copes and Hochstetler point out, most of these concerns also apply for interviews outside the prison context. They argue that based on available data, we simply do not know whether interviews with active offenders produce more valid data than interviews with the incarcerated ones.

A similar idea about validity is expressed when Jacques and Wright (2008, p. 35) state that the "criminals who are closest in relational distance to the researcher, especially those who have done previous interviews, are the ones most likely to produce the greatest amount of valid data." Hoffer (2006) interpreted the rejection of money as a sign of emerging friendship and proposed that the increased trust gave him more valid information. Brannen (1988) however suggests that interviewees who know they will not meet the researcher again will be more sincere. The idea is that the information participants give is protected better when the researcher is an outsider, which would apply wherever they are interviewed. It may be that the positive effect of fieldwork and repeated interviews is as much about the quantity of information about a person and community, as it is about the quality. Again, it is difficult to generalize, and attempts at constructing "laws" for the interaction between researchers and research participants (see Jacques and Wright 2008) will probably fail.

A more fundamental concern about the validity of narrative as record is raised by the discussion of observation versus self-reported data. Many "hardcore" ethnographers argue that there is a large gap between behavior and attitude, or between what people say they do and what they actually do (Gobo 2008, p. 6). Some even define ethnography as "a methodology which privileges (the cognitive mode of) observation as its primary source of information" (Gobo 2008, p. 12). Interviews are thus considered to be secondary to observation, and less valid as data. While researchers doing extensive fieldwork use observation, interaction, and experience to validate narrative data, interview-studies often validate data from one interview by checking them with information from another. If responses in a sample start to get repeated, for example concerning prices of drugs or how transactions are organized, and there is no reason to suspect that the research participants have collaborated in order to respond in a certain way, they are regarded as valid.

Validity is a contested term, primarily because it represents a positivist notion of truth. Constructivists often challenge this positivist notion. They prefer the term *accountability* over validity because it demands only that the researcher publish the "empirical documentation on which his or her analysis has been based" (Gobo 2008, p. 264). In this way other researchers are able to make their own interpretations.

The intuitive difference between observation and interview is also questioned by many. Dean and Whyte (1958) emphasize that behavior cannot be used to validate attitudes, because behaviors are in flux as well. Presser (2009) argues that we need not know if a story is true in order to recognize its role in promoting criminal behavior. In Järvinen's (2000, p. 385) words, narratives act as boomerangs "thrown from the present into the past and returns with a force bearing it into the future." Narratives emerge from earlier experiences and social interaction and influences actions to come. It is therefore difficult to separate them from action or behavior.

Atkinson and Coffey (2003) more radically challenge the division between observation and interviews. Their argument is twofold. First, an event does not just happen, it is made to happen. It has a beginning, middle, and an end. Its structure and the observer's capacity to recognize it are essentially narrative in form. Moreover, in participant observation, events are narrated by observers, and hence rely on the same culturally shared categories of memory, account, narratives, and experience (Atkinson and Coffey 2003, p. 119–121). As everybody else, researchers do not see phenomena objectively during observation, but structure them according to the interpretative schemes and discursive repertoires they already possess.

The fieldwork-note at the beginning of this paper can serve as an example. The choice to categorize the young men as "drug dealers," instead of "poor" or "marginalized," is decisive. Both categories are true, but which one is used influences the way we understand the phenomenon. Moreover, a student once commented that the whole extract sounded more like a detective story than a scientific text. Ethnographic work particularly, and scientific articles and books more generally, borrow narratives and language from other literary genres, also when it is not a conscious choice by the author. Bakhtin (1981) famously called this *intertextuality*. Observations are thus embedded in narratives in the same way as interview-research, also when it is less obvious than in the fieldwork-note above.[4] Events have to be narrated and they are therefore embedded in our common pool of interpretative resources, described by Foucault as the "archive" (Foucault 1972) or "the order of discourse" (Foucault 1978).

A Framework between Ethnomethodology and Discourse Analysis

When developing a framework of narrative criminology, insights from ethnomethodology (see Garfinkel 1967), conversation analysis (see Silverman 1998), and narrative psychology (see Crossley 2000) must play an essential part. However, such a framework should also include insights from more post-structural discourse analysis (see Laclau and Mouffe 1985) and the postmodern trend in qualitative research. Themes in the latter literature include uncontroversial concerns about the blurring of the boundary between interviewers and interviewees, the introduction of new forms of communication and new topics of inquiry, more concern about whose stories are told, and an increasing concern with interviewees' own understanding (Fontana 2003). More radical themes from the postmodern trend include experimenting with forms used to report findings (Fontana 2003), radically changing the center of attention from the research participant to the researcher (Gubrium and Holstein 2003b), and an increasing politicization of research (Denzin and Lincoln 2005).[5]

---

4. The scientific article is also a genre that limits what can be said.
5. There are great differences within postmodern approaches to qualitative method, as illustrated between the different "brick" handbooks. Gubrium and Holstein's anthology (2001, see also 2003a) is, for example, less radical and political than Denzin and Lincoln's (2005).

Borrowing from this vast, and at times quite technical and complicated literature, has its disadvantages. To make it straightforward, and avoid narrative criminology turning into some kind of theory exercise, it really comes down to two points. First, narrative criminologists must *analyze talk as action.* Ethnomethodology emphasizes that speech acts must be analyzed as symbolic resources "used to perform specific tasks" (Potter and Wetherell 1987, p. 73). In his study of the use of inmate codes, Wieder's (1974) concern, for example, is not whether or not a statement is "true," but rather what is achieved by using it and what function it has in concrete interactions. This idea can be illustrated with the data from my own research. Ali, who was introduced in the fieldwork-note at the beginning of this paper, knew I was only interviewing drug dealers. When he said he did not "sell drugs anymore" it can be understood as a way to get rid of me. More than being true or false, his speech act performed a specific task: dismissing me. Moreover, like everybody else, research participants construct themselves as particular kinds of moral agents when they speak (Atkinson and Coffey 2003, p. 116). Ali's comment may also be interpreted as a form of self-presentation. Framing his earlier drug dealing as "out of character" (Presser 2008, p. 78) functions to present a morally decent self.

Second, and at the same time, as pointed out by discourse analytical studies inspired by Foucault (1972, 1978), narrative criminologists should recognize that *narratives are enacted and identities constructed through "shared narrative formats"* (Atkinson and Coffey 2003). Ali's "out of character" narrative was told by him and effective because it is a widespread cultural narrative. Meaning is constructed locally, from minute to minute, but always in a way that reflects "discursive environments" and "families of language games" (Gubrium and Holstein 2003c). It can thus be argued that narratives used in an interview, or elsewhere, are taken from, and illustrative of, the social context. Research participants cannot choose from an infinite pool of language and meaning. Instead they rely on ways of self-presenting and thinking that they have learned and used elsewhere. In this way, no matter what kind of stories are told, or whether they are true or false, they tell us something important about values, identities, cultures, and communities.

Doing Narrative Criminology

Narrative criminology is situated in the classical opposition between agency (what is the teller trying to accomplish?) and structure (which narratives are available?). The different ways of doing narrative criminology can be illustrated with extracts from interviews with offenders. Let us take a closer look at three examples: Thomas, Moa, and Daniel.[6]

---

6. The interviews with Thomas, Moa, and Daniel were done in Norwegian and tape-recorded. They were translated by the author.

Thomas: Three Conflicting Stories

I met Thomas while I was engaged in an on-going project interviewing drug smugglers and large-scale drug dealers in prison. Throughout the interview, he kept returning to an episode where he had retaliated violently against a friend who had stolen from him. He had reflected a lot around this event, and it was an important part of his self-narrative. Towards the end of the interview, Thomas presented three conflicting stories about the incident within three minutes. The following was the first of the three:

> Thomas: It went too far. I should've stopped beating him earlier. But I ended up ... [describes the grave violence in detail]. That's just completely unnecessary. He's down, so that's just completely unnecessary.

Thomas' self-criticism demonstrates that he is aware of a "code of honor" which says that fighting can be acceptable, but it ends when one of the fighters is down. In this way he justifies the fight itself, but not the severe violence he administered. The quote could have been used to argue that there is an "honor culture" among violent offenders, but that practice does not always follow ideology. We could also emphasize how Thomas takes responsibility for his actions by self-criticism, and yet how he still manages to argue that there was some fairness and integrity involved. In this way he presents a "morally decent self" (Presser 2004); an important part of this presentation of self is taking responsibility for one's own actions (Sandberg 2009b).

Only a minute later however, literally speaking, he presented a different version of the event. In his words, "If I hadn't been wasted on GHB that night, I would never have gone to his place. So that wasn't a very rational moment. From there on it all went wrong." Now Thomas claims that the main problem with his actions began the moment he decided to approach his friend. He also rejects responsibility for everything that happened that night by blaming it on the use of drugs. This version is the one that is closest to views about violence portrayed by conventional others (i.e., fights are wrong and drugs are destructive). The naïve methodological criticism of such statements is that they are merely attempts to justify or excuse behavior when talking to representatives of the prison or mainstream society. Such accounts should, therefore, be regarded as untrue. A more sophisticated interpretation would see it as a neutralizing technique (i.e., denial of responsibility) (Sykes and Matza 1957) or form aligning action (Stokes and Hewitt 1976) where Thomas frames his actions in a way to make it easier for him to commit the violence, or at least justify it later. It is a "not my fault" narrative (Green, South, and Smith, 2006), where the drugs and not him are framed as responsible for the incident. Interpreted in this manner, the truth of whether drugs led to his decision or not is irrelevant. What matters is that Thomas frames his story in this manner.

The emphasis upon agency, or what the teller is trying to accomplish, is common in narrative analysis inspired by symbolic interactionism, ethnomethodology, and narrative psychology. Such a "rational" approach to the interview with Thomas, however, is not only challenged by the fact that he already has presented two different accounts, but further challenged when he less than a minute later presents yet another version of the episode.

> Thomas: Well, that's the way it goes right. I didn't say this in court, but I would have done the same thing again. Only this time, instead of treating him like a friend, and try to talk to him first, I would have beaten him so bad that he wouldn't be able to go to the police, right. It would have been worth it. (...) [getting increasingly aggressive, both in body language and verbally, listing reasons to kill this person]
>
> Sveinung: To make a point?
>
> Thomas: Yes, yes
>   [Ca. four seconds break]
>
> Sveinung: Well, the smartest thing would probably have been just to leave it?
>
> Thomas: Of course [both laugh]. Of course! Hell. That's what I had planned to do as well.

The obvious methodological observation in the quote above is that interview data are co-created and that the interviewer influences which stories are told.[7] The less obvious is that Thomas is presenting a repertoire of narratives, which all says a great deal about him and his social context. During a short period, Thomas changes between three rather contrary understandings of the same episode. In the first one he thinks he was right to give his friend a beating, but that it became too severe. In the next he blames the drugs and describes the whole incident as irrational and not what he intended. In the third he states that he would do it again, but this time even more brutally. The final version is the one most dedicated to what has previously been conceptualized as "street masculinity" (Mullins 2006), "the code of the street" (Anderson 1999), or "street capital" (Sandberg and Pedersen 2009). Here, Thomas even takes it further and explicitly "neutralizes being good" (Topalli 2005).

We can understand each of these narratives by emphasizing what is achieved by using it, and what function it has in concrete interactions (Wieder 1974). The first one presents a morally decent self, the second denies responsibility, and the third boosts an image as "bad." To understand the sum of them however, we need to add a less "rational" and voluntaristic understanding of the way language works. If Thomas was any kind of rational actor he would choose one narrative and stick to it.

---

7. From years of interviewing violent offenders I am used to this kind of talk, but this time I became uncomfortable. Was I encouraging a story about the rationale in killing a guy? And more importantly, was he talking about the past or the future? As a result, after long a period of silence, I confronted him with a different interpretation of what would be the "smart thing" to do. This was a very tense moment, and I was not sure what to expect. He could have seen this as an attempt by me to correct him and gotten angry. He was already quite aggressive. Fortunately, he only laughed and returned to the first narrative.

When Foucault (1970) announced the often misunderstood "death of man," he was trying to capture the way narratives are not only *spoken by* individuals but also *spoken through* them. This is the more radical stand of seeing narratives as the unit of analysis, and not individuals. Thomas' talk, for example, is not so much rational stories with an attempt to accomplish something (conscious or not), as it is a display of the set of narratives his social context offers him to understand his present situation. Even though Thomas' narratives differ, none of them are necessarily "lies" or deception.

Some ethnographers may argue that behavior more accurately measures commitment to subculture. Thomas retaliated violently, which means that he must have been committed to "the code of the street" (Anderson 1999), and afraid of losing face. What he has to say about it afterwards does not matter. But Thomas' behavior supports both claims. First he waited for months before retaliating, which supports the second narrative, but in the end he finally ended up doing it, which indicates a strong commitment to subcultural values. Dean and Whyte (1958) argue that behavior, opinions, and values are in flux and that the conflict among them may be the most important information obtained. Thomas' devotion to a criminal subculture is obviously in fluctuation. The next two examples further elaborate on the importance of such an observation for narrative criminology.

Moa: Between Conventional Culture and Subculture

Moa was one of the drug dealers I met during fieldwork at a street drug market. We were in a pub, when I asked him:

> Sveinung: You said before, you got away with it [crime] most of the time. What exactly did you get away with?
>
> Moa: Back then, it was fruit machines [slot machines]. We're talking millions. There could be as much as 20-30,000 kroner in a machine. We did a couple of machines every day. While the shops were open. We broke in from behind. Cleaned them out for every penny. And fed in banknotes, took them out again. Then we raised our credit limit to 10,000 and sat and played till we dropped. It was petty crime alright. And so easy! The penalties were pitiful. Still are. Theft, you don't get punished for it. It's like rape, grown-up men raping young girls, no punishment at all. That's really bad. It's sick! They get off so fucking lightly. That's the system of justice in Norway for you, plain as day. If you want to be a criminal, and you know the rules and what to expect, you can earn a million before you're caught. They'll lock you up for a year or two, and you're sitting there with a million stashed away some place. All my older friends have done it.

Without recording the interview, I would probably have written down the kinds of crime Moa had committed, and how he committed them. The parts on punishment and rape could easily have been considered as chaotic nonsense that was difficult to understand and thus left out. After all, in real-time, it is all over in 15 seconds. In retrospect, however, what is most interesting about this interview is not the details of the crimes Moa committed, but the way he talks about them.

When Moa states that he has made millions of kroner, it is likely an exaggeration. We do not know and maybe we do not need to know. What is interesting is that by telling the story in this way, Moa manages to link his petty theft with the activity of some of the big guys in Oslo's criminal underworld. The emphasis on knowing people with millions "stashed away" surely has this effect. With this narrative Moa becomes an important, experienced, smart, and fascinating person, and emphasizing his friendship with some of the people higher up in the hierarchies makes the story convincing. His "older friends" are well-known Oslo gang leaders, which he in other parts of the interview mentions by name. These kinds of stories are typical for offenders involved in a violent street culture. They are typically embedded in the *gangster discourse* of a violent street culture (Sandberg 2009a, 2009b). Gangster discourse includes a series of personal narratives emphasizing how hard, smart, and sexually alluring the speakers are. Exaggerations are common, and criminal activity is bragged about.

Street culture is not the young men's only cultural influence however, and in the middle of the flow of gangster discourse Moa merges a highly conventional story about how the penalties for crime are too low, especially for sexual offences. This sudden change can be interpreted as an attempt to justify criminal activity towards mainstream society. Moa justifies it both by stating that he *knows* that penalties should be higher and by comparison: at least robbing a fruit machine is not as bad as grown men raping young girls. This is what Cromwell and Thurman (2003) describe as "justification by comparison" (see also Presser 2008, p. 93). Moa is acknowledging some criminal participation, but distances himself from "real" criminals and sick people like rapists. This distancing himself from others is similar to the way, for example, hustlers try to distance themselves from crackheads, who are considered weak, dirty, and unworthy of respect (Copes, Hochstetler, and Williams 2008).

Many of the drug dealers we interviewed tended to brag about their criminal activity. At the same time however, literally speaking, they felt obliged to justify or excuse these same crimes. Moa manages to merge these different narratives more elegantly than Thomas, but even in his story the narratives represent quite different rationales. Both Hochstetler, Copes, and Williams (2010) and Presser (2008) describe complex identity constructions among violent men similar to the one Moa is presenting. Presser described it as "elastic" narratives. Many did, for example, resist being labeled as authentically violent and told narratives that made them both potentially violent and morally decent. This should not come as a surprise. According to Goffman (1963), stigmatized people will more than others participate in such "two-headed roleplaying." They feel excluded from mainstream society, but still seek recognition from it.

Daniel: Two-Headed Role-Playing

An interview with Daniel, another drug dealer, illustrates similar "artful" (Garfinkel 1967) combinations of conventional and subcultural narratives. We were discussing drug use when I mentioned chasing the optimal high:

> Sveinung: To chase the optimal high, is that common?
>
> Daniel: [...] Time just floats. That's the same about everything, everything you see and do, you come to a certain "supreme" [in English] superiority, see? If you manage to keep it there. You don't manage to keep it there. I understand your concept, I know what you are trying to get at. It's like a spiritual experience. Like the Indians, they used hashish to come to, to get to ....
>
> Sveinung: Another place?
>
> Daniel: Another place. Yes, generally. When you do amphetamines for many days, so many weeks, then it's not the same anymore. Cause amphetamines is chemical, so it's not the same. [...]
>
> Interviewer: How are the highs different?
>
> Daniel: It depends on the person. Depends upon how your body can handle it. A guy can smoke hashish for 10 years and never experience shit. He can take amphetamines once and become so high that he flies. It's tricky to answer that. Everybody experience it differently. Except for ecstasy [MDMA], then you fly. You can be so happy that you say "I love you" to anyone. Everything is good, see. You live in a world of dreams. As long as it lasts. The high usually doesn't last more than 12 hours. Those that didn't land ended up at Gaustad [a well-known mental hospital]. Maybe they only tried it once.

Notice how Daniel emphasizes the difference between cannabis and "chemical" drugs, a widespread way to justify cannabis. The paradox is that he himself uses more cocaine than cannabis, but this is probably harder to justify, so he does not try. He also introduces a more implicit narrative about "Indians" and their use of drugs. Evoking Native Americans brings up associations to a celebrated indigenous group and similarly fortifies the "natural" status of cannabis without even completing the story.

Another interesting aspect about the quote is to see the way the frame story is a rather conventional one, where it only takes one use of drugs for some to end up in mental hospital. Later, he even speculates about the percentage of people getting into trouble due to the use of drugs. Such a statement can be interpreted in two ways. It can be seen as a way of pointing out that these types of consequences of drugs are random and not necessarily signs of weakness on the part of users.[8] Daniel thus protects his identity from any negative consequences from the use of drugs. This understanding emphasizes his agency (what is he trying to accomplish?). At the same time we could also present a more structural understanding (which narratives are at his disposal?). The frame story is the main narrative about drug use both in drug rehabilitation centers, in

---

8. Thanks to Heith Copes for pointing this out.

media, and in society as a whole. His use of it could indicate the power of mainstream society and dominant discourses. Even though Daniel uses a lot of drugs, he cannot avoid framing it in an overall negative narrative.

The interview extract demonstrates that Daniel has two narratives at his disposal, one subcultural (illegal drugs gives great experiences, makes you stand out from conventional society, and can be managed by some) and another more conventional (it is dangerous and will go wrong in the end). He is not sure which story to stick to. The latter may be the frame story because he is speaking to a person he sees to be a representative of the welfare state apparatus, because he tries to communicate something about his identity, or because the "order of discourse" (Foucault 1978) does not allow him to say anything else. All of these interpretations make sense, and the one should not exclude the other. It illustrates how narrative criminology is situated in an on-going tension between the active use of language (agency) and the language available (structure).

Concluding Remarks

Flexibility and being able to change research strategy is one of the main advantages of qualitative research. In narrative criminology, it is therefore more difficult than in other types of research to suggest "best practices." Based on the discussion above, some advice can still be offered. The choice of methodological approach should depend upon practical concerns and interests of the researchers: if the primary interest is facts (e.g., of certain types of crimes, prices of drugs, etc.), a positivist notion of truth and a traditional understanding of validity may not be problematic. One still has to remember that events and facts have to be narrated, and that narratives are constitutive of social life. If the researcher's primary interest is in cultures and value-systems, however, questioning the truthfulness of research participants may be unnecessary.

Like social science more generally, criminology often uses self-reported data. This has often come with a concern about whether or not research participants are lying, and been followed by speculative and common-sense questioning of the accuracy of statements. This is often described as "methodological criticism." For example, "you met him in a prison, that means he must be lying in order to get his sentence reduced" or "you met her in rehab, that means she must have taken you for one of the staff there" or "you talked to him on the street, he must have been showing off in front of his friends." But who tells stories independent of whom they are talking to and environmental context? The narratives we tell differ, but this does not make them less interesting or valuable as sources of data. At the same time the stories people tell will always reflect a rather limited repertoire of narratives.

Interviews are an effective way to reveal offenders' repertoire of narratives because they, as illustrated above, often trigger a set of otherwise context-specific stories. Some positivist researchers promote the use of standardized interview guides (e.g., life history calendars) even when conducting ethnographic interviews (Freedman, Thornton, Camburh, Alwin, and Young-DeMarco 1988). The objective is to minimize variation. This may be a fundamental mistake when studying cultures and value-systems. Instead of standardizing, we should do our best to get the multitude of stories present in a social and cultural context. Instead of always searching for consistency and rationality in the stories people tell, we should, sometimes, explore fragmentation and flux in language use. Thus, the interviewer should try to record the interviews (to reduce loss of data), probe from different angles, follow what seems interesting, and most importantly, let the research participant speak as freely as possible. The best way to capture research participants' repertoires of narratives is to let them be carried away by their own stories.

Moreover, why must we necessarily know whether or not a story is true for it to be worth studying? Even obvious lies can be interesting, and the natural inclination to minimize lying may not always be the best approach. Research participants do not even always know the truth themselves, which makes a positivist notion of truth, and the traditional idea of validity and of narrative as record suspect. In the interviews with Thomas, Moa, and Daniel, it would have added little to the analysis presented above. However, one could still ask how important these changes between narratives are. What can criminological theory learn from them?

The complex discursive work where Thomas, Moa, and Daniel balance different interpretative frameworks reveals some of the complexity of social life, and challenges the homogeneity of culture and the consistency of identity assumed by much social scientific theory. More specifically, it challenges the ideas of isolated deviant subcultures described by both the Chicago- and the Birmingham-school (for an overview, see Plummer 1997; Turner 1990) and common-sense categorizations of people into, for example, "street" or "decent" (Anderson 1999). It also challenges Presser's emphasis on the *one* "unified life story" (Presser 2008). Many of Presser's narratives and the interview extracts presented above indicate a set of fundamentally different narratives. In order to *substantially* challenge the inherent individualism and rational actor model in criminology, it is probably better to describe such changes as interdiscursivity or as indicative of a repertoire of narratives (Sandberg 2009a). These narratives are sometimes in conflict, other times creatively combined, but always taken from the social context.

Instead of always searching for "the truth" one should appreciate the multitude of stories present in a social context, whether these are the product of years of fieldwork, a few meetings on the street, or interviews arranged by others or in prisons. Not only offenders, but everybody tells a multitude of stories. Instead of damning our data, these complex narratives teach us a great deal about people, culture, and society. By seeking answers to what narrative repertoire is available, why particular people emphasize particular stories, and how they go about doing this, we shed light on both them and their social context. The most common question in ethnographic research (do research participants lie?) can thus be turned on its head with a more important one: what can "lies" tell us about life?

Acknowledgments

Thanks to Heith Copes for encouragement, edits, and comments on several versions of this paper. Also thanks to anonymous referees from JCJE.

References

Anderson, E. 1999. *Code of the street: Decency, violence, and the moral life of the inner city*. New York: W.W. Norton.

Atkinson, P., and A. Coffey. 2003. Revisiting the relationship between participant observation and interviewing. In J. F. Gubrium and J. A. Holstein (Eds.), *Postmodern interviewing* (pp. 109–122). London: Sage.

Bakhtin, M. 1981. *The dialogic imagination*. Austin, TX: University of Texas Press.

Bourgois, P. 1996. *In search of respect: Selling crack in El Barrio*. Cambridge: Cambridge University Press.

Brannen, J. 1988. The study of sensitive topics. *Sociological Review* 36: 552-563.

Copes, H., and A. Hochstetler. 2010. Interviewing the incarcerated: Pitfalls and promises. In W. Bernasco (Ed.), *Offenders on offending: Learning about crime from criminals* (pp. 49-67). Cullompton, UK: Willan.

Copes, H., A. Hochstetler, and J. P. Williams. 2008. "We weren't like no regular dope fiends:" Negotiating hustler and crackhead identities. *Social Problems* 55: 254-270.

Cromwell, P., and Q. Thurman. 2003. The devil made me do it: Use of neutralization by shoplifters. *Deviant Behavior* 24: 535-550.

Crossley, M. L. 2000. *Introducing narrative psychology: Self, trauma, and the construction of meaning*. Buckingham: Open University Press.

Dean, J. P., and W. F. Whyte. 1958. How do you know if the informant is telling the truth? *Human Organization* 17: 34-38.

Denzin, N. K., and Y. S. Lincoln (Eds.). 2005. *The Sage handbook of qualitative research*. London: Sage.

Fontana, A. 2003. Postmodern trends in interviewing. In J. F. Gubrium and J. A. Holstein (Eds.), *Postmodern interviewing* (pp. 51-66). London: Sage.

Foucault, M. 1970. *The order of things*. London/New York: Tavistock/Pantheon Books.

Foucault, M. 1972. *The archaeology of knowledge and the discourse on language*. New York: Pantheon Books.

Foucault, M. 1978. *The history of sexuality* (Vol. 1). New York: Pantheon Books.

Freedman, D., A. Thornton, D. Camburh, D. Alwin, and L. Young-DeMarco. 1988. The life history calendar: A technique for collecting retrospective data. *Sociological Methodology* 18: 37-68.

Garfinkel, H. 1967. *Studies in ethnomethodology*. Englewood Cliffs, NJ: Prentice-Hall.

Gobo, G. 2008. *Doing ethnography*. London: Sage.

Goffman, E. 1963. *Stigma*. Englewood Cliffs, NJ: Prentice-Hall.

Green, G., N. South, and R. Smith. 2006. They say that you are a danger but you are not: Representations and construction of the moral self in narrative of dangerous individuals. *Deviant Behavior* 27: 299-328.

Gubrium, J. F., and J. A. Holstein (Eds.). 2001. *Handbook of interview research*. London: Sage.

Gubrium, J. F., and J. A. Holstein (Eds.). 2003a. *Postmodern interviewing*. London: Sage.

Gubrium, J. F., and J. A. Holstein. 2003b. Postmodern sensibilities. In J. F. Gubrium and J. A. Holstein (Eds.), *Postmodern interviewing* (pp. 3-20). London: Sage.

Gubrium, J. F., and J. A. Holstein. 2003c. In J. F. Gubrium and J. A. Holstein (Eds.), *Postmodern interviewing* (pp. 21-50). London: Sage.

Hammersley, M. 1987. Some notes on the terms "validity" and "reliability." *British Educational Research Journal* 13: 73-81.

Hochstetler, A., H. Copes, and P. Williams. 2010. "That's not who I am:" How offenders commit violent acts and reject authentically violent selves. *Justice Quarterly* 27 (4): 492-516.

Hoffer, L. D. 2006. *Junkie business: The evolution and operation of a heroin dealing network*. Belmont: Thompson Wadsworth.

Jacobs, B. 2000. *Robbing drug dealers: Violence beyond the law*. New York: Aldine de Gruyter.

Jacques, S., and R. Wright. 2008. Intimacy with outlaws: The role of relational distance in recruiting, paying, and interviewing underworld research participants. *Journal of Research in Crime and Delinquency* 45: 22-38.

Järvinen, M. 2000. The biographical illusion: Constructing meaning in qualitative interviews. *Qualitative Inquiry* 6: 370-391.

Laclau, E., and C. Mouffe. 1985. *Hegemony and socialist strategy: Towards a radical democratic politics*. London: Verso.

Maruna, S., and H. Copes. 2005. What have we learned from five decades of neutralization research. *Crime and Justice: A Review of Research* 32: 221-320.

Mullins, C. W. 2006. *Holding your square: Masculinities, streetlife and violence*. Devon: Willan.

Pearson, G., and D. Hobbs. 2004. "E" is for enterprise: Middle level drug markets in ecstasy and stimulants. *Addiction Research and Theory* 12: 565-576.

Plummer, K. 1997. *The Chicago school* (Vols. 1-4). London: Routledge.

Potter, J., and M. Wetherell. 1987. *Discourse and social psychology: Beyond attitudes and behaviour*. Los Angeles, CA: Sage.

Presser, L. 2004. Violent offenders, moral selves: Constructing identities and accounts in the research interview. *Social Problems* 51: 82-101.

Presser, L. 2008. *Been a heavy life: Stories of violent men*. Urbana, IL: University of Illinois Press.

Presser, L. 2009. The narratives of offenders. *Theoretical Criminology* 13: 177-200.

Sandberg, S. 2009a. Gangster, victim, or both? Street drug dealers' interdiscursive construction of sameness and difference in self-presentations. *British Journal of Sociology* 60: 523-542.

Sandberg, S. 2009b. A narrative search for respect. *Deviant Behavior* 30: 487-510.

Sandberg, S., and W. Pedersen. 2008. "A magnet for curious adolescents:" The perceived dangers of an open drug scene. *International Journal of Drug Policy* 19: 459-466.

Sandberg, S., and W. Pedersen. 2009. *Street capital: Black cannabis dealers in a white welfare state*. Bristol: Policy Press.

Scott, M. B., and S. M. Lyman. 1968. Accounts. *American Sociological Review* 33: 46-62.

Silverman, D. 1998. *Harvey Sacks: Social science and conversation analysis*. Oxford: Oxford University Press.

Stokes, R., and J. P. Hewitt. 1976. Aligning actions. *American Sociological Review* 41: 838-849.

Sykes, G., and D. Matza. 1957. Techniques of neutralization: A theory of delinquency. *American Sociological Review* 22: 664-670.

Topalli, V. 2005. When being good is bad: An expansion of neutralization theory. *Criminology* 43: 797-836.

Turner, G. 1990. *British cultural studies: An introduction*. London: Unwin-Hyman.

Venkatesh, S. 2006. *Off the books: The underground economy of the urban poor.* Cambridge, MA: Harvard University Press.

Venkatesh, S. 2008. *Gang leader for a day: A rogue sociologist takes to the streets.* New York: Penguin.

Ward, J. 2008. Researching drug sellers: An 'experimental' account from 'the field'. *Sociological Research Online* 13(1): 14.

Wieder, D. L. 1974. *Language and social reality: The case of telling the convict code.* Lanham, MD: University Press of America.

Wright, R. T., and S. H. Decker. 1994. *Burglars on the job.* Boston, MA: Northeastern University Press.

Wright, R. T., and S. H. Decker. 1997. *Armed robbers in action.* Boston, MA: Northeastern University Press.

Exploring Strategies for Qualitative Criminological and Criminal Justice Inquiry Using On-Line Data

Thomas J. Holt

Qualitative research methods in criminology have been supplanted in recent years by advanced statistical inquiries into various quantitative data sources. There is, however, an emerging body of qualitative analyses using data generated from various sources available on-line. As the Internet and computer-mediated communications (CMCs), such as email and instant messaging, are rapidly adopted by all manner of criminals and deviants, it is critical that qualitative criminologists recognize how this data may be examined in order to understand social phenomena. This article considers the utility of the Internet, websites, and various forms of CMCs as a source for traditional qualitative criminology inquiry. Each type is addressed in detail, along with the unique methodological and ethical concerns present in Internet-based explorations.

Empirical assessments of deviance and crime lie at the core of the criminological discipline. In recent years, there has been increasing significance placed on quantitative inquiry into both victims and offenders using advanced statistical techniques (Hagan and McCarthy 1997; Miller 2005). Traditional qualitative research on street crime and offending has become less prominent in the field despite its central role in many early explorations of crime and deviance in urban environments (Adler and Adler 1987; Buckler 2008; Kleck, Tark, and Bellows 2006; Miller 2005; Tewksbury, Dabney, and Copes 2010; Tewksbury, DeMichele, and Miller 2005). There has, however, been a revival of qualitative inquiry in criminology in the last two decades. A number of studies within this resurgence have utilized the development and adoption of the Internet and computer-mediated communications (CMCs) since the mid-1980s as a means to understand human behavior (see Garcia, Standlee, Bechkoff, and Cui 2009; Hine 2005; Jewkes and Sharpe 2003; Meyer 1989).

The rapid growth and use of email, e-commerce, and virtual communities have had a significant impact on social life, both on- and off-line (see Baudrillard 1998; Burkhalter 1999; Ebo 1998; Garcia et al. 2009; Miller and Slater 2000;

Turkle 1995). A great deal of information is shared in public settings about individuals, communities, and groups through websites and social networking sites like Facebook and MySpace (Patchin and Hinduja 2007; Taylor, Fritsch, Liederbach, and Holt 2010). Forums and chat rooms that enable near-real time exchanges of information for communities centered around everything from dating and romance (see Jerin and Dolinsky 2001), politics (Ebo 1998), to health care and addiction support groups (Eysenbach and Till 2001).

The unprecedented social impact of these technologies has also caused a shift in the formation, persistence, and social organization of criminal communities and exchanges (DiMarco and DiMarco 2003; Holt 2009; Quinn and Forsyth 2005). Newsgroups, web forums, and similar sites allow individuals to exchange all sorts of information almost instantaneously (DiMarco and DiMarco 2003; Durkin 2007; Taylor et al. 2010). Deviant and criminal peers can communicate on-line across great distances, facilitating the global transmission of subcultural knowledge without the need for physical contact with other members of the subculture (see Holt 2007a; Taylor et al. 2010). Unique forms of offending have emerged as a direct consequence of computer technology, such as computer hacking and malicious software creation (see Holt 2007a; Holt, Soles, and Leslie 2008; Taylor 1999), while on-line communities have emerged to facilitate real world crimes including prostitution and pedophilia (see Blevins and Holt 2009; Holt and Blevins 2007; Holt, Blevins, and Kuhns 2008, 2009; Jenkins 2001; Sharpe and Earle 2003). As a consequence, criminologists have increasingly begun to adapt traditional research methods to examine these phenomena in virtual environments and through the use of CMCs (see Blevins and Holt 2009; Durkin and Bryant 1999; Jenkins 2001; Mann and Sutton 1998; Sharpe and Earle 2003; Taylor 1999).

While social science researchers have provided some benchmarks on the use of email and other forms of on-line data in qualitative inquiry (Cherny 1999; Garcia et al. 2009; Herzog, Dinoff, and Page 1997; Hessler et al. 2003; Hine 2005; Hookway 2008; Kendall 2004; Leung 2005; Silverman 2004; Walker 2000), there is a relatively limited knowledge base for how these sources may be prac-tically examined by criminologists. Thus, I consider the utility of the Internet, websites, and various other CMCs as sources of data for qualitative criminology and criminal justice inquiries. Each form will be considered in detail using examples from various studies, as well as the methodological issues evident in on-line data collection. In addition, I will present some of the unique ethical concerns present in Internet-based explorations.

Data Sources

Forums, Bulletin Boards, and Newsgroups

There are myriad data sources that may be mined for qualitative inquiry, each with their own strengths and weaknesses. One of the most common resources for Internet-based qualitative research are forums (see Blevins and Holt 2009;

Holt 2007a, 2009; Holt and Blevins 2007; Holt, Blevins et al. 2008; Holt et al. 2009; Malesky and Ennis 2004; Mann and Sutton 1998; Taylor 1999; Williams and Copes 2005), Bulletin Board Systems (BBS; Jenkins 2001; Landreth 1985; Meyer 1989), and newsgroups (Durkin and Bryant 1999; Gauthier and Forsyth 1999; Loper 2000; Wilson and Atkinson 2005). Generally speaking, these different forms of CMC enable individuals to discuss topics and interact with others in real time, or revisit them later for comment. An individual creates a post within a forum, asking a question or giving an opinion. Other people respond to the remarks with posts of their own that are connected together to create strings. Thus, strings are composed of posts that center on a specific topic under a forum's general heading.

Since posters respond to the ideas of others, the exchanges presented in the strings of a forum may "resemble a kind of marathon focused discussion group" (Mann and Sutton 1998, p. 210). Additionally, this data may be treated as naturally occurring conversation based on the nature of the discussion as ongoing and between multiple participants (Holt 2007a; Jenkins 2001). Thus, forum, BBS, and newsgroup discussions constitute a form of social interaction, providing information about the social world of forum users.

The value in this type of CMC data as a resource is that they exist in both open and closed formats. Open forums do not require registration to access posts and content, thus large amounts of data can be accessed with little difficulty or interaction with the group (Mann and Sutton 1998). Within on-line communities, individuals who engage in such a practice are often referred to as lurkers or leeches, as they do not contribute to the larger community but simply draw down information provided by others (see Cooper and Harrison 2001; Rutter and Smith 2005). Such data collection processes reduce the potential for researcher contamination or bias that may arise through partici-pant observation or other naturalistic research methods (Lofland and Lofland 1995). A number of studies have utilized data derived from open forums, including research on digital pirates (see Cooper and Harrison 2001; Holt and Copes 2010), hacker communities (Holt 2007a, 2009; Mann and Sutton 1998; Taylor 1999), identity thieves (Franklin, Paxson, Perrig, and Savage 2007; Holt and Lampke 2010; Honeynet Research Alliance 2003; Thomas and Martin 2006), malicious software creators (Chu, Holt, and Ahn 2010), pedophilia (Durkin and Bryant 1999; Holt, Blevins, and Burkert 2010; Jenkins 2001), and prostitution (Blevins and Holt 2009; Holt and Blevins 2007; Holt, Blevins et al. 2008; Holt et al. 2009).

By contrast, closed forums require registration and the creation of a user-name and password in order to access content (Jenkins 2001; Landreth 1985). Additionally, closed forums may require that a user post within the board in order to maintain their account and access certain posts. This raises several ethical dilemmas on the part of the researcher, including the development of a user identity and the need for deception on the part of the researcher (see Hine 2005; Rutter and Smith 2005). Any social scientist undertaking such a research project must carefully consider if they will reveal their identity as a researcher within a closed community or operate anonymously in order to conceal their activities (Rutter and Smith 2005).

There is value in both lurking and participating in any forum or interactive CMC as various ethnographic strategies can be employed. Covert observations can be undetected by the larger population of forum or BBS users. Such a method may be particularly useful in sites where there are significant populations of offenders or illegal behavior in order to reduce the likelihood of researcher contamination (see Holt 2007a; Loper 2000; Mann and Sutton 1998). The ethics of lurking are questioned by some researchers, as the population of users may feel spied on or unfairly treated as a consequence of data collection without recognition (see Bell 2001; Kendall 2004; Miller and Slater 2000; Sveningsson 2004).

Thus, some argue that researchers should actively engage in participant observation in forums and BBS to understand a phenomenon and encourage an understanding of group dynamics and norms (Bell 2001; Kendall 2004; Miller and Slater 2000; Sveningsson 2004). Engaging an on-line community enables researchers to ask users pointed questions and observe interactions between participants. Follow-up questions can be posted to probe a specific issue of interest to the researcher. A long-term ethnographic exploration of forum communities could also be conducted to understand the enculturation process and dynamics of on-line communities (see Miller and Slater 2000; Rutter and Smith 2005). Posting within a forum community can, however, introduce the potential for researcher contamination or bias (Silverman 2004). Actively engaging offenders in conversation may negatively affect the tenor of discussions and the dynamics between posters. Thus, there is a significant need to consider the way that a researcher will engage a forum or BBS community.

Regardless of the form of CMC selected these data sources provide almost instantaneous access to weeks or months of posts. Researchers can examine a phenomenon of interest over time using forum or BBS information without the need for actual long-term entrenchment within a community. For example, Cunningham and Kendall (2009) used posts from on-line prostitution review sites to analyze changes in sex work, including prices, activities, and demographic composition of providers, from 1999 to 2008. In order to conduct such a study in the real world, the researchers would have required a massive investment of time and resources. Thus, CMCs provide access to longitudinal data that enable the exploration of changes in group dynamics and behavior over time, while significantly reducing the costs of data collection (see Jenkins 2001; Loper 2000).

Forum user populations may also include a variety of individuals with different skill levels and knowledge of a subculture or certain form of deviance (see Blevins and Holt 2009; Holt 2007a; Jenkins 2001). For example, Holt (2007a) developed a data set of forum posts based on several criteria, including size, traffic, and public accessibility. Forums with both large and small user populations were identified to represent the range of forums currently operating on-line. Additionally, high traffic forums with a large number of existing posts were included, as frequent posts suggest high activity (Holt 2007a). This sort of sampling framework can help to examine social interactions within on-line environments.

A variety of research questions can be addressed using posts from forums and BBS, particularly explorations of deviant or criminal subcultures (see Blevins and Holt 2009; Chu et al. 2010; Cooper and Harrison 2001; Durkin and Bryant 1999; Holt 2007a; Holt and Lampke 2010; Holt et al. 2010; Mann and Sutton 1998; Taylor 1999). For example, the text-based exchanges in CMCs lend themselves to explorations of the argot, or specialized language of deviant communities, which help communicate the structure, norms, and values of a given subculture to its members and demonstrate membership and status within a community (see Blevins and Holt 2009; Holt 2009). In addition, studies have considered the development and demonstration of subcultural identity in on-line environments among straightedge groups (Copes and Williams 2007; Williams and Copes 2005; Wilson and Atkinson 2005), computer hackers (Holt 2007a, 2009; Taylor 1999), the customers of prostitutes (Blevins and Holt 2009), and pedophiles (see Durkin and Bryant 1999; Holt et al. 2010; Malesky and Ennis 2004). Thus, CMCs provide invaluable data to address a variety of criminological research questions to understand crime and deviance on- and off-line.

Email and Instant Messaging

Emails and instant messaging chat sessions have also become a source of data for some researchers as both a source of offending (see Wall 2004), and as a means of communicating with research participants (see Holt 2007a; Holt and Copes 2010; Jordan and Taylor 1998; Pruitt 2008; Taylor 1999). First, it is necessary to consider this form of CMC as a means of criminal activity. Email and instant messaging chats can be used to engage in fraud or entice individuals to be victimized (see Taylor et al. 2010; Wall 2004). Spam messages, or unsolicited bulk emails, involve multiple messages that offer illicit or counterfeit services and information (Wall 2004). Some estimates suggest that over half of all the email traffic directed toward commercial entities today constitutes spam and pose a significant nuisance for computer users (see Gartner Group 2003). A substantial number of individuals around the world receive and fall victim to various email scams (Taylor et al. 2010; Wall 2004). A small body of research has analyzed the content of these messages in order to understand the methods and practices of email fraudsters (see Edelson 2003; Holt and Graves 2007; King and Thomas 2009; Wall 2004). These studies suggest that the format of fraudulent emails are consistent across disparate senders and use various linguistic techniques to increase the likelihood of victim responses (see Edelson 2003; Holt and Graves 2007; King and Thomas 2009; Wall 2004). As email driven cybercrimes increase in frequency and severity, the opportunities for criminological inquiry through this form of CMC will expand (see Taylor et al. 2010).

The second way that email and instant messaging can be used by qualitative researchers is through direct communications with others for interviews or focus groups (see Kivits 2005; Selwyn and Robson 1998). There are various instant messaging systems, Internet Relay Chat, and webcam-based communication systems that allow researchers to engage in real-time synchronous discussions with multiple individuals across great distances (Dillman 2000; Garcia et al. 2009; Kivits 2005; Mann and Stewart 2002; Williams and Copes 2005). Alternatively, discussions can be held with individuals via email or forums through asynchronous communications. These tools are a massive aid to researchers, as certain forms of deviance may be more greatly distributed and require significant travel and investment in order to develop a representative sample of respondents (for a discussion, see Silverman 2004). For example, Taylor (1999) utilized email interviews with hackers living in the Netherlands as a means of understanding a computer hacker subculture. This had significant value for the researcher as he resides in the UK where laws related to hacking are particularly harsh. Thus, respondents living abroad were much more likely to answer questions posed in the course of an interview than those in the UK (Taylor 1999).

The use of email or instant messaging protocols, however, enables a researcher to identify and interview individuals in much the same way as traditional face-to-face encounters with some additional benefits (see Kivits 2005; Selwyn and Robson 1998). Interviews can be conducted at any time for the convenience of the respondent, thereby potentially increasing the response rate of any given sample size (see Copes and Williams 2007; Williams and Copes 2005). Email-based interviews allow respondents to take their time and formulate a response to certain questions that may otherwise be briefly addressed off the cuff in face-to-face interactions (see Dillman 2000; Kivits 2005). The comments made during an on-line interview may be more candid as individuals may be less concerned about maintaining a certain impression of self (see Riva 2002). For instance, Williams and Copes (2005) used IRC and instant messaging as a means to interview young members of a "straight edge" subculture, where youths do not use drugs or alcohol. The researchers found significant success as their sample population regularly used this technology and preferred to communicate in this fashion.

An important and distinct methodological advantage of using email or instant messaging protocols for interviews is that this technology provides an immediate and accurate transcript of the discussion between the participants (Mann and Stewart 2002). The exchanges and content in this form of CMC can be either copied and pasted into a word document, or saved via other means for later analysis. This is a considerable advantage over audio- or video-taped interviews that must be transcribed by researchers with some cost and investment of time. Additionally, this reduces the potential for errors that can develop during the transcription process, particularly with muffled or garbled speech by participants (Mann and Stewart 2002; Silverman 2004).

This process of interviewing does pose some unique methodological concerns for the researcher. Specifically, the non-verbal cues revealed in the course of an in-depth interview conducted in person, such as facial expressions or posture, are not evident in CMCs (Garcia et al. 2009; Kivits 2005; Silverman 2004). A respondent may be using sarcasm to express themselves, though this may go unnoticed by the interviewer. Additionally, respondents may grow tired of typing over the course of a long interview, and greatly reduce the length or thought given to an answer. As a consequence, a great deal of care must be taken when interpreting an individual's comments, and a researcher may have to ask for clarification in order to ensure they appropriately document what is being said (Garcia et al. 2009; Kivits 2005; Silverman 2004).

In addition, technological complications beyond the researchers' control may negatively impact the interview process. For example, a loss of Internet connectivity or a system crash on either the researcher or respondent computers may disrupt an interview completely (Hine 2005). Additionally, the transient nature of on-line chat and email may make it difficult to follow up with a respondent after an interview is complete (Dillman 2000; Kivits 2005; Selwyn and Robson 1998). Scheduling times to speak with an individual or remind them that you need further assistance can help to ensure a continuous line of open communication.

Finally, malicious respondents can attempt to attack the interviewer in the course of data collection if they feel they are being mistreated, or as a means to demonstrate their ability or skill. For instance, a respondent in the sample developed by Holt and Copes (2010) attempted to send malicious software to one of the researchers because they were dissatisfied with the questions asked during the interview. Thus, it is imperative that researchers who are not well versed with this sort of CMC should also consider spending time orienting to this environment so that they understand how to appropriately use the technology (see Garcia et al. 2009). Despite these issues, there is significant value in the use of email and other rapid communication methods for criminological inquiry.

Websites, Blogs, and Texts

A number of qualitative criminologists have utilized the content of websites for their research as these sites provide a wealth of information in various formats. Websites enable individuals to express their thoughts and beliefs through text, images, and video, and provide links to other groups and entities that share their interests (Hine 2005). As a consequence, a researcher need simply identify these websites and materials in order to analyze the documents contained therein. For example, websites can act as an advertising space, enabling individuals to sell products and services that may be less than legitimate (see Grov 2004; Lee-Gonyea, Castle, and Gonyea 2009; Sharpe and Earle 2003; Soothill and Sanders 2005; Tewskbury 2003, 2006; Thomas and Martin 2006). Lee-Gonyea et al. (2009) utilized a rigorous sampling framework to identify websites used by male escorts to advertise their services. The content of each website was examined and a content analysis performed to understand the ways that escorts used the Internet to share information about themselves, their services, and the process of solicitation on-line. A number of studies have examined bugchasing, where HIV negative individuals actively seek out sex with HIV positive partners for the purposes of becoming infected, using data from dating and personal ad websites (Gauthier and Forsyth 1999; Grov 2004; Tewksbury 2003, 2006). This research suggests that there are some differences in the ads of individuals actively pursuing HIV infection, and may vary from the larger population of users in these sites.

Web logs, or blogs, also provide an important, though underutilized form of qualitative data (Hookway 2008). Blogs typically consist of a series of user-created posts listed in reverse chronological order on a single page that can be updated and tracked over time. The contents of blogs are often personal, and may constitute a sort of diary that can be explored over time. Blog content is often openly accessible, though some require registration in order to access information.

Regardless, few criminologists have examined blog content as a means to understand crime and deviance. Holt, Soles, et al. (2008) are notable excep-tions, as they used a small sample of active blogs used by malicious software writers as a case study to understand their motives and activities. There is, however, a great deal of information that can be derived from blog content, making them "a valid addition to the qualitative researcher's toolkit" (Hookway 2008, p. 93). For example, examining multiple blog sites longitudinally could be used to facilitate social construction research. The ability of citizens, organiza-tions, and governmental agencies to post and maintain blogs could be useful in exploring the ways that criminal justice issues are framed and developed by various claimsmakers, from the use of tasers to racial profiling. Thus, blogs can prove to be "a valid addition to the qualitative researcher's toolkit" (Hookway 2008, p. 93).

Qualitative researchers can also mine websites for information that can be used to develop a sample of potential interviewees. For example, Pruitt (2008) collected the email addresses provided on a single website that acts as a national ad space for male escorts in order to assess the variation in response rates to different email solicitations among this population. Similarly, Cunning-ham and Kendall (2009) used the email addresses provided on multiple national advertising spaces to survey female escorts about their sexual activity and practices with clients. Taylor (1999) also solicited interviewees via web forums to examine the norms and values of the computer hacker subculture. Thus, there are a variety of ways that websites can be successfully used as a data source for the qualitative researcher.

Data Triangulation

In light of the data sources discussed, qualitative researchers may find it beneficial to develop multiple data sets to understand a phenomenon with greater depth. The use of data triangulation, or examining a phenomenon using multiple data sources, could assist in expanding a researcher's understanding of a social setting or behavior (see Denzin 1970; Silverman 2004). For instance, a series of threads from a forum may give some insights into a certain form of crime or deviance, though this data could be augmented by structured inter-views with individuals who actively participate in deviance or the related on-line community (see also Hine 2005; Holt 2007a). Thus, collecting data from various outlets enables the researcher to combine these sources to examine a social phenomenon from different perspectives (Denzin 1970; Silverman 2004).

In addition, data triangulation can be used to examine crime and deviance from different contexts to understand how events or actions are constructed and situated (Silverman 2004). Specifically, triangulation has particular utility for behaviors that have both on- and off-line components, such as criminal behavior that takes place in the real world driven in part by social relationships that emerge in forums or other CMCs. For instance, Adler and Adler (2007) utilized interviews conducted via email and face-to-face exchanges as well as data from on-line forums as a means to understand the behavior of self-injurers. Similarly, Holt (2007a) utilized forum data, on- and off-line interviews, and participant observations in order to understand how the computer hacker subculture is affected by virtual and real experiences. Developing data sources in virtual and real social environments allow researchers to consider how individual identity and action are structured as a result of experiences in each setting (Holt 2007a; Wilson and Atkinson 2005).

Using data collected from multiple on-line sources can also help to further explicate a research question, particularly for phenomena that are unusual or difficult to access. Durkin (2007) conducted a study of cyber-shrews, women who humiliate or degrade men on-line in exchange for money, using four years of data collected from websites, forums, and newsgroups. Additionally, Holt and Copes (2010) used forum data and interviews conducted via instant messaging protocols to consider the practices of persistent digital pirates. Through analyses of different resources, a researcher may be able to better situate social phenomena in a virtual environment (see Silverman 2004). Thus, there is significant empirical value for the qualitative criminologist to consider data triangulation when dealing with on-line data.

Methodological Concerns

In light of the variety of data available on-line, most type of qualitative analysis can be applied to Internet-based data. There are, however, several critical issues that are common across on-line data that must be considered from the point of data collection through analysis. One of the most significant method-ological concerns that on-line researchers must address is the representative nature of information presented over the Internet. Some forms of offending, such as computer hacking or credit card theft, immediately lend themselves to on-line environments since offenders can share information and solicit or engage in criminal activity through forums and other CMCs (see Chu et al. 2010; Holt 2007a; Holt and Lampke 2010; Thomas and Martin 2006). Other criminal groups, such as burglars and robbers, may not utilize the Internet as a means of planning and executing the offence. Thus, scientific inquiry into these behaviors via on-line data may prove extremely limited. Should a pocket of offenders be found in a message board or blog, the content must be taken with some degree of trepidation as it is most likely not a representation of the larger population of offenders. Additionally, researchers must consider how representative their data is of a given group of deviants or a certain behavior. For example, research may identify a sample of gang members using MySpace as a means to communicate with one another and broadcast threats to rival gangs (see King, Walpole, and Lamon 2007). Such an examination would be unique for its contribution to our larger understanding of gang activity, though it begs the question how these individuals differ from the larger pool of gang members generally.

Once a researcher recognizes that they can reasonably examine a form of deviance or crime through on-line data, they must begin to identify their data sources. To that end, it is important to understand how a sample of forums, blogs, or websites is initially identified on the World Wide Web. The most immediate way to find any content is through the use of a search engine, such as Google, Yahoo, or Bing. There are a variety of search engine options available, and the most practical recommendation is to carefully select the engine used at the outset of a project. Google is the number one search engine used, though the algorithm that determines placement in search results can be affected by various factors, referred to as search engine optimization. Essentially, this means that a website may artificially inflate its placement in search results through the repeated use of a term or phrase rather than because it is the primary outlet used by a community.

One way to validate the results of a search is through the use of carefully chosen search terms and triangulation through multiple search engines. For example, Lee-Gonyea et al. (2009) crafted a rigorous sampling framework to identify and examine websites used by male escorts. They used Google as a primary search engine, and cross-referenced the results against four other popular engines as a means of validation. The authors utilized multiple search strings using common phrases, including "escorts and male," "male escorts," "escorts male for women," and "escort agencies male" (Lee-Gonyea et al. 2009). These terms generated over two million hits in Google, and the sites included in their final sample appeared across multiple search engines. Researchers who employ similar strategies may find their search results improve and give an additional methodological weight to their research.

In addition, scholars engaging in international data collection may also consider using country specific search engines to generate results. For example, South Korean web users commonly prefer the use of Naver to Google when accessing the World Wide Web (Park, Lee, and Bae 2005). This also has some importance within deviant communities as research suggests Russian hackers utilize ICQ instant messenger to chat rather than other services (Chu et al.

2010; Holt 2007b). Culturally sensitive researchers must recognize this issue and use appropriate communication methods and tools in order to obtain more relevant results than by simply choosing Google. Such a practice may otherwise limit the results of any search.

An additional issue with search engine results is the potential for deviant and criminal groups to shield their websites from detection. Specifically, search engines capture information about the existence and last appearance of a website through the use of spider programs that span web pages for information (Steel 2006). Spider programs will not, however, be able to capture information about a web page if the author removes the robots.txt function (Steel 2006). Pages related to deviance and crime with this function turned off may be completely removed from search results. In order to combat this issue, researchers can use a sort of snowball sampling procedure based on search results and examinations of websites. Snowball samples are often used in qualitative research as a way to create a sample based on specific criteria when it is difficult to determine the presence of given elements in a population (see Silverman 2004).

One way that researchers may apply snowball sampling techniques to on-line data sources is to examine a site initially identified through search string results for any links to other websites (e.g., Damphouse 2009; Holt 2007a). The structure of html web pages and the networked nature of the Internet allow individuals to easily chain disparate resources together, thereby establishing connections between groups. Examining the links provided in a web page or forum can expand a sample beyond the limited results that may turn up in search engine results and potentially provide access to hidden communities. For example, Damphouse (2009) utilized snowball sampling techniques over the course of 12 years to examine the relationships and nature of terror and extremist groups in the USA. By linking multiple sites together to create an expanded database, it appears that groups such as the KKK have become more connected to one another through the use of the Internet. Similarly, Holt (2009) identified a sample of web forums by clicking through links provided in two sites provided in search engine results. Such techniques may not always be necessary, but can help to increase the sample size of a data set.

Once a researcher has conducted a search through their preferred engine, they must begin to narrow their results and identify an appropriate sample population. This can be challenging given the variations in Internet use among offender populations, and the research question generally. The sampling framework employed by a researcher should focus on saturation and representativeness, which can be considered through repeated appearances in search results (e.g., Lee-Gonyea et al. 2009), forum population sizes (e.g., Holt 2007a), or representative populations (e.g., Blevins and Holt 2009; Cunningham and Kendall 2009). Regardless of the strategies employed, it is critical that researchers new to on-line data collection realize the massive amount of data that can be generated from even a small number of websites. For example, Gauthier and Chaudoir (2004) conducted an examination of multiple websites, chat rooms, and other on-line groups from 2000 to 2002. This data set produced over 1000 pages of printed material. In addition, Blevins and Holt (2009) generated over 2500 printed pages of data from a 10-city sample of forums run by and for the customers of prostitutes. Thus, researchers must give some consideration as to how to appropriately winnow their sampling criteria, while at the same time recognizing the volume of information that may be generated.

Throughout the course of data collection and analysis, researchers must continuously question the validity of information that is provided in on-line environments. There are myriad undercover operations conducted by law enforcement agencies to understand and investigate criminal behavior in online environments, particularly in pedophile communities and prostitution (see Hinduja 2007). It is possible that the information posted in certain sites may be falsified in order to attract offenders. Alternatively, individual users may over-exaggerate their actions or lie for the sake of status or clout within a community (see Cherny 1999; Mann and Stewart 2002; Meyer 1989 for discussion).[1] There are no immediate ways to rectify this issue, though previous research provides some guidance on techniques that can be employed within forums. For instance, many forums provide Frequently Asked Questions (FAQs) that detail the rules and structure of forum interactions. Moderators in these sites act as place managers and may ban or restrict the rights of an individual who provides false information (see Holt 2007a; Holt, Blevins, et al. 2008). Additionally, individuals within forums may single out and deride users who appear to disrupt exchanges by providing deliberately poor information or give indications that they may be connected with law enforcement (see also Holt 2007a; Holt and Blevins 2007; Mann and Sutton 1998). Thus, the internal processes of forums can give some direction as to the validity of exchanges between participants. Similar strategies can be employed within websites and blogs by observing comments made by those viewing the site. If a preponderance of negative comments or feedback is present, then the content of the site may be questionable. Additionally, a site that has high placement in search engine results across multiple engines may be more recognized and acknowledged than lower ranked pages.

On-line data also poses a distinct challenge for collection and analysis due to the mutability of websites and their content. A website or forum that facilitates criminal behavior may be short-lived due to the inherent risk of detection (see Gauthier and Chaudoir 2004; Holt 2007a; Lee-Gonyea et al. 2009; Mann and Sutton 1998). As a consequence, researchers must carefully document all facets of their data set. Numerous qualitative studies using on-line data recognize that information is lost during the process of data collection (see Damphouse 2009; Gauthier and Chaudoir 2004; Lee-Gonyea et al. 2009), which is perhaps one of

---

1. The use of lies and exaggerations can be critical elements in the construction of identity in online environments, and would prove useful in any examination of the formation of a subcultural identity in cyberspace (see Copes and Williams 2007; Williams and Copes 2005).

the most significant challenges for the qualitative researcher using on-line data (see Garcia et al. 2009; Hine 2005).

There are several steps that may be taken to reduce data loss or website attrition. Qualitative researchers in the real world regularly document as much information as is possible through field notes and video and audio recordings (see Lofland and Lofland 1995; Silverman 2004). On-line researchers must take similar steps, such as taking screenshots or saving a webpage as it appeared on the screen at a certain point in time on their local hard disk so that they may later retrieve the content (see Garcia et al. 2009; Hine 2005; Kendall 2004). Others may simply copy and paste web content into a word document or other text file so that it can be analyzed. Some researchers question the ethnics of capturing data in such a fashion, as it may affect the anonymity of the partici-pants (see Garcia et al. 2009 for a discussion). At the same time, researchers must maintain some sort of documentation of data or risk losing sensitive information. As a consequence, qualitative researchers must determine an appropriate solution to enable continuous analysis of data in some format.

A final concern lies in the potential response rate to an interview solicitation using a population developed on-line. Individuals whose contact information is posted in a public place on-line may reasonably expect to receive unsolicited emails. They may also, however, be inclined to delete unsolicited messages that they believe to be spam or potentially fraudulent. This poses a methodological dilemma, as email surveys from a researcher could be marked as spam based on keywords in a message, or ignored due to an inability to validate the credentials of the sender. Research in this area suggests several tactics to increase the like-lihood of responses. For example, sending emails out to a single individual at a time can help to reduce the likelihood that a message is perceived as spam, and increase the perceived and actual confidentiality of a message to your respon-dent (Dillman 2000; Heerwegh 2005). Using legitimate email domains, such as a university or known service provider can help to establish credibility. Finally, using clear and brief subject headings and introductions that establish the researcher and the study can help to increase the likelihood of a response (Dillman 2000).

The unique dynamics of on-line interviewing and research methods with deviance and crime are evident in a study by Pruitt (2008). He reported signifi-cant variation in the response rate to survey questions provided in a sample of male escorts advertising on-line based on the type of email address used by the researcher; one from a university account and the other from an AOL account. After collecting a sample of 448 email addresses for male escorts advertising on-line, 107 were undeliverable, reducing the sample to 341 total addresses (Pruitt 2008). From that subset, only 15% of the sample actually responded to the questions sent from the university email account compared to 60% who answered to the AOL account (Pruitt 2008). This example demon-strates that research protocols in on-line environments can be affected by myriad factors outside of the usual considerations necessary in face-to-face interactions.

Ethical Issues in On-Line Research

In light of the various data sources available on-line, it is critical to consider the ethical dilemmas that can develop from a research protocol. Given that most information available on-line is publicly accessible, researchers have questioned the relative nature of privacy in virtual environments (see Marx 1998; Reid 1996). Individual posts in an open website, blog, or other form of CMC place their information in a technically public sphere where there is less privacy than in a real world setting. In addition, many individuals who participate in deviant communities on-line take steps to hide their actual identity, such as the use of a nickname or pseudonym. It is also difficult to impute race, age, gender, and other identifying characteristics to an individual based solely on comments made in on-line exchanges. Thus, some researchers argue the use of on-line data is acceptable in that the individuals who post and comment in public settings are protected from personal identification (see Garcia et al. 2009; Marx 1998 for further discussion).

It is, however, critical to consider what steps can be taken to appropriately protect the identities of participants in research projects using on-line data. One of the most immediate and simple measures a researcher can take is to replace actual usernames with pseudonyms in the data. Additionally, scholars may not identify the websites where their data originated as a means of protecting the respondents (see Garcia et al. 2009; Holt 2007a). This provides some degree of insularity for the participants who may not know they were actively incorporated into a study. At the same time, using quotes from on-line data can obviate the protection afforded by a false name (see Bell 2001; DiMarco and DiMarco 2003; Garcia et al. 2009; Hine 2005; Kendall 2004; Miller and Slater 2000; Rutter and Smith 2005; Sveningsson 2004). Specifically, web pages from forums can be captured and indexed through search engines, thereby allowing individuals to potentially find the source of a quote provided in an academic publication. Thus, the privacy of a respondent is difficult to maintain in qualitative research using on-line data (see Garcia et al. 2009; Hine 2005). At the same time, it is important to note that individual forum users may take multiple steps to maintain their anonymity through the use of fake names or email addresses. This ensures that any individual who provides information in a forum or study has a degree of protection that enables a researcher to quote that individual.

An additional ethical concern lies in researcher identification. Some researchers argue it is necessary to announce themselves and their professional credentials within an on-line community as a means of building trust and establishing ethical boundaries within on-line environments (see Garcia et al. 2009; Turkle 1995). This raises a challenge for criminological research, as a group of individuals engaging in crime or deviance on-line may be less inclined to communicate, or change their behavior entirely due to the presence of an outsider (see Chu et al. 2010; Mann and Sutton 1998). This sort of contamination bias is possible in virtual environments, and could lead some groups to disband entirely due to fear over detection by law enforcement. As a consequence, many researchers engage in surreptitious observations and data collection to ensure that they do not affect the natural exchanges between participants (see Blevins and Holt 2009; Holt 2007a; Holt et al. 2009; Lee-Gonyea et al. 2009; Mann and Sutton 1998). Researchers must, however, consult their Institutional Review Board to obtain appropriate guidance on the nature of their study.

In addition, researchers must consider how to protect themselves from potential risks that develop in the course of on-line qualitative research. Qualitative researchers who study various forms of behavior in the real world are cognizant of the threats and prospective harms that they may incur, including injury, physical assault, and police harassment (see Jacobs 1998; Wright, Decker, Redfern, and Smith 1992). These risks are diminished in Internet-based research, though there are some pertinent dangers that can occur. Specifically, websites and forums can be attacked and compromised by computer hackers as a means of infecting computer systems that visit the site (see Chu et al. 2010). This is often an indiscriminant act designed to affect as many computer users as possible, often through the use of common web browsers like Internet Explorer and Mozilla Firefox (see Chu et al. 2010 for discussion). As a consequence, researchers who regularly engage in on-line research must carefully secure their computer through the use of constant security patches and active antivirus scanning software to protect the user in real time from web-based attacks.

In addition, researching certain types of deviant groups can increase the risk of computer attacks. For example, skilled computer users, such as those actively engaged in digital piracy and computer hacking, may be inclined to attack a researcher as a demonstration of their ability or dissatisfaction over the research experience (see Holt and Copes 2010; Taylor 1999). Researchers investigating markets that facilitate the sale and trade of stolen information or malicious software may also face significant risk of attack as these entities generate massive profits and do not want to be compromised by outsiders (see Chu et al. 2010; Franklin et al. 2007; Holt and Lampke 2010; Thomas and Martin 2006). Thus, it is critical that researchers secure their computer from attack through the use of computer security software.

In addition, savvy researchers may benefit from engaging in data collection from computers that do not contain sensitive information, such as personal financial data, student information, or data sets for unrelated projects. This will drastically reduce the likelihood of data compromise should an attack occur. Finally, when searching for websites and gathering data, researchers may want to consider using an Internet connection outside of their university in an attempt to reduce attribution to their educational institution. This can help to reduce the likelihood of a university being targeted for attack, as well as minimize any compromise or attack from spreading across university systems.

A final issue to consider before conducting research is the way that criminological research using on-line data may generally impact virtual deviant communities over time. Though academics are careful to protect the anonymity and privacy of a population, especially through unobtrusive observations, the publication and dissemination of their research may reach their subjects. The practical policy implications of criminological studies for law enforcement may also facilitate increased investigations into certain forms of behavior with unique ties to the Internet. As a consequence, criminal groups that regularly discuss illegal behavior in open forums may recognize an increased risk in communicating in public settings and change their practices. For example, increasing attention from law enforcement and academic researchers caused a shift in the market dynamics of stolen credit card and identity documents on-line (see Chu et al. 2010; Franklin et al. 2007; Holt 2007b; Holt and Lampke 2010; Thomas and Martin 2006). Specifically, these communities once operated in clear text in publicly accessible forums and Internet Relay Chat, but now operate overseas in closed sites where participants communicate in foreign languages to reduce the risk of detection and infiltration. As more researchers adopt virtual methods to examine deviance and crime, it is critical that they give some consideration as to how the overall landscape of Internet use may change.

Applying On-Line Methods in the Classroom

In light of the tremendous value in utilizing on-line data for qualitative analysis, academic instructors may benefit from adopting these methods in the class-room. One of the inherent challenges in teaching qualitative methods is the process of data collection, which can be extremely labor-intensive and difficult to complete in the course of a single semester (see Wright and Stein 1996). The process of identifying prospective respondents, completing interviews, and transcribing these materials can take a significant amount of time, and may limit the focus placed on analysis techniques and strategies (see Buckler 2008; Wright and Stein 1996). The dearth of qualitative data sets available for second-ary analyses through ICPSR also hinders access to existing data. Thus, encourag-ing students to develop data sets from on-line resources may streamline the collection process. For instance, students are now regularly exposed to, and familiar with, the use of various CMCs, making it easier for them to conduct simple interviews and practice this technique. Additionally, the innovative nature of on-line data and the range of research questions that can be addressed may increase the likelihood that a student could develop a publish-able manuscript from their research. These benefits emphasize the need to incorporate on-line data collection techniques into existing methods courses as a means of fostering student development.

An instructor could also prepare a data set from forums or BBS that can be used by all students as a means to practice various analytic techniques. The variety of offenses and deviant communities that operate in on-line environ-ments would allow students to perform content analyses, discourse analyses, and various ethnographic examinations. This would enable a focused course examining analysis strategies without the need for a more protracted focus on data collection (see Wright and Stein 1996). The use of a single data set would also allow students to address various topics independently over the course of a semester with greater depth than might otherwise occur with data collected individually. Thus, qualitative methods instructors should consider adopting on-line data collection and analysis in their courses due to the significant benefits they can have for students' development as researchers and scholars.

Conclusions

Though there has been some decline in the amount of qualitative scholarship in criminology, this manuscript has examined the emerging body of qualitative scholarship using data developed from the Internet and CMCs. The ubiquity and global connectivity afforded by the Internet enables criminals and deviants to connect with others socially and communicate subcultural knowledge and information on methods of offending (see DiMarco and DiMarco 2003; Jewkes and Sharpe 2003; Wall 2001). This shift poses a unique research opportunity for criminologists to understand deviance from a different social perspective and assess the impact of technology on human behavior.

The degree to which criminal groups use CMCs vary (see Taylor et al. 2010), though there are a variety of outlets that can be used as a source of qualitative data. Forums, BBSs, and newsgroups provide a great deal of information on social relationships between offenders and the possible subcultural dynamics of criminal groups (see Adler and Adler 2007; Blevins and Holt 2009; Durkin and Bryant 1999; Holt 2007a; Holt et al. 2009; Jenkins 2001; Mann and Sutton 1998; Meyer 1989; Williams and Copes 2005). Web pages also provide copious information that can be used for textual and visual analyses, and mined to develop sample populations for interviews (see Cunningham and Kendall 2010; Durkin 2007; Gauthier and Chaudoir 2004; Gauthier and Forsythe 1999; Hookway 2008; Lee-Gonyea et al. 2009; Sharpe and Earle 2003; Soothill and Sanders 2005; Tewksbury 2003, 2006). Furthermore, email and instant messaging systems can provide a simple, yet effective means of interviewing distributed populations of offenders with some ease (see Holt and Copes 2010; Pruitt 2008; Taylor 1999; Williams and Copes 2005).

Regardless of the form of CMC used, researchers must give careful consideration to the ethical and methodological challenges of on-line data collection and analysis. The lack of consistency in on-line environments coupled with different definitions of public and private make it difficult to define standards for data collection and protection of subjects. Variations in the use of CMCs by deviant and criminal groups call to question the representative nature of information posted in on-line communities. The continuous shift in the technologies used in on-line environments also requires researchers to be cognizant of the ways that social interactions may change. As individuals become more connected through cell phones, blogs, and social networking sites, these resources will define social interactions and provide increased opportunities for qualitative explorations. Thus, criminologists must recognize that the ease of access to on-line data is tempered by critical questions of validity, representativeness, and scientific rigor in much the same way as qualitative studies of real world offending (see Silverman 2004).

References

Adler, P. A., and P. Adler. 1987. *Membership roles in field research*. Newbury Park, CA: Sage.

Adler, P. A., and P. Adler. 2007. The demedicalization of self-injury: From psychopathology to sociological deviance. *Journal of Contemporary Ethnography* 36: 537-570.

Baudrillard, J. 1998. *Jean Baudrillard: Selected writings*. Stanford, CA: Stanford University Press.

Bell, D. 2001. *An introduction to cyberculture*. New York: Routledge.

Blevins, K., and T. J. Holt. 2009. Examining the virtual subculture of johns. *Journal of Contemporary Ethnography* 38: 619-648.

Buckler, K. 2008. The quantitative/qualitative divide revisited: A study of published research, doctoral program curricula, and journal editor perceptions. *Journal of Criminal Justice Education* 19: 383-403.

Burkhalter, B. 1999. Reading race online: Discovering racial identity in Usenet discussions. In M. A. Smith and P. Kollack (Eds.), *Communities in cyberspace* (pp. 60-74). New York: Routledge.

Cherny, L. 1999. *Conversation and community: Chat in a virtual world*. Stanford, CA: CSLI.

Chu, B., T. J. Holt, and G. J. Ahn. 2010. *Examining the creation, distribution, and function of malware on-line*. Technical Report for National Institute of Justice. NIJ Grant No. 2007-IJ-CX-0018. Retrieved April 20, 2010, from http://www.ncjrs.gov/pdffiles1/nij/grants/230112.pdf

Cooper, J., and D. M. Harrison. 2001. The social organization of audio piracy on the Internet. *Media, Culture, and Society* 23: 71-89.

Copes, H., and P. Williams. 2007. Techniques of affirmation: Deviant behavior, moral commitment, and resistant subcultural identity. *Deviant Behavior* 28: 247-272.

Cunningham, S., and T. Kendall. 2009. *Prostitution 2.0: The changing face of sex work*. Retrieved June 1, 2009, from http://www.toddkendall.net/Pros20_Final.pdf

Cunningham, S., and T. Kendall. 2010. Sex for sale: Online commerce in the world's oldest profession. In T. J. Holt (Ed.), *Crime on-line: Correlates, causes, and context* (pp. 40-75). Raleigh, NC: Carolina Academic Press.

Damphouse, K. 2009. The dark side of the web: Terrorists' use of the Internet. In F. Schmalleger and M. Pittaro (Eds.), *Crimes of the Internet* (pp. 573-592). Upper Saddle River, NJ: Pearson Prentice Hall.

Denzin, N. 1970. *The research act in sociology*. London: Butterworth.

Dillman, D. 2000. *Mail and Internet surveys: The tailored design method*. New York: John Wiley.

DiMarco, A. D., and H. DiMarco. 2003. Investigating cybersociety: A consideration of the ethical and practical issues surrounding online research in chat rooms. In Y. Jewkes (Ed.), *Dot.cons: Crime, deviance and identity on the Internet* (pp. 164-179). Portland, OR: Willan.

Durkin, K. F. 2007. Show me the money: Cybershrews and on-line money masochists. *Deviant Behavior* 28: 355-378.

Durkin, K. F., and C. D. Bryant. 1999. Propagandizing pederasty: A thematic analysis of the on-line exculpatory accounts of unrepentant pedophiles. *Deviant Behavior* 20: 103-127.

Ebo, B. 1998. *Cyberghetto or cybertopia: Race, class, and gender on the Internet.* Westport, CT: Praeger.

Edelson, E. 2003. The 419 scam: Information warfare on the spam front and a proposal for local filtering. *Computers and Security* 22: 392-401.

Eysenbach, G., and J. E. Till. 2001. Ethical issues in qualitative research on Internet communities. *British Medical Journal* 323: 1103-1105.

Franklin, J., V. Paxson, A. Perrig, and S. Savage. 2007, October-November. *An inquiry into the nature and cause of the wealth of Internet miscreants.* Paper presented at the 14th ACM conference on Computer and Communications Security, Alexandria, VA.

Garcia, A. C., A. I. Standlee, J. Bechkoff, and Y. Cui. 2009. Ethnographic approaches to the Internet and computer-mediated communication. *Journal of Contemporary Ethnography* 38: 52-84.

Gartner Group. 2003. *Gartner says marketers must differentiate e-mail marketing from spam.* Retrieved July 14, 2006, from www4.gartner.com/5_about/press_releases/pr29sept2003a.jsp

Gauthier, D. A. K., and N. K. Chaudoir. 2004. Tranny boyz: Cyber community support in negotiating sex and gender mobility among female to male transsexuals. *Deviant Behavior* 25: 375-398.

Gauthier, D. K., and C. J. Forsyth. 1999. Bareback sex, bug chasers, and the gift of death. *Deviant Behavior* 20: 85-100.

Grov, C. 2004. Make me your death slave: Men who have sex with men and use the Internet to intentionally spread HIV. *Deviant Behavior* 25: 329-349.

Hagan, J., and B. McCarthy. 1997. *Mean streets: Youth crime and homelessness.* Cambridge: Cambridge University Press.

Heerwegh, D. 2005. Effects of personal salutations in e-mail invitations to participate in a web survey. *Public Opinion Quarterly* 69: 588-598.

Herzog, H. A., B. Dinoff, and J. R. Page. 1997. Animal rights talk: Moral debate over the Internet. *Qualitative Sociology* 20: 399-418.

Hessler, R., L. Downing, C. Beltz, A. Pelliccio, M. Powell, and W. Vale. 2003. Qualitative research on adolescent risk using email: A methodological assessment. *Qualitative Sociology* 26: 111-124.

Hinduja, S. 2007. Computer crime investigations in the United States: Leveraging knowledge from the past to address the future. *International Journal of Cyber Criminology* 1: 400-420.

Hine, C. (Ed.). 2005. *Virtual methods: Issues in social research on the Internet.* Oxford: Berg.

Holt, T. J. 2007a. Subcultural evolution? Examining the influence of on- and off-line experiences on deviant subcultures. *Deviant Behavior* 28: 171-198.

Holt, T. J. 2007b, August. *The market for malware.* Paper presented at the Defcon 15 conference, Las Vegas, NV.

Holt, T. J. 2009. Examining the role of technology in the formation of deviant subcultures. *Social Science Computer Review.* doi:10.1177/0894439309351344

Holt, T. J., and K. R. Blevins. 2007. Examining sex work from the client's perspective: Assessing johns using online data. *Deviant Behavior* 28: 333-354.

Holt, T. J., K. R. Blevins, and N. Burkert. 2010. Considering the pedophile subculture online. *Sexual Abuse* 22: 3-24.

Holt, T. J., K. R. Blevins, and J. B. Kuhns. 2008. Examining the displacement practices of johns with on-line data. *Journal of Criminal Justice* 36: 522-528.

Holt, T. J., K. R. Blevins, and J. B. Kuhns. 2009. Examining diffusion and arrest avoidance practices among johns. *Crime and Delinquency.* doi:10.1177/0011128709347087

Holt, T. J., and H. Copes. 2010. Transferring subcultural knowledge online: Practices and beliefs of persistent digital pirates. *Deviant Behavior* 31: 625-654.

Holt, T. J., and D. C. Graves. 2007. A qualitative analysis of Advanced Fee Fraud schemes. *International Journal of Cyber-Criminology* 1: 137-154.

Holt, T. J., and E. Lampke. 2010. Exploring stolen data markets on-line: Products and market forces. *Criminal Justice Studies* 23: 33-50.

Holt, T. J., J. B. Soles, and L. Leslie. 2008, April. *Characterizing malware writers and computer attackers in their own words.* Paper presented at the 2008 International Conference on Information Warfare and Security, Peter Kiewit Institute, University of Nebraska at Omaha, NE.

Honeynet Research Alliance. 2003. Profile: Automated credit card fraud. *Know Your Enemy Paper series.* Retrieved July 20, 2008, from http://www.honeynet.org/papers/profiles/cc-fraud.pdf

Hookway, N. 2008. Entering the blogosphere: Some strategies for using blogs in social research. *Qualitative Research* 8: 91-113.

Jacobs, B. A. 1998. Researching crack dealers: Dilemmas and contradictions. In J. Ferrell and M. S. Hamm (Eds.), *Ethnography at the edge: Crime, deviance, and field research* (pp. 160-177). Boston, MA: Northeastern University Press.

Jenkins, P. 2001. *Beyond tolerance: Child pornography on the Internet.* New York: New York University Press.

Jerin, R., and B. Dolinsky. 2001. You've got mail! You don't want it: Cyber-victimization and on-line dating. *Journal of Criminal Justice and Popular Culture* 9: 15-21.

Jewkes, Y., and K. Sharpe. 2003. Crime, deviance and the disembodied self: Transcending the dangers of corporeality. In Y. Jewkes (Ed.), *Dot.cons: Crime, deviance and identity on the Internet* (pp. 1-14). Portland, OR: Willan.

Jordan, T., and P. Taylor. 1998. A sociology of hackers. *Sociological Review* 46: 757-780.

Kendall, L. 2004. Participants and observers in online ethnography: Five stories about identity. In M. D. Johns, S.-L. S. Chen, and G. J. Hall (Eds.), *Online social research: Methods, issues, and ethics* (pp. 125-140). New York: Peter Lang.

King, A., and J. Thomas. 2009. You can't cheat an honest man: Making ($$$ and) sense of the Nigerian e-mail scams. In F. Schmalleger and M. Pittaro (Eds.), *Crimes of the Internet* (pp. 206-224). Upper Saddle River, NJ: Pearson Prentice Hall.

King, J. E., C. E. Walpole, and K. Lamon. 2007. Surf and turf wars online: Growing implications of Internet gang violence. *Journal of Adolescent Health* 6: 66-68.

Kivits, J. 2005. Online interviewing and the research relationship. In C. Hine (Ed.), *Virtual methods: Issues in social research on the Internet* (pp. 35-50). Oxford: Berg.

Kleck, G., J. Tark, and J. J. Bellows. 2006. What methods are most frequently used in research in criminology and criminal justice? *Journal of Criminal Justice* 34: 147-152.

Landreth, B. 1985. *Out of the inner circle.* Washington, DC: Microsoft Press.

Lee-Gonyea, J. A., T. Castle, and N. E. Gonyea. 2009. Laid to order: Male escorts advertising on the Internet. *Deviant Behavior* 30: 321-348.

Leung, L. 2005. *Virtual ethnicity: Race, resistance and the World Wide Web.* Burlington, VT: Ashgate.

Lofland, J., and L. H. Lofland. 1995. *Analyzing social settings: A guide to qualitative observation and analysis.* Belmont, CA: Wadsworth.

Loper, D. K. 2000. The criminology of computer hackers: A qualitative and quantitative analysis (Unpublished doctoral dissertation, Michigan State University, 2000).

Malesky Jr., L. A., and L. Ennis. 2004. Supportive distortions: An analysis of posts on a pedophile Internet message board. *Journal of Addictions and Offender Counseling* 24: 92-100.

Mann, C., and F. Stewart. 2002. Internet interviewing. In J. A. Holstein and J. F. Gubrium (Eds.), *Handbook of Internet research: Context and method* (pp. 603-628). London: Sage.

Mann, D., and M. Sutton. 1998. Netcrime: More changes in the organisation of thieving. *British Journal of Criminology* 38: 201-229.

Marx, G. 1998. An ethics for the new surveillance. *Information Society* 14: 171–185.

Meyer, G. R. 1989. The social organization of the computer underground (Master's thesis, Northern Illinois University, 1989).

Miller, D., and D. Slater. 2000. *The Internet: An ethnographic approach.* New York: Berg.

Miller, J. 2005. *The status of qualitative research in criminology.* Retrieved May 17, 2006, from http://www.wjh.harvard.edu/nsfqual/Miller%20Paper.pdf

Park, S., J. H. Lee, and H. J. Bae. 2005. End user searching: A Web log analysis of NAVER, a Korean web search engine. *Library and Information Science Research* 27: 203–221.

Patchin, J., and S. Hinduja. 2007. What kids do on MySpace. *Technology and Learning* 27: 7–27.

Pruitt, M. V. 2008. Deviant research: Deception, male Internet escorts, and response rates. *Deviant Behavior* 29: 70–82.

Quinn, J. F., and C. J. Forsyth. 2005. Describing sexual behavior in the era of the Internet: A typology for empirical research. *Deviant Behavior* 26: 191–207.

Reid, E. M. 1996. Informed consent in the study of online communities: A reflection on the effects of computer-mediated social research. *Information Society* 12: 169–174.

Riva, G. 2002. The sociocognitive psychology of computer-mediated communication: The present and future of technology-based interactions. *CyberPsychology and Behavior* 5: 581–598.

Rutter, J., and G. W. H. Smith. 2005. Ethnographic presence in a nebulous setting. In C. Hine (Ed.), *Virtual methods: Issues in social research on the Internet* (pp. 81–92). Oxford: Berg.

Selwyn, N., and K. Robson. 1998. E-mail as a research tool. *Social Research Update* 21. Retrieved November 14, 2005, from http://www.soc.surrey.ac.uk/sru/SRU21.html

Sharpe, K., and S. Earle. 2003. Cyberpunters and cyberwhores: Prostitution on the Internet. In Y. Jewkes (Ed.), *Dot.cons: Crime, deviance and identity on the Internet* (pp. 36–52). Portland, OR: Willan.

Silverman, D. 2004. *Interpreting qualitative data: Methods for analyzing talk, text, and interaction* (3rd ed.). Thousand Oaks, CA: Sage.

Soothill, K., and T. Sanders. 2005. The geographical mobility, preferences and pleasures of prolific punters: A demonstration study of the activities of prostitutes' clients. *Sociological Research On-Line* 10 (1). Retrieved from http://www.socresonline.org.uk/10/1/soothill/soothill.pdf

Steel, C. 2006. *Windows forensics: The field guide to corporate computer crime investigations.* Somerset, NJ: Wiley.

Sveningsson, M. 2004. Ethics in Internet ethnography. In E. A. Buchanan (Ed.), *Virtual research ethics: Issues and controversies* (pp. 45–61). Hershey, PA: Information Science.

Taylor, P. A. 1999. *Hackers: Crime in the digital sublime.* New York: Routledge.

Taylor, R. W., E. J. Fritsch, J. Liederbach, and T. J. Holt. 2010. *Digital crime and digital terrorism* (2nd ed.). Upper Saddle River, NJ: Pearson Prentice Hall.

Tewksbury, R. 2003. Bareback sex and the quest for HIV: Assessing the relationship in Internet personal advertisements of men who have sex with men. *Deviant Behavior* 24: 467–482.

Tewksbury, R. 2006. Click here for HIV: An analysis of Internet-based bug chasers and bug givers. *Deviant Behavior* 27: 379–395.

Tewksbury, R., D. Dabney, and H. Copes. 2010. The prominence of qualitative research in criminology and criminal justice scholarship. *Journal of Criminal Justice Education* 21: 391–411.

Tewksbury, R., M. T. DeMichele, and J. M. Miller. 2005. Methodological orientations of articles appearing in criminal justice's top journals: Who publishes what and where. *Journal of Criminal Justice Education* 16: 265–279.

Thomas, R., and J. Martin. 2006. The underground economy: Priceless. *login* 31: 7-16.

Turkle, S. 1995. *Life on-screen: Identity in the age of the Internet.* New York: Simon & Schuster.

Walker, K. 2000. It's difficult to hide it: The presentation of self on Internet home pages. *Qualitative Sociology* 23: 99-120.

Wall, D. S. 2001. Cybercrimes and the Internet. In D. S. Wall (Ed.), *Crime and the Internet* (pp. 1-17). New York: Routledge.

Wall, D. S. 2004. Digital realism and the governance of spam as cybercrime. *European Journal on Criminal Policy and Research* 10: 309-335.

Williams, P., and H. Copes. 2005. How edge are you? Constructing authentic identities and subcultural boundaries in a Straightedge Internet forum. *Symbolic Interaction* 28: 67-89.

Wilson, B., and M. Atkinson. 2005. Rave and Straightedge, the virtual and the real: Exploring online and offline experiences in Canadian youth subcultures. *Youth and Society* 36: 276-311.

Wright, R. T., S. H. Decker, A. K. Redfern, and D. L. Smith. 1992. A snowball's chance in hell: Doing field research with residential burglars. *Journal of Research in Crime and Delinquency* 29: 148-161.

Wright, R. T., and M. Stein. 1996. Seeing ourselves: Exploring the social production of criminological knowledge in a qualitative methods course. *Journal of Criminal Justice Education* 7: 65-77.

The Case for Edge Ethnography

J. Mitchell Miller and Richard Tewksbury

Whereas the teaching of qualitative research has long been sacrificed for instruction on quantitative approaches, alternative fieldwork orientations are rarely professed. Edge ethnography represents a strain of qualitative inquiry employing atypical qualitative fieldwork strategies characterized by: (1) the conduct of research within the context of the immediacy of social action, (2) atypical researcher involvement in research settings and activities intentionally maximizing the value of deep involvement, and (3) potential risk to researchers and subjects, as well as related ethical issues raised by close association with active criminals and knowledge of ongoing criminal activity. Despite the strategic value of unconventional qualitative strategies based in full immersion into fieldwork environments, such as entrée to closed and esoteric study settings and contact with otherwise inaccessible subjects, they are seldom employed. Ostensibly, limited application is a function of a lack of coverage in graduate-level research methods courses—a neglect fostered by multiple issues, including ethical objections. After briefly reviewing the two major forms of alternative qualitative fieldwork, the principal advantages and ethical justification for engaging edge ethnography are presented.

The issue of philosophy of science is central to a methodological discourse in the social sciences. While discussion over the paradigmatic correctness and superiority of positivism versus subjectivism is a longstanding and seemingly never-ending debate in many disciplines (e.g., sociology, political science, and psychology), the implications of the nature of knowledge and its presuppositions and foundations have been neglected by criminology and criminal justice (CCJ) in favor of research methods instruction *per se*. The matter of the nature of social reality and the capabilities of social science to capture data through measurement, for example, is barely addressed in general methods or qualitative focused texts (e.g., Babbie 2009; Berg 2006; Hagan 2010). Whereas training in more established social science disciplines comprehends *methodology* as a philosophical framework shaping the development of inquiry strategies through theory-methods symmetry and *methods* as data collection and analysis techniques, these terms are basically synonymous within CCJ. Indifference to philosophy of science in CCJ arises, in part, from the general applied and technocratic orientation of a professional school rather than social science discipline identity (Shover 1979), a lingering effect of the LEAA Act origins of academic criminal justice.

Focus on enhancing the effectiveness of prevention, enforcement, and rehabilitation services delivery directs considerable research interest and activity to accountability documentation and performance specification, primarily through hypothetic-deductive driven evaluative processes entailing measurement, variable analysis, and causality determination (i.e., quantitative research). While it is understandable that policy and practice effectiveness demands necessitate numerical confirmation derived from statistical analysis, hyper-focus on causality generally limits pure and qualitative research opportunities. Comparison and contrast of quantitative and qualitative techniques in research methods courses, however, provides a platform for epistemological ideation and consideration of possibilities for scientific advancement.

This paper presents the advantages of engaging in qualitative research, specifically, edge ethnography—an approach to social science that emphasizes understandings via full immersion and the taking of risks (whether physical, social, or legal) so as to attain a detailed understanding of marginalized and typically inaccessible via traditional methods populations, activities, and (sub)cultural settings (also see Ferrell 1997; Tewksbury 2009). Our hope is to expose newer generations of scholars to seldom address inquiry options, and to possibly invigorate a new wave of scholars to consider and employ such approaches. Because teaching the "how-to" differs minimally between traditional and alternative qualitative methods as observational and interactive data collection and analysis goals are similar, professing edge ethnography primarily involves consideration of a range of issues related to entre, self-presentation and ethics inherent to studying crime and deviance in natural settings. These issues, which have led to major objections to deep fieldwork immersion, are thus reviewed and refuted with the hope that present-day scholars will see the value of engaging emerging scholars in an examination of the benefits of such approaches.

The Challenge of Qualitative Inquiry

Review of any representative sample of CCJ research confirms a majority-minority balance regarding the relative use of quantitative and qualitative methods and, for methodological and practical reasons, this dominance is likely permanent (Buckler 2008; Tewksbury, Dabney, and Copes 2010; Tewksbury, DeMichele, and Miller 2005). First, paradigmatic conflict between positivism and subjectivism, while not likely to ever be fully resolved, has clearly shifted to near categorical preference for causal logic model-driven science as indicated by statistical significance observed through variable analysis (Bryant 1985; Gottfredson and Hirschi 1987; Higgins 2009; Worrall 2000). The general message communicated to new generations of scholars is that a positivism-quantitative research orientation to social science is an objective, well-defined, systematic approach to inquiry that is more scientific than subjectivism-qualitative strategies. This message is evidenced by the common description of qualitative approaches in general as "alternative." However, the "alternative" nature of qualitative methods is far from accepted, and within the population of qualitatively oriented investigators certain data collection and analysis techniques are more likely to be seen as "alternative"—such is the case with edge ethnographic methods. And, as the "different" or "extreme" of what the larger genre already seen by some as alternative, approaches such as edge ethnography may be perceived as inaccessible, dangerous or simply "too much or too far" for scholars early in their careers.

The majority of CCJ researchers are employed in academe where they must regularly generate research productivity vital to career success that is assessed at multiple junctures such as initial hire, annual merit, third year review, tenure, and promotion (see Holmes, Tewksbury, and Holmes 2000). Those employed in private and non-profit contexts similarly face accountability and necessarily direct energy toward opportunities for perceived success. The axioms of the dominant positivistic paradigm (e.g., generalizability through random sampling and causality determination through temporal ordering of influences and effects, correlation, and lack of spuriousness) drive a formulaic research process utilizing quantitative methods that are far less time-consuming than qualitative interaction with numerous people which, in CCJ contexts, may be difficult to locate and approach.

Those engaging qualitative fieldwork, especially at an early career stage, can ill afford failed projects, lengthy delays due to hurdles in the approval process, greater time investment required for data collection and analysis or stigmatization. Engaging quantitative work that can be executed more quickly (and safely) is a safer bet for bringing a greater number of research pieces to publication, especially given the general increase in research productivity throughout the discipline that has significantly affected employment and professional development performance expectations (Jennings, Schreck, Sturtz, and Mahoney 2008).

The applied nature of CCJ, particularly criminal justice, is derived partly from the need to demonstrate accountability, performance effectiveness, and efficiency—matters assessed against known best practices and with dichotomous success determinations indicated clearly through measureable behavior. Criminal justice research, then, is oriented toward helping the system. Accordingly, the vast majority of available funding is geared toward quantitative research. For all these reasons, it is understandable that quantitative designs are the preferred approach throughout CCJ.

Qualitative methods are taught and employed far less frequently than quantitative designs and analysis. Including at the level of doctoral training, qualitative methods courses are especially rare; Buckler (2008) reported that only 56% of criminal justice doctoral programs offer a course in qualitative methods, and only 16% require a qualitative methods course. If looking beyond traditional qualitative approaches courses, edge ethnography is all but absent from doctoral training in CCJ, surviving only at the level of occasional readings, typically presented as "alternatives" to the already "alternative" approach of qualitative methods generally. As a result, actual instances of edge ethnographic methods used in the discovery and elaboration of knowledge regarding crime, deviance, and criminal justice are exceptionally rare (Miller 1995).

Alternative Qualitative Fieldwork Methods

Edge ethnographic methods are best understood as variants of traditional qualitative methods, such as participant observation and in-depth interviewing, more so than unique methods (Ferrell and Hamm 1998; Gold 1958; Miller and Tewksbury 2001, 2006). There are few differences in terms of research goals (exploration, discovery, description, and assessment) or design steps (data collection, management, and analysis). Through alternative strategies, though, the limitations inherent to mainstream qualitative research (especially fieldwork) processes can be averted or minimized so that substantive knowledge bases may be extended. What is different about edge ethnography and largely defines it as an independent inquiry subfield is the nature of the researcher role in terms of depth of involvement in study environments and intensity of interaction with human subjects. These elements contrast with conventional fieldwork protocols and form the conceptual basis for a qualitative sub-paradigm demonstrating the relevance and linear connectivity between subjectivist philosophy of science and variant fieldwork (Ferrell 1997; Tewksbury 2009). It is important to acknowledge, however, that many of the endeavors and inquiries that exemplify and illustrate the edge ethnographic approach do not self-identify as edge ethnography. For some this is undoubtedly a matter of historical development, as the term was not available until the late 1990s, for others it may be a lack of recognition or engagement with the methodology literature and for others it may be a conscious dissociation with the "extreme" label of edge ethnography.

Regardless of the labels attached to one's own work, the goals of those working within a subjectivist/interpretivist philosophy of science are exploration and description of the elements, actors, actions, and interactions of study settings. Such are often difficult accomplishments when dealing with those labeled as "criminals" and the criminal justice system. Traditional qualitative methods may be employed to better understand the nature of crime, but closer consideration of the covert and confidential nature of crime suggests that overt qualitative fieldwork strategies invite, and often likely ensure, a validity threatening Hawthorne effect wherein observations and interview data are tainted by researcher presence. To the extent that subjects behave differently than normal and withhold or alter information in response to the presence of research activity, collected data is apt to be contaminated and undermine the study (see Tewksbury 2009).

The problems of Hawthorne effect and, more fundamentally, access to research subjects are sufficiently fatal that most variable analysis and traditional qualitative designs are not viable options for many research topics of interest to criminal justice and criminology. Whereas a researcher interested in attorney perception of judicial bias might randomly sample from a local or state bar association list, no such database exists for identifying prostitutes, drug dealers, burglars, or arsonists. Samples can be developed through convenience opportunities and snowball strategies, but even after identifying a subject pool, issues remain. First, there is no way to ascertain the generalizabilty of findings based on data obtained from convenience samples drawn from unknown populations. Also, there is the problem of data quality.

Those labeled as and typically considered "criminals" in our society are most often vested in secrecy and disclosure of their behavior carries literal legal, financial, and possible physical risks. Accordingly, it is altogether rational and utilitarian to avoid criminal labeling made possible through association with risky others, particularly authorities perceived as threatening. Because of suspicion inherent to crime and presumed criminals, generally, and possible harm associated with inquiry, specifically, accessing and exploring criminal, deviant and/or stigmatized, secretive environments can be an uphill challenge. First, professional titles such as criminologist, criminal justice scientist, social scientist, and especially grant titles of principal investigator or evaluator may be erroneously defined and misunderstood as roles being part of, or aligned with, the criminal justice system. After all, both detectives and field researchers ask a lot of specific questions about sensitive topics, often in cultural settings where citizen non-cooperation with legal authorities is normative. Thus, openly announced research with formal researcher-subject relations is often unlikely to be effective for establishing a viable position to observe normal illegal behavior committed by individuals actively engaged in law violating behaviors.

Assuming subjects can be identified that are willing to participate in a research project, other concerns remain. "Criminals" are most easily identified for research purposes by their official status as indicated by prior convictions, incarcerated status, and other involvement with the system, as indicated by sampling strategies in the general CCJ literature. A seldom considered but important characteristic of data obtained from system identified offenders is that surveys and, especially, secondary analysis of official information are based on past behavior recollection involving memory accuracy, and legal, social, and psychological (i.e., guilt) influences on veracity. Most people reinterpret and remember events so as to minimize their culpability and responsibility for wrongful behavior (Benson 1985; see Maruna and Copes 2005 for review of this literature). So, simply getting qualitative data does not ensure that it will accurately reflect the individuals, social interaction, or settings being investigated. It is illogical to think that individuals engaged in behaviors subject to social sanctions are reliably forthright when knowingly being observed or interviewed; they have compelling reasons to act otherwise. Researcher presence suppresses behavior subject to penalties from witnesses through the removal of the advantage of secrecy. Few would argue, for example, that participant observation via police patrol ride-alongs would be a good means by which to examine excessive use of force (however, see Engel, Sobol, and Worden 2000).

Fortunately, edge ethnography encompasses options that facilitate the study of backstage social settings and environments, including deviant and criminal subcultures. More broadly, it is well-suited for social science examination of a wide range of phenomena involving those disenfranchised from, and in conflict with, the larger society. As individuals and groups become further alienated, they posture and behave in ways that accentuate underclass, anti-social, deviant, and criminal traits, including mistrust and secrecy—norms reinforced through collective consciousness. In order to address and get beyond the removed and clandestine nature of crime, edge ethnographers, through various combinations of fieldwork techniques, employ one of two general approaches: *full participation* or *covert participant observation*.

Full Participation

Full participation has been employed from the perspective of various subjectivist and critical theoretical frameworks (e.g., symbolic interactionism, cultural criminology, and conflict perspectives). Essentially, this research process entails engaging in a degree of immersion in study settings and group dynamics sufficient to develop rapport to the point of being able to exercise free movement and open discourse. By meeting subjects on their terms and in their environments in a non-judgmental manner, edge ethnographers gain access to the people and settings of research interest. Frequently, edge ethnographers share the ideological viewpoints of subject groups and justify their activities, including criminal behavior, a part of the risk of "going native" (e.g., Ferrell and Hamm 1998; Kraska 1998; Tunnell 1998; Van Maanen 1988). For some, identification and rapport development is altogether natural as researcher perspective and behavior may already parallel those of subjects.

Whether natural or assumed, the related concepts of trust (from the perspective of group members) and confidentiality (from the perspective of research) are vital to the full participation process. Ethnographers must find a way to "fit in" so as to not significantly alter activity over time and, ideally, not affect behavior any longer than would any new group member. Prominent examples of full immersion include Adler's (1985) assumption as a regular member of a drug dealing network, Wallace's (1964) life on skid row, Scarce's (1994) supportive involvement with animal rights activists, and Ferrell's (1993) vandalistic participation with urban graffiti artists.

The full immersion form of edge ethnography, then, means research subjects are made aware of the researcher's true identity (to the extent that any participant's true identity is known), purpose, and objectives. However, research activity is typically a byproduct occurrence tangential to and overshadowed by normal activities in which the researcher's full participation masks dual roles as both group member and social scientist (e.g., Asch 1951; Formby and Smykla

1981). There are clear advantages to working with confederates who can facilitate entrée, expedite understanding of subcultural jargon and behavioral norms, and minimize risks in dangerous situations (Tewksbury and Gagné 1997). Full participation research success is thus dependent to some degree on winning the trust and acceptance of those being studied. Reliance on confederates may be counterproductive, though, because, while active participant observation may be generating data, the issue of whether researcher–subject relations have truly developed beyond the threat of Hawthorne effects cannot really be known, only perceived. If only a few individuals in a research site know a person's presence is for research rather than natural purposes, it becomes probable that interaction will be artificial and restricted. Announcing research activity, then, may result in "data distortion" (Miller 1995) and leave well-intended and labor-intensive full participation research susceptible to some of the same problems of addressing crime and deviance research topics through traditional approaches. The second major form of edge ethnography avoids problems inherent to overt research techniques by further extending the boundaries of edge ethnography.

Covert Participant Observation

Covert participant observation has been used rather synonymously with other terms, such as "secret observation" (Roth 1962), "investigative social research" (Douglas 1976), "sociological snooping" (Von Hoffman 1970), and particularly "disguised observation" (Denzin 1968; Erikson 1967). Each of these forms of undercover research involves hiding the presence of research activity for the purpose of interacting with subject groups (i.e., entrée and rapport). A distinguishing feature is that the researcher's intent to conduct research is not made known to subjects within the field setting so as to gain access and conduct research within the immediacy of crime/deviance. While successful rapport development with the full participation approach enables research to be conducted in real-time settings, covert orientations are sometimes necessary for access and natural environment preservation. This is perhaps the only strategic approach to directly observe crime/deviance and eliminate dependency on others' recollection of events.

Covert designs assume different forms, especially in regard to the nature of disguise employed. Disguised observation typically refers to those who simply keep research activity secret through forms of hiding or role misrepresentation, such as Stein's (1974) observation of prostitutes servicing customers via a hidden two-way mirror, Calvey's (2000) study of bouncers, and Tewksbury's (1990, 2002) ethnographic accounts of adult bookstore patronage or gay bathhouse sexual activities from the vantage point of a "regular" customer. While covert participant observation also involves disguise for observational purposes, researchers are immersed in field settings and thus interact with subjects. Defining characteristics include intentional misrepresentation, interpersonal deception, and assumption and maintenance of a false identity, often for prolonged periods of time (Jorgensen 1989). *Covert participant observation* is therefore a more intense form of edge ethnography than both full participation and other disguised observation strategies because it better encapsulates and captures the active nature of the fieldwork essential to the technique (Miller 1995). Leading examples include Steffensmeier and Terry's (1973) study of the relationship between personal appearance and suspicion of shoplifting involving students dressed either conservatively or as hippies, Stewart and Cannon's (1977) masquerade as thieves, Tewksbury's (1990, 2002; Douglas and Tewksbury 2008) descriptions of sexual deviance, Miller and Selva's (1994) infiltration of drug enforcement operations, and, most notably, Laud Humphreys' (1970) infamous study of homosexual behavior in public places.

Aspects of the covert participant observation research process are unconventional. The most pronounced controversial point is gaining entry to a setting through misrepresentation. The closed nature of backstage settings and the criminal behavior of subject groups may preclude announcement of the researcher's objectives and leave role deception as the only means by which to access social phenomena. Assuming a covert role means full—or nearly full (see Tewksbury 2006)—participation in various group and individual activities that can pose certain risks to the researcher and to the inquiry. Assuming a role either as one who violates the law or one who is in close proximity to crime does not absolve the researcher from culpability; thus, moral decisions and even the possibility of arrest and legal sanction must be considered prior to entry into the field.

The Ethical Basis for Professing the Edge

The ethicality of edge ethnography has long been debated, as evidenced by the "deception debate" and the "native controversy" (Bulmer 1980; Galliher 1973; Humphreys 1970; Miller 1995; Roth 1962). Participants in these controversies have tended to assume one of two polarized positions: moralistic condemnation or responsive justification. Critics explicitly equate full immersion and deception with immorality—so unconscionable that some would have edge ethnography banned from social science research altogether (Erikson 1967). Major objections include the question of at what point are edge ethnographers so immersed in criminal activities that their behavior is no longer absolved, if it ever was, by a research agenda. And, for covert researchers, there is the challenge of justifying why deceptive techniques that violate the principle of informed consent, constitute invasion of privacy, and risk bringing harm to subjects are acceptable.

Critics contend that full immersion and misrepresentation not only harm subjects, but also the researcher and science by provoking negative public scrutiny and making subject populations wary of future researchers (Polsky 1967). Risk to the researcher, though, is seemingly a personal decision, much like a subject consents to participate in studies, wherein the presence of some risk is acceptable as long as subjects are informed to possible harm and agree. Surely, researchers should be entitled to afford themselves the same license of participation. There are risks for edge ethnographers, especially professional risks. The edge ethnographer:

> is often seen as a person of questionable moral value, or at the very least "different" from the mainstream of social scientists. The edge ethnographer is one who acknowledges, usually accepts, and often embraces the stigma (as a form of social danger) that comes from being known as one who is comfortable with and at ease being in, around, and a part of the deviant and illicit worlds that provide him or her real data and perspectives. Scholars working with vulnerable, disreputable, and/or socially ostracized populations are often considered by other scholars as sharing in the stigma (and perhaps deviant activities) of those whom they study. (Tewksbury 2009, p. 409)

Setting restrictions on academic investigations in an *a priori* fashion based on potential harm is at odds with both the values of an open, democratic society (including individual freedom and autonomy) and the traditional academic standard of free inquiry.

One of the important challenges that confront the edge ethnographer is gaining approval for one's endeavors from an institutional review board (IRB). There may be two sets of issues working against the edge ethnographer seeking approval for a research project from an IRB. First are the inherent dangers in the setting, activities, and approaches of the edge ethnographic enterprise. Second, as argued by Jacques and Wright (2010), IRBs are more likely to disapprove research proposed by lower status researchers. Therefore, for the edge ethnographer who is both already seen as "extreme" and marginal by method, topic, and association, and working in a by definition dangerous setting/population, it is likely that an IRB will be reluctant to endorse or approval such work. When such is the case, the edge ethnographer is put in a quandary: do not do the work being proposed or sidestep, avoid or ignore the IRB. To not do the work is to be muzzled, restricted, and quashed. To do the work without seeking or obtaining approval—or in defiance of an IRB's unwillingness to approve such a project—is professionally and perhaps personally, dangerous.

However, in actuality the fact that an IRB disapproves a proposed research project does not mean that said project will necessarily not be conducted (Katz 2006). As outlined by Katz (2006), qualitative fieldwork in general has a nearly insurmountable challenge in gaining IRB approval—when researchers are required to know beforehand whom they will encounter, where, when, under what conditions, and in the presence of whom else—it is not possible to meet the structured conditions of an IRB. When such conditions cannot be fully and accurately predicted, the ethnographic researcher (and especially the edge ethnographer) is left to either abandon their work or be condemned to an "underground existence" (Katz 2006, p. 500). While such a response is clearly not ideal, nor desired, it is likely to be seen as a last resort—so as to accommodate the pursuit of science. When IRB review is not included in an endeavor there are risks involved for the researcher, for those being studied, for the researcher's institution, and anyone with whom the researcher comes into contact. However, for some edge ethnographers—who have already demonstrated their willingness to take risks by their adopting an edge ethnographic approach to begin with—going underground (or conducting "guerilla research" (Taylor and Tewksbury 1995, p. 126) may be perceived as the best, or only, option.

The argument that edge ethnography will hinder future research also is unsound. Many settings of interest to criminologists already are restricted and typically occupied by subjects suspicious of strangers due to the threat of legal penalties associated with disclosure. Because *all* outsiders—including researchers—routinely are distrusted and excluded from such settings, future researchers using overt approaches will not be able to gain entry into the field, regardless of the outcome of previous research in general and especially apart from the more specific issue of whether a particular study involved a covert dimension.

The use of deceit and the potential harm that subjects may encounter from covert research are more troubling problems. From the debate over the use of deception in social science research, one might think the maneuver to be limited to covert designs. The common use of prevarication in overt qualitative research, however, is guised in less alarming labels and thus ignored. An excellent example of this point is Carl Klockars' (1974) well-known *The Professional Fence* that involved considerable duplicity, despite its status as an overt study. This life history of the 30-year career of Philadelphia fence Vincent Swaggi was made possible by an intentionally misrepresentative letter wherein Klockars admittedly lied about: (1) his academic credentials, (2) his familiarity and experience with the subject matter of fencing, (3) the number of other thieves he had interviewed, and most seriously (4) Swaggi's possible legal risks from participating in the project (Klockars 1974). Klockars' book and similar projects avoid much of the controversy associated with edge methods by evoking a "positivised" jargon consistent with mainstream research design. Despite various levels of duplicity, the terms "case history" and "in-depth interview" simply do not provoke the interest and suspicion generated by "covert" and "disguise."

There are practical arguments for edge ethnography, most basically that those engaged in illegal or unconventional behavior—such as drug dealers and users—simply will not agree to participate in a study using overt methods, fearing possible exposure, arrest, and prosecution. Likewise, offenders and practitioners in powerful and authoritative positions are secretive and difficult to observe openly (Shils 1975). Because white-collar criminals, police chiefs, prison wardens, drug enforcement agents, and various others benefit from the existing power structure, they resist the study of their behavior in these official roles. A covert design is often the only way to conduct qualitative evaluation research of enforcement and intervention programs closed to the public (and thus, the research community).

Theoretical justification for covert participant observation can be found in both dramaturgical and conflict perspectives. If Goffman (1959) is to be taken seriously, then all researchers should be viewed as wearing masks and the appropriateness of any inquiry viewed in its situational context. Following Goffman, Denzin (1968, p. 502) argued that ethical propriety depends upon the situation: "the sociologist has the right to make observations on anyone in any setting to the extent that he does so with scientific intents and purposes in mind." Dramaturgy, then, suggests that the duplicity of roles already present in any setting, including criminal settings—such as those adopted by undercover cops, police informants, fences, racketeers—is only multiplied, not introduced, when the role of covert researcher is adopted.

The well-known consensus-conflict debate also provides support of covert research. Conventional field methods, such as in-depth interviewing and overt observation, are heavily based on a consensus view of society where respondents or subjects are cooperative and willing to share their points of view and experiences with the researcher (Patton 2001). This assumption is suspect, however, in stratified and culturally diverse societies. Because acute conflicts over interests, values, and actions saturate modern social life, leaving some more advantaged than others, covert methods could help expose institutionally embedded class disjuncture and correlated elite deviance.

Perhaps the most compelling basis for the use of disguise in research is "the ends and the means" position first stated by Roth (1962), then Douglas (1976) and Homan (1980), and more recently Miller and Selva (1994). Employing this justification in support of covert observation, Douglas (1976, pp. 8–9) notes: "exceptions to important social rules, such as those concerning privacy and intimacy, must be made only when the research need is clear and the potential contributions of the findings to general human welfare are believed to be great enough to counterbalance the risks."

That the ends of research may absolve the means also has been acknowledged by the British Sociological Association, which since 1973 has acknowledged that "the use of covert methods may be justified in certain circumstances ... Covert methods ... should be resorted to only where it is impossible to use other methods to obtain essential data" (British Sociological Association 2002, pp. 4-5). Certainly this is the case in many criminal and criminal justice research settings. The benefits of investigating and reporting on expensive, dysfunctional, unethical, and even illegal facets of the criminal justice system may outweigh potential costs. When the actions of criminal justice agencies are inconsistent with their stated legitimate objectives, the failure to study and expose how various initiatives and strategies are implemented on the streets could subject citizens to additional misfortune and abuse.

The ends and the means rule, of course, requires some subjective interpretation of plausible harm to subjects, and some consideration of who will benefit from the research. Because anticipating and validly and reliably weighing harms and benefits are near impossible, most practical applications of the ends and the means formula will result in painful choices and controversial decisions by the researcher. Covert research carries more ethical baggage than other qualitative methods, yet its ethicality can be supported through careful and detailed reasoning, purpose, and design.

Conclusion

Edge ethnography is essentially "opportunistic research" (Ronai and Ellis 1989) conducted by "complete-member researchers" (Adler and Adler 1987) who study phenomena in settings where open knowledge is limited to full members. Admission to otherwise inaccessible settings is gained by assuming a natural position that allows unrestricted dialogue and observation through trust and covert posture. The studies of crime and clandestine criminal justice interventions invite and sometimes require the use of covert participant observation. How other than through a covert research design can topics such as the criminal calculus, undercover policing, and inmate-correctional officer interaction be fully understood or analyzed? Criminals, as well as criminal justice officials, have vested interests in maintaining high levels of autonomy and secrecy. This is evident in such terms as "snitch," "confidential informant," and "police fraternity."

Topics that largely have gone unexplored in conventional criminological and criminal justice studies often preclude overt research. Ironically, this absence of research makes these topics particularly desirable for academic investigation. Full and covert participant observations are useful techniques for extending research into new and unusual areas. The most difficult problems confronting this method always will be ethical concerns that too often bring negative scrutiny and disregard from colleagues and funding agencies. But these concerns are matters that must be dealt with on a case-by-case basis. We believe the problems inherent to this method usually can be overcome with caution, conviction, and adherence to established scientific guidelines for qualitative research—including qualitative fieldwork. High quality social science research requires the selection of methods on the grounds of technical merit and relevance to research objectives, not on rigid ethical posturing. Hopefully, the practical and methodological observations presented here will prompt reconsideration of alternative qualitative fieldwork strategies and associated pedagogical opportunities to illustrate multiple related major research methods concepts such as informed consent, confidentiality, entrée, and rapport development.

References

Adler, P. A. 1985. *Wheeling and dealing: An ethnography of an upper-level dealing and smuggling community*. New York: Columbia University Press.
Adler, P. A., and P. Adler. 1987. The past and future of ethnography. *Contemporary Ethnography* 16: 4-24.

Asch, S. E. 1951. Effects of group pressure upon the modification and distortion of judgment. In H. Guetzkow (Ed.), *Groups, leadership and men* (pp. 177-190). Pittsburgh, PA: Carnegie Press.

Babbie, E. 2009. *The practice of social research* (12th ed.). Belmont, CA: Wadsworth.

Benson, M. L. 1985. Denying the guilty mind: Accounting for involvement in white collar crime. *Criminology* 23: 583-607.

Berg, B. L. 2006. *Qualitative research methods for the social sciences* (6th ed.). Boston: Allyn & Bacon.

British Sociological Association. 2002. *Statement of ethical practice for the British Sociological Association*, section 32. Retrieved May 26, 2010, from http://www.brit-soc.co.uk/equality/Statement+Ethical+Practice.htm

Buckler, K. 2008. The quantitative/qualitative divide revisited: A study of published research, doctoral program curricula, and journal editor perceptions. *Journal of Criminal Justice Education* 19: 383-403.

Bulmer, M. 1980. Comment on the ethics of covert methods. *British Journal of Sociology* 31: 59-65.

Bryant, C. G. A. 1985. *Positivism in social theory and research*. London: MacMillan.

Calvey, D. 2000. Getting on the door and staying there: A covert participant observational study of bouncers. In G. Lee-Treweek and S. Linkogle (Eds.), *Danger in the field: Risk and ethics in social research* (pp. 43-61). London: Routledge.

Denzin, N. 1968. On the ethics of disguised observation. *Social Problems* 115: 502-504.

Douglas, B., and R. Tewksbury. 2008. Theaters and sex: An examination of anonymous sexual encounters in an erotic oasis. *Deviant Behavior* 29: 1-17.

Douglas, J. D. 1976. *Investigative and social research: Individual and team field research*. Beverly Hills, CA: Sage.

Engel, R. S., J. J. Sobol, and R. E. Worden. 2000. Further exploration of the demeanor hypothesis: The interaction effects of suspects' characteristics and demeanor on police behavior. *Justice Quarterly* 17: 235-258.

Erikson, K. T. 1967. Disguised observation in sociology. *Social Problems* 14: 366-372.

Ferrell, J. 1993. *Crimes of style: Urban graffiti and the politics of criminality.* New York: Garland.

Ferrell, J. 1997. Criminological verstehen: Inside the immediacy of crime. *Justice Quarterly* 14: 3-23.

Ferrell, J., and M. S. Hamm. 1998. *Ethnography at the edge: Crime, deviance and field research*. Boston: Northeastern University Press.

Formby, W. A., and J. Smykla. 1981. Citizen awareness in crime prevention: Do they really get involved? *Journal of Police Science and Administration* 9: 398-403.

Galliher, J. F. 1973. The protection of human subjects: A reexamination of the professional code of ethics. *The American Sociologist* 8: 93-100.

Goffman, E. 1959. *The presentation of self in everyday life*. New York: Doubleday.

Gold, R. L. 1958. Roles in sociological field observation. *Social Forces* 36: 217-222.

Gottfredson, M. R., and T. Hirschi. 1987. *Positive criminology*. Newbury Park, CA: Sage.

Hagan, F. E. 2010. *Research methods in criminal justice and criminology* (8th ed.). New York: Prentice Hall.

Higgins, G. E. 2009. Quantitative versus qualitative methods: Understanding why quantitative methods are dominant in criminology and criminal justice. *Journal of Theoretical and Philosophical Criminology* 1. Retrieved May 21, 2010, from http://jtpcrim.org/archives.htm

Holmes, S. T., R. Tewksbury, and R. M. Holmes. 2000. Do I need to publish? Or, if I don't will I perish? *Humanity & Society* 24: 375-438.

Homan, R. 1980. The ethics of covert methods. *British Journal of Sociology* 31: 46-59.

Humphreys, L. 1970. *Tearoom trade: Impersonal sex in public places*. New York: Aldine.

Jacques, S., and R. Wright. 2010. Right or wrong? Toward a theory of IRBs' (dis)approval of research. *Journal of Criminal Justice Education* 21: 42-59.

Jennings, W., C. Schreck, M. Sturtz, and M. Mahoney. 2008. Exploring the scholarly output of academic organization leadership in criminology and criminal justice: A research note on publication productivity. *Journal of Criminal Justice Education* 19: 404-416.

Jorgensen, D. L. 1989. *Participant observation: A methodology for human studies.* Newbury Park, CA: Sage.

Katz, J. 2006. Ethical escape routes for underground ethnographers. *American Ethnologist* 33: 499-506.

Klockars, C. B. 1974. *The professional fence.* New York: The Free Press.

Kraska, P. 1998. Enjoying militarism: Political/personal dilemmas in studying U.S. police paramilitary units. In J. Ferrell and M. S. Hamm (Eds.), *Ethnography at the edge: Crime, deviance and field research* (pp. 88-110). Boston: Northeastern University Press.

Maruna, S., and H. Copes. 2005. What have we learned from five decades of neutralization research? *Crime and Justice: A Review of Research* 32: 221-320.

Miller, J. M. 1995. Covert participant observation: Reconsidering the least used method. *Journal of Contemporary Criminal Justice* 11: 97-105.

Miller, J. M., and L. H. Selva. 1994. Drug enforcement's double-edged sword: An assessment of asset forfeiture programs. *Justice Quarterly* 11: 313-335.

Miller, J. M., and R. Tewksbury (Eds.). 2001. *Extreme methods: Innovative approaches to social science research.* Boston, MA: Allyn & Bacon.

Miller, J. M., and R. Tewksbury (Eds.). 2006. *Research methods: A qualitative reader.* Upper Saddle River, NJ: Prentice Hall.

Patton, M. Q. 2001. *Qualitative research & evaluation methods* (3rd ed.). Newbury Park, CA: Sage.

Polsky, N. 1967. *Hustlers, beats and others.* New York: Anchor Books.

Ronai, C. R., and C. Ellis. 1989. Turn-ons for money: Interactional strategies of the table dancer. *Journal of Contemporary Ethnography* 18: 271-298.

Roth, J. A. 1962. Comments on secret observation. *Social Problems* 9: 283-284.

Scarce, R. 1994. (No) trial (but) tribulations: When courts and ethnography conflict. *Journal of Contemporary Ethnography* 23: 123-149.

Shils, E. A. 1975. *Essays in macrosociology.* Chicago, IL: University of Chicago Press.

Shover, N. 1979. *A sociology of American corrections.* Homewood, IL: Dorsey Press.

Steffensmeier, D. J., and R. M. Terry. 1973. Deviance and respectability: An observational study of reactions to shoplifting. *Social Forces* 51: 417-426.

Stein, M. L. 1974. *Lovers, friends, slaves: The nine male sexual types.* Berkeley: Berkeley Publishing Corp.

Stewart, J. E., and D. Cannon. 1977. Effects of perpetrator status and bystander commitment to a simulated crime. *Journal of Police Science and Administration* 5: 318-323.

Taylor, J. M., and R. Tewksbury. 1995. From the inside out and the outside in: Team research in the correctional setting. *Journal of Contemporary Criminal Justice* 11: 119-136.

Tewksbury, R. 1990. Patrons of porn: Research notes on the clientele of adult bookstores. *Deviant Behavior* 11: 259-271.

Tewksbury, R. 2002. Bathhouse intercourse: Structural and behavioral aspects of an erotic oasis. *Deviant Behavior* 23: 75-112.

Tewksbury, R. 2006. Acting like an insider: Studying hidden environments as a potential participant. In J. M. Miller and R. Tewksbury (Eds.), *Research methods: A qualitative reader* (pp. 3-11). Upper Saddle River, NJ: Prentice Hall.

Tewksbury, R. 2009. Edge ethnography. In J. M. Miller (Ed.), *21st century criminology: A reference handbook* (pp. 406-412). Thousand Oaks, CA: Sage.

Tewksbury, R., D. Dabney, and H. Copes. 2010. The prominence of qualitative research in criminology and criminal justice scholarship. *Journal of Criminal Justice Education* 21: 391-411.

Tewksbury, R., M. DeMichele, and J. M. Miller. 2005. Methodological orientations of articles appearing in criminal justice's top journals: Who publishes what and where. *Journal of Criminal Justice Education* 16: 265-279.

Tewksbury, R., and P. Gagné. 1997. Assumed and presumed identities: Problems of self-presentation in field research. *Sociological Spectrum* 17: 127-155.

Tunnell, K. D. 1998. Honesty, secrecy, and deception in the sociology of crime: Confessions and reflections from the backstage. In J. Ferrell and M. S. Hamm (Eds.), *Ethnography at the edge: Crime, deviance and field research* (pp. 206-220). Boston: Northeastern University Press.

Van Maanen, J. 1988. *Tales of the field: On writing ethnography.* Chicago: University of Chicago Press.

Von Hoffman, N. 1970, January 30. Sociological snoopers. *The Washington Post*, p. 177.

Wallace, S. E. 1964. *Skid row as a way of life.* New York: Harper & Row.

Worrall, J. L. 2000. In defense of the "quantoids": More on the reasons for the quantitative emphasis in criminal justice education and research. *Journal of Criminal Justice Education* 11: 353-360.

Dangerous Intimacy: Toward a Theory of Violent Victimization in Active Offender Research

Scott Jacques and Richard Wright

Active offender research contributes to criminology, but a major concern for active offender researchers is that they will be victimized in the course of their work. With that concern in mind, experienced criminologists have recommended strategies for minimizing danger during research, but they have done so in a largely atheoretical manner. This paper calls for the development of a theory of violent victimization in active offender research, and poses the question: What determines the amount of violent victimization in such research? Answering this question is important because it has the potential to provide practical strategies for reducing victimization and, in turn, increasing the amount of research conducted and the number of insights that flow from it. This paper theorizes that active offender researchers are less likely to be threatened or physically harmed as they become more familiar with recruiters, criminals, and their relational ties. The paper concludes with a set of theoretically situated, practical tips for how criminologists might reduce the amount of violent victimization in active offender research.

Active offender research has provided criminology with unique and important insights into crime (see, among many others, Copes, Forsyth, and Brunson 2007; Decker and Van Winkle 1996; Jacobs 1999, 2000; Jacobs and Wright 2006; Jacques 2010; Jacques and Wright 2008a, 2008b; Miller 2001; Piquero and Rengert 1999; St. Jean 2007; Topalli 2005; Venkatesh 2006; Williams 1989, 1992). Despite the substantial benefits of research with active offenders, this methodological strategy is potentially dangerous (Wright and Decker 1994, p. 29). Active offender researchers have been threatened, stalked, robbed, and murdered in the course of their research (Jacobs 2006; Lee 1995). As observed by an experienced group of criminologists, "[a] serious problem confronting many social scientists is assuring the physical safety of ethnographers and other staff conducting research among potentially violent persons who are active in dangerous settings" (Williams, Dunlap, Johnson, and Hamid 1992, p. 343).

"But danger must be accommodated if we are to make the strides we need to make to really understand offender behavior" (Jacobs 2006, p. 167). Recognizing the dangers inherent in studying active offenders, researchers have recommended various strategies for avoiding violent victimization (see, e.g., Jacobs 1998, 2006; Sluka 1990; Williams et al. 1992). Although the value of this work is undeniable, its limitation is its *atheoretical* orientation (see Jacques and Wright 2008c; Venkatesh 1999, p. 285).

Without theory, scientific progress is slowed. Yet criminologists often have failed to view their methodological experiences through a *theoretical lens*, thereby rendering their recommendations difficult to falsify (see Popper 2002). What is needed, then, is a *theory of violent victimization in active offender research*. Although elements of that preliminary theory may turn out to be incorrect, the long-term goal should be to develop an empirically tested, tried-and-true theory of method that allows criminologists to reduce *their* probability of being violently victimized in the course of active offender research. Such a theory would not only have the potential to reduce violent crimes against researchers, it may also increase criminological research by providing scientists with the tools needed to safely collect data that are fundamental to documenting, explaining, and reducing crimes of all sorts.

The purpose of this paper is to stimulate discussion among criminologists seeking to understand variability between individual researchers, groups of researchers, and research situations in the rate and magnitude of violent victimization. To do so, the paper provides a definition of "violent victimization in active offender research," suggests an explanation of it that is built on existing theories (Black 1998; Cooney 2006; Jacques and Wright 2008b), then illustrates the theory by describing the experiences of active offender researchers (Arias 2006; Jacobs 2006; Mieczkowski 1988), and concludes by discussing future directions for criminology and offering a set of theoretically situated, practical recommendations for reducing the likelihood of violent victimization in active offender research. In the end, the hope is that developing a theory of victimization in research will lead to practical strategies for crime control that increase the amount of research that occurs and the number of insights that flow from it.

Violent Victimization in Active Offender Research: Concepts and Assumptions

The first step in the development of a theory of violent victimization in active offender research is to specify what that behavior "is." How is it defined? How is it measured empirically? What definitionally distinguishes violent victimizations relevant to "active offender research" from violent events that are not relevant to that process? The second step in developing such a theory is to lay bare the reasons for why studying such a behavior is an important endeavor.

A Definition of Active Offender Research

Active offender research is defined here as the process of obtaining information about criminals through conversation with or observation of unincarcerated persons involved in crime. There are at least three distinct components of active offender research: recruitment; remuneration; and data collection (Jacques and Wright 2008c, 2010; also see Dunlap and Johnson 1999; Wright, Decker, Redfern, and Smith 1992).

Recruitment is defined as the process of interacting with criminals and convincing them to provide data (Jacques and Wright 2008c). This is a quantitative variable measurable by the amount of social interaction spent convincing criminals to participate in research. For example, the more times a researcher asks a particular offender or group of offenders to participate in research, the greater is recruitment.

Remuneration is defined as the payment for participation in research (Jacques and Wright 2008c). This is a quantitative variable measurable by the amount of objects or services provided to subjects and recruiters for participation in research. For example, the more a participant is paid for cooperation in research, the greater is remuneration.

Data collection or *data quality* is defined as the process whereby knowledge about crime is ascertained by criminologists through conversation with or observation of criminals (Jacques and Wright 2008c). Data collection is a quantitative variable measurable by the *quantity* of *valid* information obtained. For instance, the more truthful information an offender provides, the greater is data collection/quality.

Defined as such, active offender research is a social, empirical, and quantifiable variable measured by (1) the number of recruitments or the amount of effort (e.g., time) spent on recruitment, (2) the number of remuneration payments or the amount of remuneration provided, and (3) the number of data collection sessions (e.g., interviews) or the amount of valid data collected. *More recruitment, remuneration, or data collection* is equivalent to *more research*.

A Definition of Violent Victimization

Violence is defined as "the use of physical force against people or property, including threats and attempts" (Black 2004, p. 146). Violence is a quantitative variable measurable by any consistent indicator of damage and destruction, such as the number of murder threats, shots fired, punches thrown, or the number of bruises or gunshot wounds. There are two prominently studied forms of violence: *predatory* and *retaliatory* (Cooney and Phillips 2002; Felson 1993; Jacques and Wright 2008a).

"*Predatory violence* is [defined as] the use of force in the acquisition of wealth or other resources," whereas *retaliatory violence* is defined as "the handling of a grievance with aggression" (Black 2004, p. 146, italics in original). A person has been *violently victimized* when someone else threatens or uses physical force against them as a means of resource acquisition (predation) or social control (retaliation).

A Definition of Violent Victimization in Active Offender Research

The above definitions of active offender research and violence suggest that *violent victimization in active offender research* is defined as threats or physical force against a researcher that occurs during or due to the recruitment of, remuneration of, observation of, or conversation with unincarcerated lawbreakers. Violent victimization in active offender research is a quantitative variable measurable by (1) the amount of physical harm experienced, and (2) the number of threats received.

The Interplay of Active Offender Research and Violent Victimization

There are two implicit assumptions in the criminological literature that deserve discussion because they lie at the very heart of the debate surrounding violent victimization in active offender research: (1) the more criminologists do research with active offenders, the greater is violent victimization in active offender research; and (2) the greater is violent victimization in active offender research, the less active offender research occurs (see Jacobs 2006; Williams et al. 1992).

In other words, common sense tells us that when criminologists come into contact with persons known to be involved in crime, especially violent kinds such as robbery or murder (see Jacobs and Wright 2006; Wright and Decker 1994), then of course there is a greater opportunity for victimization among criminologists. If, for instance, there is only one interview with an active offender conducted by one researcher, then there is only one opportunity for victimization. But if, say, there are 100 interviews with 100 active offenders conducted by a researcher, then there are 100 opportunities for victimization.

Common sense also suggests that the more often a criminologist is victimized in the course of research and the more serious are such events (as measured by injury or other factors), then there is less active offender research conducted. It stands to reason, for instance, that criminologists would be less likely to conduct active offender research if the likelihood of victimization during that activity is one in ten rather than one in a hundred or one in a thousand.

Although the above ideas are common sense, there are theoretical reasons why active offender research might attract victimization, and also why victimization repulses research (see, e.g., Gottfredson and Hirschi 1990; Hindelang, Gottfredson, and Garofalo 1978). Opportunity theory suggests, for example, that the more often a potential target (e.g., a researcher) comes into contact with a motivated offender (e.g., a potential participant) in the absence of a capable guardian (such a jail or prison guard) the more chance there is for victimization/crime (see, e.g., Cohen and Felson 1979). Deterrence/rationality theory explains behavior as the outcome of choices intended to maximize benefits and minimize costs; this perspective therefore predicts that active offender research decreases as victimization related to this work increases because it represents an increase in costs (see, e.g., Clarke and Cornish 1985). The danger associated with obtaining data from active offenders is not surprising to criminologists because the logic of various theoretical perspectives suggests that interacting with criminals and seeking information about outlawed behavior increases the odds of personal victimization.

In short, there are many good reasons why violent victimization is integrally intertwined with active offender research. These reasons provide the basis for two predictions, that are likely explainable with many different theoretical perspectives: (1) violent victimization in active offender research increases as the amount of active offender research increases; and (2) active offender research decreases as the amount of violent victimization in active offender research increases.

Although those ideas are on some level nothing more than common sense, they are empirical predictions that can be falsified or supported through the collection and analysis of data that bear on the interplay between active offender research and violent victimization.

If those predictions are verified, then it becomes clear that maximizing criminology's potential depends on the development of a theory that explains why there is variability between active offender researchers (individuals and groups) and research situations in the rate and seriousness of violent victimization. The development of a valid theory of this kind is important because its logic can be used to develop practical strategies for increasing active offender research—and the criminological knowledge that comes from it—by reducing the likelihood and magnitude of violent victimization in the course of such work.

All of the above raises the question: *Holding constant the amount of active offender research, what factors affect the amount of violent victimization in active offender research?*

Toward a Theory of Violent Victimization in Active Offender Research

The third key step in developing a theory of violent victimization in active offender research is to view that behavior through a particular *theoretical lens*, and then make falsifiable predictions regarding how variability in specific factors influences the behavior in question. Specifically, between situations, people, or groups, what factors affect the amount of violent victimization in active offender research?

Although many theoretical perspectives may be able to answer this question, the present paper looks at this phenomenon through the lens of *pure sociology* (see Black 1976, 1995, 1998; Cooney 2006). The goal of pure sociology is to use sociological variables to explain sociological behavior (Black 1976, 1995).

There are at least five variables of interest to pure sociologists: wealth, relationships, organization, culture, and social control (Black 1976, 1998). Pure sociologists attempt to specify how variability in any of those factors explains the others and itself. For instance, a pure sociologist might ask, "How does any given act of social control (e.g., incarceration) affect relationships (e.g., marriage), organization (e.g., gang membership), culture (e.g., educational attainment), wealth (e.g., income), or subsequent acts of social control (e.g., further incarceration)?"

At present, there are three purely sociological theories with direct relevance to developing an understanding of violent victimization in active offender research: Jacques and Wright's (2008c) preliminary theory of active offender research; Black's (1983, 1998) theory of self-help; and Cooney's (2006) theory of predation.

Jacques and Wright's Theory of Active Offender Research

In an attempt to transcend the limits of atheoretical methodology and move criminology toward a more scientific understanding of the knowledge production process in active offender research, Jacques and Wright (2008c) have begun to develop a preliminary "theory of method" nested in the paradigm of pure sociology (also Jacques and Wright 2010).

They have proposed a preliminary theory of active offender research that, in part, uses *relational distance*, or intimacy, to explain variation in recruitment, remuneration, and data collection (quality). Relational distance is defined as the degree to which people participate in each other's lives (Black 1976, p. 40). "It is possible to measure relational distance in many ways, including the scope, frequency, and length of interaction between people, the age of their relationship, and the nature and number of links between them in a social network" (1976, p. 41).

In short, the relational distance between two people decreases as the quantity of social interaction between them and their relational ties (e.g., friends, family, neighbors, and associates) increases.

> All else equal, for example, two persons who have traded drugs are closer in relational distance than two people who have never traded, ... and two persons who have talked together about drugs are closer in relational distance than two persons who have never communicated. (Jacques and Wright 2008c, p. 26)

There are at least three key roles in active offender research: researcher; recruiter; and, active criminal. *Researcher* is defined as an actor who records data about crime obtained through conversation with or observation of active criminals. *Recruiter* is defined as an individual who attempts to convince active criminals to participate in research, but who does not record data. *Active criminal* is defined as an unincarcerated person who is involved in crime.[1] Researchers, recruiters, and criminals vary in the amount of time they have spent in each other's company. By definition, the more researchers, recruiters, and criminals have interacted with each other or each other's relational ties, the closer they are in relational distance.

Jacques and Wright (2008c) asked the question: "How does relational distance between researchers, recruiters, and criminals affect subject recruit-ment, resource expenditure, and the quantity and quality of data produced?" (p. 26). In offering a tentative answer to that question, they deduced three falsifiable propositions: As the relational distance between a researcher, recruiter, and criminal decreases (1) the probability that the criminal will be recruited increases, (2) the amount of remuneration provided to the criminal decreases, and (3) the quantity and validity of data provided by the criminal increases. This theory suggests, for example, that a researcher's or recruiter's criminally involved friend or family member is more likely than a stranger to be recruited for active offender research, to receive less remuneration, and to provide a plentiful amount of truthful information.

Black's Theory of Self-Help

Black (1983, 1998) has developed a theory of self-help that has direct relevance for understanding violent victimization in active offender research. Self-help is defined as "the handling of a grievance by unilateral aggression ... It ranges from quick and simple gestures of disapproval ... to massive assaults resulting in numerous deaths" (Black 1998, p. 74). Thus, retaliatory violence is one kind of self-help, but not the only kind. Violent retaliation is defined as the use of threats or physical force in punishing a wrongdoer (Black 1983, 2004).

Black's (1998, pp. 74-79) theory of self-help argues that retaliatory violence is affected by several different sociological variables, one of which is relational distance. According to Black's theory, "as the relational distance between persons grows smaller, the likelihood of retaliatory violence between them declines" (pp. 76-77). Black's theory suggests, for instance, that friends are less likely than strangers to solve disputes with violence.

Cooney's Theory of Predation

Violence, however, is not always moralistic (Cooney and Phillips 2002; Jacques and Wright 2008a). Cooney (2006) has begun to construct a theory of predation that also is useful in explaining violent victimization in active offender research. Preda-tion is broadly defined as "the non-moralistic seizure of the person or property

---

1. Note that while a criminal simultaneously can be a recruiter *or* researcher, a recruiter cannot simultaneously be a researcher because, by definition, a researcher *records* data but a recruiter does not. If the "recruiter" records data, then that recruiter is a researcher (even if the researcher "recruits" criminals for research).

of another" (Cooney 2006, p. 58), and includes many acts of fraud, burglary, auto-theft, robbery, kidnapping, and murder (see Cooney 2006; Cooney and Phillips 2002; Jacques and Wright 2008a). Thus, predation is sometimes violent, but not always. Violent predation is defined as the use of threats or force to take an actor's property for non-moralistic reasons (Cooney and Phillips 2002, p. 81).

Cooney's (2006) theory of predation holds that violent predation is affected by the relational distance between prey and predators. According to Cooney's theory, as two persons become closer in relational distance, the likelihood that they will prey on one another declines. Cooney's theory predicts, for example, that two persons who are strangers are more likely to violently prey on each other than are friends.

A Theory of Violent Victimization in Active Offender Research

When combined, the logic of Jacques and Wright's (2008c) theory of active offender research, Black's (1998, pp. 76-77) theory of self-help, and Cooney's (2006) theory of predation suggest that violent victimization in active offender research may behave as a function of the relational distance between research-ers, recruiters, and criminals. Stated as a formal proposition:

> Violent victimization in active offender research decreases as the relational distance between researchers, recruiters, and criminals decreases.

In other words, and all else equal, the more often researchers interact with recruiters, criminals, and their associates (e.g., friends and family), the less likely they are to be violently victimized for reasons related to recruiting, remunerating, and collecting criminological data from active offenders (also see Jacobs 2006, p. 164; Williams et al. 1992, pp. 350-357).

The above proposition predicts, for instance, that a researcher who is friends with *many* criminals is less likely to be violently victimized while conducting active offender research than one who has spent time with just *one* criminal, but that person is less likely to be victimized than a researcher *without any* social links to the underworld. In addition, the proposition predicts that the more intimate a researcher is with a recruiter, the less likely that researcher is to be assaulted, robbed, raped, or killed during the course of research. The proposition further suggests that the more intimate a researcher is with the relational ties of a recruiter or criminal (i.e., their friends or family), the less likely that researcher is to be victimized for reasons related to active offender research.

Descriptions of Violent Victimization in Active Offender Research

Do the experiences of active offender researchers provide empirical support for the above proposition? Below, the paper provides descriptions of violent victimization in active offender research culled from the extant literature (Arias 2006; Jacobs 1998; Mieczkowski 1988). These experiences illustrate how the amount of intimacy between researchers, recruiters, and criminals affects the likelihood that researchers are violently victimized for reasons related to the recruitment of, remuneration of, observation of, or conversation with active criminals.

Arias' Study of Drug Traffickers in Rio de Janeiro

Arias' (2006) study of drug trafficking in Rio de Janeiro, Brazil, demonstrates how closer relational distance can deter violent victimization in active offender research. Brazil has a longstanding reputation for criminal violence, and Arias contributes to criminology by examining how politics and networks intertwine to influence lawbreaking. His study is based on findings from qualitative data obtained in conversations with and observations of law-abiding and criminal persons living in Rio's shantytowns, or *favelas*.

The relational distance between Arias and criminals

In the beginning of his study, Arias (2006) "sought to build individual ties that would help [him] gain access to favelas" (p. xi). Eventually, he came into contact with an employee of a non-governmental organization, who provided him "with a long list of names and phone numbers of civic organizers in favelas around the city" (2006, p. xii). Arias spent time in three favelas, and in each community sought to "establish strong connections with leaders of the local Associação de Moradores (Residents' Association, AM), the civic organization that generally mediates relations between outsiders and the community. In two of the three favelas" that Arias studied, the AM leaders "had very close ties to the local drug gang" (p. xii). Thus, we might say that, over time, Arias closed relational distance with the AM leaders, who were close in relational distance to members of the local drug gang.

Relational distance and violent victimization in active offender research

Does Arias' experience bear out the theory that violent victimization in active offender research decreases as the relational distance between researchers, recruiters, and criminals decreases? According to Arias, he experienced fewer confrontations while conducting research as he increasingly interacted with community members. It is theoretically interesting that as Arias became closer in relational distance to favela residents, the number of confrontations between them grew smaller. In Arias' own words:

> When I started work, drug dealers often challenged me as I walked by their *bocas*. I always responded that I was visiting one of my connections in the AM, and they invariably let me in without further problems. After awhile if an inexperienced lookout stopped me, others would just say something like, "Oh, he's a friend of Josias, its cool," and let me go by. In one community, the adolescent gang member who kept watch became friendly and joked with me as I went to work. (2006, p. xii)

On one occasion, Arias was threatened by a drug dealer, but his close connections with the godfather of a drug trafficker's child deterred his violent victimization. As Arias recounts:

> The following event drives home the usefulness of ... connections [to the AM]. One night I was working very late in the favela of Tubarão, one of my research sites, interviewing a drug addict and his girlfriend, when a dealer decided that I looked like an X-9 (undercover informant) that gang members suspected operated in the favela. If he and other traffickers decided this was true they would have brutally murdered me. The addict I had interviewed tried to explain things but did not get anywhere. Despite all of this, I was never really nervous since I had the protection of the AM president who was also the godfather of an important drug trafficker's child. On other occasions this had always worked to resolve potential problems. After I explained myself and my work, the trafficker apologized, suggested I take care and that I, perhaps, should not stay out on the street so late. (2006, p. xii)

In sum, what we see from Arias' experience in studying criminal behavior in Brazilian shantytowns is that violent victimization is affected by the relational distance between researchers and criminals, which is in part dependent on their common relational ties. Had Arias been less well connected with AM members or less familiar with drug gang members (i.e., further in relational distance from them), the threats against him *may have* escalated to assault, robbery, kidnapping, or even murder. And had Arias' experience with victimization been more common or serious, then he *may have* conducted less subsequent research.

Mieczkowski's Study of Heroin Dealers in Detroit

Mieczkowski's (1988) study in Detroit, Michigan, provides further support for the theory that the amount of intimacy between researchers, recruiters, and criminals affects the amount of violent victimization in active offender research. "Starting in the 1970s, the major newspapers and other media in the city of Detroit began reporting on groups of teenage street-level heroin dealers ... These heroin-selling units were collectively referred to as 'Young Boys, Inc.' (YBI)" (1988, p. 40). Mieczkowski (1986, 1988) made methodological and theoretical contributions to criminology by interviewing heroin dealers operating as part of the YBI.

> The Detroit study was based on the interview technique, coupled with observation and description of the subjects within their own natural setting. It involved

meeting contacts on the street ... and meeting subjects in various settings such as dope houses. (Mieczkowski 1988, p. 40)

Relational distance between Mieczkowski and criminals

Mieczkowski's (1988) "major procedural problem was how to gain access to YBI drug dealers A plausible and nonthreatening entrée was needed" (p. 40). Access to the underworld came through one of Mieczkowski's connections, a student named "Dave":

> Attempts to establish an initial contact with Young Boys operatives came about through the voluntary work of a contact named Dave...[,] a student in a criminal justice course who became familiar with my research ambitions. He said that he could put me in touch with numerous drug operatives of the Young Boys type. Dave was able to help me for several reasons. First, he was a resident in the Jeffries Housing Project, a major center of heroin activity. He was not only a resident but had lived there since birth. Second, although Dave was not a drug dealer or user, his two brothers were both drug dealers. Third, he knew nearly all of the major dealers in the Jeffries. (1988, p. 41)

As relates to measuring the intimacy between persons involved in the Detroit project, Mieczkowski initially had no direct ties to heroin dealers and so was far away from them in relational distance. However, his student, Dave, bridged that distance. Dave's close relational distance to criminals gave Mieczkowski access to the information held by them (also see Jacques and Wright 2008c, pp. 28-29). Because all of the dealers who participated in the study were unknown to Mieczkowski prior to the interview, his relational distance from each of them depended wholly on Dave's relational distance from each individual; the less well Dave knew a participant, the further in relational distance that participant was from Mieczkowski.

Relational distance and violent victimization in active offender research

Does Mieczkowski's study of heroin sellers indicate whether or not violent victimization in active offender research diminishes as the relational distance between researchers, recruiters, and criminals lessens? Two "frightening" incidents experienced by Mieczkowski suggest that victimization is affected by relational distance. As recounted by Mieczkowski:

> Consideration was given to the potential dangers and risks involved in approaching and sustaining contact with heroin vendors ... To those knowledgeable about the street heroin trade and those familiar with the city of Detroit, fear of violence is not an unfounded concern ... Dave felt that there was some inevitable risk to us, but he was confident that his supervision and prior solicitation of informants would obviate extreme risk ... Thus, the problem of violence was not

eliminated, but it was reduced to a reasonable degree … In fact, there were only two experiences which were frightening.

Cruising sometimes led to interviewing on the steps of a housing unit … Sometimes we would sit and talk as a group. While engaged in one such scene, *with Dave absent*, I was harassed by an *unknown* individual who was very belligerent and demanded money from me. He jostled me several times and continued to demand money. Eventually, he departed after receiving some money from me …

[In a separate frightening incident,] Dave had hastily set up an interview with a recently released convict who had a heavy background in drug dealing. Dave told me the person had just been released from prison where he did time for "taking a dude out"—killing him. One of Dave's sisters was dating the individual, and through that route Dave had made contact with him. *Since he was not a neighborhood person, Dave had no firsthand knowledge of his credibility* … Dave had briefed him on the project … as we were introduced … At the start of the interview, the person became quite upset and insisted that he had nothing to do with drugs … As time wore on, the person became increasingly agitated. Attempts at terminating the interview were met with his insistence that I sit down, shut up, and listen to him. (1988, pp. 41–43, italics added)

In short, Mieczkowski's lack of direct ties to drug dealers meant that his relational distance from research participants was mostly dependent on Dave's relational distance from them. The greater Dave's relational distance from the participant, the greater was Mieczkowski's relational distance from the participant. The theory of violent victimization in active offender research proposed in this paper suggests that as researchers, recruiters, and criminals become less intimate, the quantity of victimization increases. During the course of his research, the most "frightening" incidents experienced by Mieczkowski involved individuals who were, in comparison to other participants, further away from Dave in relational distance. Had Dave known the "individual who was very belligerent," then Mieczkowski may have not been harassed. Conversely, had Dave been further in relational distance from the murderer (e.g., by not being the brother of his girlfriend), Mieczkowski *may have* been murdered or otherwise violently victimized. And had Mieczkowski been more often or more seriously victimized, then he *may have* conducted less subsequent research.

Jacobs' Study of Crack Dealers in St. Louis

Jacobs (1998, 2006) was robbed and then stalked for reasons related to his criminological research in St. Louis, Missouri (see Jacobs 1999). In a groundbreaking study, Jacobs explores the world of street-corner crack-cocaine dealing. What motivates crack selling? What is the social organization of crack selling? What is the role of predation in crack markets? How do the police affect crack dealing? What is the future of crack selling? Jacobs addresses these questions and others with qualitative data obtained during interviews with 40 active crack dealers.

Relational distance between Jacobs and criminals

Jacobs gained access to the information possessed by active crack dealers by building social ties with them, their friends and family, and fellow community members. Jacobs describes his initial attempts at accessing the underworld:

> I began frequenting a neighborhood known for open street-level crack sales... For weeks, I would either walk or slowly drive through the area to try to be recognized, attempt to capitalize on what Goffman has called second seeings... Unfortunately, this process did not go as easily as Goffman suggests... A few more weeks passed and more trips, but I had yet to make any direct contacts. (1999, p. 13)

In need of data and apparently out of better options, Jacobs turned to a more dangerous approach (also see Jacobs 2006):

> Finally, I decided to get out of my car and approach the individuals I had seen dealing ... I told the dealers who I was and that I wished to take a few minutes out of their day to interview them about street life. Predictably they scoffed, accused me of being the "poh-lice," and instructed me to "get the hell out of here." Two days later, I tried again. I showed the dealers my university identification and told them that the interviews would be confidential ... and that they would be paid for their time and effort. (Jacobs 1999, p. 14)

This second interaction with the street dealers was a positive turning point in the study, as it opened up the collection of valid and plentiful data. The individuals who Jacobs initially approached served as recruiters for the study, and from that point onward the sample began to snowball:

> The first five respondents were recruited directly from the dealers I initially approached. Four of these five became contacts and provided six additional referrals. Three of these six then referred nine additional respondents. This chain referral method was carried out to secure a forty-person sample. (Jacobs 1999, pp. 19-20)

As relates to measuring the relational distance between Jacobs and street criminals, his description of the recruitment process suggests that Jacobs is closer in relational distance to the crack dealers he "initially approached" than he is to the dealers contacted thereafter since he has known the former group of dealers longer.

Relational distance and violent victimization in active offender research

Does Jacobs' experience provide any supporting or counter evidence for the theory that violent victimization in active offender research decreases as the relational distance between researchers, recruiters, and criminals decreases? To this point, little has been said about why it is necessary to distinguish

128

between predatory victimization and retaliatory victimizations. Jacobs' (1998) case shows why such a distinction has important theoretical implications.

Recall that the difference between predation and retaliation is that the latter is social control, or conflict management, whereas the former is exploitation (Cooney and Phillips 2002; Jacques and Wright 2008a). If a criminologist is violently victimized for reasons related to active offender research, the victimization is deemed predatory if it did not result from a pre-existing grievance. Conversely, if the researcher's perceived wrongdoing prompted their victimization, then the incident is deemed retaliatory.

Jacobs (1998) was violently victimized by a crack dealer, known as Luther. This victimization began as a robbery but escalated to more than a month of stalking. Jacobs' description of his research-related, violent victimization is perhaps the most lucid such account available in the extant literature:

"Yo, Bruce, come on down the set [neighborhood]. Meet where we usually do," Luther said, and hung up the phone. A trusted contact for an ongoing study on street-level crack dealers and a crack dealer himself, I had no reason to question him. "Just another interview," I thought... I went to the bank, withdrew fifty dollars for subject payments, and drove fifteen minutes to the dope set I was coming to know so well.

Luther flagged me down as I turned the corner. The seventeen-year-old high school drop-out opened the door and jumped in. "Swerve over there." He pointed to a parking space behind the dilapidated three-story building he called home. "Stop the car—turn it off."... He produced a pistol from under a baggy white T-shirt. "Gimme all your fuckin' money or I'll blow your motherfuckin' head off!"

"What the fuck is your problem?" I said, astonished that someone I trusted had suddenly turned on me. The gun was large, a six-shooter, probably a long-barrel .45 ... Why was he doing this? How did I get myself into the situation? It was the kind of thing you hear about on the evening news but don't expect to confront, even though I knew studying active offenders risked such a possibility.

I frantically pondered a course of action as Luther's tone became more and more hostile. He was sweating. "Just calm down, Luther, just calm down—everything's cool," I trembled. "Don't shoot—I'll give you what you want. "Gimme all your fuckin' money!" he repeated. "I ain't fuckin' around—I'll waste you right here!" I reached in my left-hand pocket for the fifty dollars and handed it over. As I did so, I cupped my right hand precariously an inch from the muzzle of his gun, which was pointing directly into my abdomen. I can survive a gunshot, I thought to myself, as long as I slow the bullet down.

He snatched the five, crisp ten-dollar bills and made a quick search of the vehicle's storage areas to see if I was holding out. "Ok," he said, satisfied there were no more funds. "Now turn your head around!" For all I knew, he was going to shoot me and run; his right hand was poised on the door handle, his left on the trigger. "Just take your money, man, I'm not gonna do anything." "Turn the fuck around!" he snapped.

As I pondered escape routes, he jammed the gun into his pants as quickly as he had drawn it, flung open the door, and disappeared behind the tenements. I hit the ignition and drove slowly and methodically from the scene, grateful to have escaped injury, but awestruck by his brazen violation of trust.

If this were the end of the story, things would have normalized, I would have learned a lesson about field research, and I would have gone about my business. But Luther was not through. Over the next six weeks, he called my apartment five to ten times a day, five days a week, harassing, taunting, irritating, baiting me.

I'd arrive home to see the answering machine lit up with messages. "I can smell the mousse in your hair—huh, huh, huh," his sinister laugh echoing through the apartment. One message ... caught my undivided attention: "897 Longacre—huh, huh, huh," he laughed as I heard him flipping through the phone book pages and identifying my address. "We'll [he and his homeboys] be over tomorrow." I didn't sleep well that night or for the next six weeks. (Jacob 1998, pp. 160-162, brackets in original)

After being robbed and stalked for six weeks, Jacobs was emotionally exhausted yet felt as though there was no end in sight to his torture. He "had to do something" (p. 162). The chance came when "the telephone rang, and Luther's number displayed on the caller ID" (p. 162). Jacobs (1998) "picked up the phone and started talking" to his victimizer (p. 162):

"What do you want?"

"Why do you keep hangin' up on me? All I want is to talk."

"What do you expect me to do, *like* you? [sardonically, on the verge of losing it.] You fuckin' robbed me and I trusted you and now you call me and leave these fuckin' messages and you want me to *talk* to you? [incredulous]"

"I only did that 'cause you fucked me over. I only ganked [robbed] you 'cause you fucked me."

"What are you talking about?"

He proceeded to explain that without him, none of the forty interviews I obtained would have been possible. True, Luther was the first field contact to believe that I was a researcher, not a cop. He was my first respondent, and he was responsible for starting a snowball of referrals on his word that I was "cool." But after he could no longer provide referrals, I moved on, using his contacts to find new ones and eliminating him from the chain. My newfound independence was inexplicable to him and a slap in the face. **He wanted vengeance; the robbery and taunting were exactly that.** (Jacob 1998, pp. 162-163, italics and brackets in original, bold added)

Jacobs' victimization clearly demonstrates why it is theoretically necessary to distinguish between acts of predation and retaliation (also see Cooney and

Phillips 2002; Jacques and Wright 2008a). Without distinguishing between predatory and retaliatory violence, his story would suggest that closer relational distance does not reduce the odds of violent victimization. Although the distinction between predation and retaliation reduces theoretical simplicity and generality, the distinction is necessary because *the nature of events preceding a situation affect (1) whether a victimization occurs, and, if it does, (2) the magnitude of that victimization.*

It makes common sense, for instance, that a researcher who "wrongs" a criminal is more likely to be violently victimized than the one who does not. In Jacobs' own words:

> Luther felt wronged, he was mad, and he took it out by robbing me. I believe the robbery would never have happened had I been more attentive to the special referral role he had come to play in my research and had I communicated my gratitude and reasons for moving on more clearly. Nobody deserves less ... but in my quest for more data, I lost sight of this. (2006, p. 160)

It is necessary to "hold constant," the nature of events preceding victimization because otherwise the *true effect* of relational distance—whatever it may be—will remain unknown or be misinterpreted.

Allow us to speculate about what might have happened if, all else equal, Jacobs (or another researcher) had either closer or further relational distance from Luther (or another person) at the time of the conflict. Put differently: If Jacobs had wronged Luther in the same way but was more (or less) intimate with that person, would he have been violently victimized? And if he was victimized, would the event have been more or less serious? The theory proposed in this paper suggests, for example, that if Jacobs and Luther had been friends or family rather than persons who met recently on a street, then Jacobs would have been less likely to be robbed or stalked as retribution for his wrongdoing. On the other hand, had Luther and Jacobs been less well acquainted (e.g., had Luther *not* been Jacobs' first respondent and recruiter, but rather his tenth or fortieth), then he *may have* been physically harmed during the robbery or stalking, perhaps even murdered as payback for his perceived betrayal. And had Jacobs' victimization been a regular or serious event, then he *may have* conducted less subsequent research.

Implications for Reducing Victimization and Increasing Research

Active offender research is an important part of qualitative criminology (see, e.g., St. Jean 2007; Topalli 2005; Venkatesh 2006; Williams 1989, 1992; Wright and Decker 1994, 1997). The benefits of active offender research, however, occasionally come at the cost of violent victimization (see, e.g., Jacobs 1998, 2006). Recognizing this, various researchers have recommended strategies for avoiding and minimizing danger during research (see, e.g., Sluka 1990; Williams et al. 1992). Although these recommendations are valuable, they have remained atheoretical, which is problematic because they are difficult to falsify (see Popper 2002).

Therefore, this paper has called for the development of a *theory of violent victimization in active offender research*. The goal is long term: to develop an empirically tested, tried-and-true theory of method that provides criminologists with practical strategies to reduce *their* probability of being violently victimized for reasons related to the recruitment of, remuneration of, observation of, or conversation with unincarcerated criminals. The value of such a theory is that reducing the amount of victimization related to research should increase research and the insights that flow from it. Thus, the question was posed: *Holding constant the amount of active offender research, what determines the amount of violent victimization in active offender research?*

This question was addressed by defining "violent victimization in active offender research" and combining the logic of three purely sociological theories (Black 1998; Cooney 2006; Jacques and Wright 2008c) to construct an empirically falsifiable proposition. For the time being, we suggest that active offender researchers are less likely to be threatened or physically harmed as they become more intimate with recruiters, criminals, and their relational ties (e.g., friends and family), holding all else constant (e.g., whether the event was predatory or retaliatory).

Effect of Relational Distance on Victimization and Research

Theorizing violent victimization in active offender research is important because such theories have implications for understanding and increasing the amount of knowledge produced by criminologists. If, as we suggested in the beginning, active offender research decreases as the amount of violent victimization in active offender research increases, then the amount of relational distance between researchers, recruiters, and criminals should have an effect on the amount of research conducted. Stated as a formal proposition:

> Violent victimization in active offender research decreases as the relational distance between researchers, recruiters, and criminals decreases, and, in turn, the amount of active offender research increases.

Stated differently, the ideas proposed in this paper suggest that researchers who have more intimate relationships with offenders and recruiters are more likely to recruit, remunerate, or collect data from criminals *because they are less likely to be violently victimized in their course of their research* (cf. Jacques and Wright 2008c).

The above proposition predicts, for instance, that a researcher who is friends with *many* criminals is more likely to do active offender research because that person is less likely to be violently victimized than a researcher who has spent time with just *one* criminal, but that person is less likely to be victimized than a researcher *without any* social links to the underworld. In addition, the proposition predicts that the more intimate a researcher is with a recruiter, the more likely research is to be conducted because the less likely that researcher is to be assaulted, robbed, raped, or killed during the course of research. The proposition further suggests that the more intimate a researcher is with the relational ties of a recruiter or criminal (i.e., their friends or family), the more likely research is to occur because the less likely that researcher is to be victimized for reasons related to active offender research.

Future Directions for Theorizing Victimization and Research

This paper has numerous theoretical limitations, including a narrowed focus on relational distance, pure sociology, violent victimization, and active offender research. Thus, much work is left to be done by theorists. They should specify the implications of various paradigms for explaining different kinds of victimization and research.

It is clear, for instance, that beyond relational distance, other aspects of social life may have relevance for explaining violent victimization in active offender research. Black's theory of self-help argues that disputants are more involved in retaliation when they are low in social status (Black 1983), equal in status, socially distant, immobile, functionally independent, and organized (Black 1998). What Black's theory implies, then, is that the researchers who are most likely to be victimized are those who are low in social status, organized, immobile, equal in status with recruiters and criminals, and socially distant and functionally independent from such persons. In addition, Cooney's (2006) theory posits that predation increases as a direct function of social distance. This paper has examined how one part of social distance, namely relational distance, affects victimization. But Cooney's theory suggests that the amount of cultural distance between researchers, recruiters, and criminals also affects violent victimization in active offender research. Theorists should further explore the relevance of purely sociological theory for understanding danger in research.

In addition, it is imperative to recognize that violent victimization in active offender research can be addressed from many different theoretical perspectives. Rational choice theory (Clarke and Cornish 1985), for instance, might address it by examining how the relative costs and benefits of victimizing an active offender researcher determine its prevalence and magnitude. Opportunity theorists (see, e.g., Cohen and Felson 1979; Hindelang et al. 1978) may explain it as a function of variability across time and space in how targets (criminologists and their wealth) and offenders (recruiters and criminals) come together in the absence of capable guardians (e.g., police). Social learning theory (Akers and Jensen 2006) would perhaps address it by specifying how violent victimization is affected by recruiters' and criminals' differential association, imitation, reinforcement, and definitions. Gottfredson and Hirschi's (1990) theory predicts that the lower a criminal's self-control, the more likely that person is to threaten or physically harm a researcher. Those theories and others (e.g., Guo, Roettger, and Cai 2008; Sampson and Laub 1993) may shed light on how violent victimization in active offender research "behaves." Thus, criminologists should specify the implications of various theoretical perspectives for understanding and reducing threats and physical harm that occur in the course of active offender research.

This paper has focused on violent victimization. An alternative theoretical approach would be to theorize not only violent but other kinds of victimization too, such as burglary, fraud, and vandalism (see Jacques and Wright 2008a). What factors, for example, affect the chance that the home or office of a researcher will be burglarized by a research participant? As relates to fraud, Jacques and Wright's (2008c) theory of method argues that criminals tell more lies as they become less intimate with recruiters and researchers, and this in turn suggests that fraud—or deceptive trading—increases in tandem with the relational distance between persons involved in the research. Theorists should specify what factors affect the likelihood of various crimes against researchers in the course of their work.

It is obvious that research-related danger is not confined to active offender research (e.g., see, Athens 1997, pp. 133-136). Among others, anthropologists, demographers, and health workers conducting research in war torn countries face the possibility that they will be violently victimized for reasons related to their work; think of the amount of danger associated with surveying households during the Iraq War (Roberts, Lafta, Garfield, Khudhairi, and Burnham 2004). The common concern among many scientists that they or their associates will be violently victimized for reasons related to research suggests that a scientific approach to understanding "violent victimization in science" is important for practical as well as academic reasons. Criminologists and other scientists should develop and test theories of violent victimization in science so that scientists can reduce their likelihood of being victimized and also so that danger does not inhibit scientific progress.

Future Directions for Researching Victimization and Research

Another limitation of this paper is that it does not attempt to falsify or support the theory through the statistical analysis of data. We hope that researchers will devote their attention to determining the validity of theories aimed at explaining violent victimization in active offender research. Such research would not only contribute to criminology by determining what factors do and do not affect violent victimization, it also would give researchers the information they need to significantly and substantially reduce the probability and magnitude of danger associated with collecting information from criminals.

Reality is complex and this makes testing almost any theory a difficult endeavor. When evaluating the validity of a theory, it is always important to control for other factors that may influence the behavior in question. It is imperative that when testing the theory proposed in this paper, the events preceding and surrounding the (absence of) victimization are controlled in analyses. For instance, recruitment, remuneration, and various forms and aspects of data collection (e.g., interviews versus unobtrusive observations) all have their own unique contingencies that likely affect the opportunity for victimization. Therefore, tests of our theory should control for whether the victimization followed from a recruitment effort, remuneration payment, or data collection session. In addition, researchers would also want to control for the factors specified by other theories and also for basic demographic variables such as age, sex, and the race/ethnicity of researchers, recruiters, and criminals.

Theoretically Situated, Practical Advice for Reducing Victimization and Increasing Research

For now, however, the validity of any theory of violent victimization in active offender research is less important than the acknowledgment that this methodological problem *can be—indeed should be—theorized*, and that, in time, this may reduce the amount of threats and physical harm experienced by criminologists in the course of their research, and, in turn, increase the amount of such research and insights that emerge from it. Atheoretical descriptions and explanations of method should be abandoned. Criminologists should always attempt to view their own behavior through a *theoretical lens*. The value of a theoretical approach to method is that theoretically situated recommendations can be constructed and then supported or falsified through empirical testing.

The theoretical proposition proposed in this paper suggests four pieces of practical, albeit tentative, advice for criminologists seeking to minimize the amount of violent victimization in active offender research and increase their involvement in such research:

1. The more time a researcher spends with *a recruiter*, the less likely they are to be threatened or physically harmed for reasons related to research, and so the more research is conducted. Researchers thus should interact more often with recruiters.
2. The more time a researcher spends with *a criminal*, the less likely they are to be threatened or physically harmed for reasons related to research, and so the more research is conducted. Researchers thus should interact more often with criminals.
3. The more time a researcher spends with *the relational ties of a recruiter*, the less likely they are to be threatened or physically harmed for reasons related to research, and so the more research is conducted. Researchers thus should interact more often with the relational ties of recruiters.
4. The more time a researcher spends with *the relational ties of a criminal*, the less likely they are to be threatened or physically harmed for reasons

related to research, and so the more research is conducted. Researchers thus should interact more often with the relational ties of criminals.

In sum, the task for criminologists is to develop and test theoretically situated suggestions for reducing violent victimization in active offender research, and to use quantitative and qualitative research to support or falsify those suggestions. Even if they are proven to be wrong, criminology and methodology will have progressed by establishing what does *not* reduce the probability of active offender researchers being victimized in the course of their research. That is often how science advances. Better yet, where the suggestions *are* supported through research, active offender researchers will have acquired an empirically proven tool for reducing *their* odds of being violently victimized and thereby increase their recruitment of, remuneration of, observation of, or conversation with unincarcerated criminals.

References

Akers, R. L., and G. F. Jensen. 2006. The empirical status of social learning theory. In F. T. Cullen, J. P. Wright, and K. R. Blevins (Eds.), *Taking stock: The status of criminological theory* (pp. 37-76). New Brunswick, NJ: Transaction Publishers.

Arias, E. D. 2006. *Drugs and democracy in Rio de Janeiro: Trafficking, social networking, and public security.* Chapel Hill: University of North Carolina Press.

Athens, L. 1997. *Violent criminal acts and actors revisited.* Champagne: University of Illinois Press.

Black, D. 1976. *The behavior of law.* New York: Academic Press.

Black, D. 1983. Crime as social control. *American Sociological Review* 48: 34-45.

Black, D. 1995. The epistemology of pure sociology. *Law and Social Inquiry* 20: 829-870.

Black, D. 1998. *The social structure of right and wrong* (Rev. ed.). San Diego, CA: Academic Press.

Black, D. 2004. Violent structures. In M. A. Zahn, H. H. Brownstein, and S. L. Jackson (Eds.), *Violence: From theory to research* (pp. 145-158). Newark, NJ: LexisNexis/Anderson.

Clarke, R. V., and D. B. Cornish. 1985. Modeling offenders' decisions: A framework for research and policy. In M. Tonry (Ed.), *Crime and justice: A review of research*, Vol. 6 (pp. 147-185). Chicago: University of Chicago Press.

Cohen, L., and M. Felson. 1979. Social change and crime rate trends: A routine activity approach. *American Sociological Review* 44: 588-608.

Cooney, M. 2006. The criminological potential of pure sociology. *Crime, Law, and Social Change* 46: 51-63.

Cooney, M., and S. Phillips. 2002. Typologizing violence: A Blackian perspective. *International Journal of Sociology and Social Policy* 22: 75-108.

Copes, H., C. J. Forsyth, and R. K. Brunson. 2007. Rock rentals: The social organization and interpersonal dynamics of crack-for-cars transactions in Louisiana, USA. *British Journal of Criminology* 47: 885-899.

Decker, S., and B. Van Winkle. 1996. *Life in the gang: Family, friends, and violence.* New York: Cambridge University Press.

Dunlap, E., and B. D. Johnson. 1999. Gaining access to hidden populations: Strategies for gaining cooperation of drug sellers/dealers and their families in ethnographic research. *Drugs and Society* 14: 127-149.

Felson, R. B. 1993. Predatory and dispute-related violence: A social interactionist approach. *Advances in Criminological Theory* 5: 189-235.

Gottfredson, M. R., and T. Hirschi. 1990. *A general theory of crime*. Stanford, CA: Stanford University Press.

Guo, G., M. E. Roettger, and T. Cai. 2008. The integration of genetic propensities into social-control models of delinquency and violence among male youths. *American Sociological Review* 73: 543-568.

Hindelang, M. J., M. R. Gottfredson, and J. Garofalo. 1978. *Victims of personal crime*. Cambridge: Ballinger.

Jacobs, B. A. 1998. Researching crack dealers: Dilemmas and contradictions. In J. Ferrell and M. S. Hamm (Eds.), *Ethnography at the edge: Crime, deviance, and field research* (pp. 160-177). Boston: Northeastern University Press.

Jacobs, B. A. 1999. *Dealing crack*. Boston: Northeastern University Press.

Jacobs, B. A. 2000. *Robbing drug dealers*. New York: Aldine de Gruyter.

Jacobs, B. A. 2006. The case for dangerous fieldwork. In D. Hobbs and R. Wright (Eds.), *The Sage handbook of fieldwork* (pp. 157-168). Thousand Oaks, CA: Sage.

Jacobs, B. A., and R. Wright. 2006. *Street justice: Retaliation in the criminal underworld*. New York: Cambridge University Press.

Jacques, S. 2010. The necessary conditions for retaliation: Toward a theory of non-violent and violent forms in drug markets. *Justice Quarterly* 27: 186-205.

Jacques, S., and R. Wright. 2008a. The relevance of peace to studies of drug market violence. *Criminology* 46: 221-253.

Jacques, S., and R. Wright. 2008b. The victimization-termination link. *Criminology* 46: 1009-1038.

Jacques, S., and R. Wright. 2008c. Intimacy with outlaws: The role of relational distance in recruiting, paying, and interviewing underworld research participants. *Journal of Research in Crime and Delinquency* 45: 22-38.

Jacques, S., and R. Wright. 2010. Apprehending criminals: The impact of law on offender-based research. In Wim Bernasco (Ed.), *Offenders on offending: Learning about crime from criminals* (pp. 23-48). Cullompton: Willan Publishing.

Lee, R. M. 1995. *Dangerous Fieldwork*. Thousand Oaks, CA: Sage.

Mieczkowski, T. 1986. Geeking up and throwing down: Heroin street life in Detroit. *Criminology* 24: 645-666.

Mieczkowski, T. 1988. Studying heroin retailers: A research note. *Criminal Justice Review* 13: 39-44.

Miller, J. 2001. *One of the guys: Girls, gangs, and gender*. New York: Oxford University Press.

Piquero, A., and G. F. Rengert. 1999. Studying deterrence with active residential burglars. *Justice Quarterly* 16: 451-471.

Popper, K. 2002. *The logic of scientific discovery*. New York: Routledge Classics.

Roberts, L., R. Lafta, R. Garfield, J. Khudhairi, and G. Burnham. 2004. Mortality before and after the 2003 invasion of Iraq: cluster sample survey. *The Lancet* 364: 1857-1864.

Sampson, R. J. and J. H. Laub. 1993. *Crime in the making: Pathways and turning points through life*. Cambridge: Harvard University Press.

Sluka, J. A. 1990. Participant observation in violent social contexts. *Human Organization* 49: 114-126.

St. Jean, P. K. B. 2007. *Pockets of crime: Broken windows, collective efficacy, and the criminal point of view*. Chicago: University of Chicago Press.

Topalli, V. 2005. When being good is bad: An expansion of neutralization theory. *Criminology* 43: 797-835.

Venkatesh, S. A. 1999. Review of *Ethnography at the edge: Crime, deviance, and field research*, edited by J. Ferrell and M. S. Hamm. *American Journal of Sociology* 105: 284-286.

Venkatesh, S. A. 2006. *Off the books: The underground economy of the urban poor.* Cambridge: Harvard University Press.

Williams, T. 1989. *The cocaine kids: The inside story of a teenage drug ring.* Cambridge: Perseus Books.

Williams, T. 1992. *Crackhouse: Notes from the end of the line.* New York: Penguin Press.

Williams, T., E. Dunlap, B. D. Johnson, and A. Hamid. 1992. Personal safety in dangerous places. *Journal of Contemporary Ethnography* 21: 343-374.

Wright, R., and S. Decker. 1994. *Burglars on the job: Streetlife and residential burglary.* Boston: Northeastern University Press.

Wright, R., and S. Decker. 1997. *Armed robbers in action.* Boston: Northeastern University Press.

Wright, R., S. Decker, A. Redfern, and D. Smith. 1992. A snowball's chance in hell: Doing fieldwork with active residential burglars. *Journal of Research in Crime and Delinquency* 29: 148-161.

In the Classroom and on the Streets: How to Teach Qualitative Field Research to Criminology/ Criminal Justice Graduate Students

Robert G. Morris and James W. Marquart

This paper presents a method for delivering a graduate seminar in qualitative methods specific to criminology/criminal justice with a goal of providing a course that is balanced between classic readings and time in the field. We provide an overview of the course structure, a sample reading list, and the means to carry out an in-class fieldwork project over the course of a single semester, including research topics that have a proven track record for first-time fieldworkers. Also discussed are bureaucratic challenges to fieldwork, physical and mental challenges, and potential dangers of fieldwork.

The richness of qualitative research is undeniable. However, it can be difficult to convince students to consider a focus in qualitative research, particularly in the study of criminal behavior or the social response to criminal behavior. Clearly, dealing with active street criminals (see Jacobs 1999), observing the culture of the prison environment (Marquart 1986), living among active drug dealers (e.g., Adler 1985), interviewing identity theft offenders (Copes and Vieraitis 2009) or car thieves and carjackers (Cherbonneau and Copes 2006; Copes and Cherbonneau 2006), or even exploring the urban underground (Ferrell 2002) can be quite dangerous and/or may not be at the top of the list for possible career paths for graduate students. Qualitative studies are mentally, and often physically, intensive and are always time-consuming; such factors are sizable hurdles as students strive to complete coursework and prepare for a thesis or dissertation. That being said, we believe that quality training and exposure to the world of qualitative research can dispel many fears students might have and aid to stimulate qualitative research initiatives. Such research is ever so critical as we seek to understand the world of crime and deviance.

Regardless of whether a criminology/criminal justice graduate student plans to focus on a career in qualitative or quantitative research, or teaching for that matter, a well laid out graduate seminar in qualitative methods can be one of the most fruitful and enriching courses he or she can take, or teach. Not only are the readings enlightening, which is certainly a plus for in-class discussion, but having the opportunity to challenge students to begin an actual fieldwork project over the course of a semester can springboard an entire career's worth of research—such was the case for Jim Marquart and Bruce Jacobs. In fact, at our university, the course garners high enrollment and interest from graduate students of many disciplines. The goal of this paper is to offer a detailed overview of *one* method for organizing and delivering such a course at the graduate level. Using this strategy, we have had much success and students have clearly benefited by developing the first steps toward completing theses, dissertations, and published articles. Certainly there are alternatives that could work equally well; however, pedagogical literature on the topic specific to criminology and criminal justice is limited.

We believe that teaching and promoting qualitative research methods classes in criminology programs is essential. First, students trained in these techniques will have an expanded methodological portfolio that will allow them to investigate multiple angles of any research problem. Second, learning these techniques will enhance the career capabilities of graduate students who will undoubtedly be called upon to teach undergraduates and perhaps graduate students and professionals in the course of their careers. If nothing else it will provide them with "war stories" of what it is like interviewing or interacting with offenders. Finally, we believe that while contemporary criminological issues require complex empirical tools, students still need a firm grounding in long-established social science techniques that involve going to the field and interacting with real people.

In the following sections, we present the structure of the qualitative methods course that we use in our graduate program. Here, we present an outline of the general course structure along with a list of key readings that we have found useful. Moreover, we present our format of carrying out an in-class qualitative field study that can be completed over the course of a single semester and review several project topic ideas and some experiences that our students have had while carrying out their research. Such a project may seem easy to implement; however, a lack of preparation and attention to time limitations can ruin a project idea and wreak havoc on semester plans. With this in mind we offer several suggestions that we think will benefit professors who offer qualitative methods courses (or intend to).

Being that our students ultimately end up leaving the classroom to go into the field, safety and ethics are paramount. We offer a detailed overview of several issues that students should be aware of before beginning a research project and discuss the hurdles that one may encounter in seeing the course through, from the perspective of the professor, as well as the student. It is important to note that what we present may have utility for many disciplines, beyond criminology/criminal justice, where qualitative inquiry can help to understand many important social issues and generally get students motivated to do this style of research.

In the end, the goal of such a course is to expose students to the world of qualitative research, beyond simply reading others' work. The trick is to find a balance between assigning and discussing readings appropriate to the course and allowing for students to get their hands dirty by carrying out a small-scale qualitative research study, related to the study of crime, justice, and/or deviance. As we will show, the experiences that students have in the field truly make the literature all the more relevant. It is our hope that this overview helps guide instructors as they develop their qualitative methods courses and guide students through the process of becoming a qualitative field researcher.

Course Structure

The structure of the graduate seminar that we outline is tailored for a standard 16-week semester but could easily be adapted for a long summer course. Since ours is a seminar in Qualitative Criminology (essentially qualitative methods), the learning outcomes surround exposing students to the qualitative criminological/deviance literature and qualitative research methods in general. Our goal is that by the end of the semester, students be able to become familiar with and synthesize the fundamental principles of qualitative research methods, become intimate with the related literature, and design and complete a qualitative fieldwork study. Essentially, the first half of the semester revolves around qualitative research methods and arranging for the fieldwork project. The second half of the course focuses on issues specific to conducting criminological qualitative research and addresses issues regarding the realities of student fieldwork projects. We recommend a general qualitative research methods text for the first section of the course. We have had success using Berg's (2009) *Qualitative Research Methods for the Social Sciences*; however, similar texts exist and likely will work equally well.

As we progress through the chapters, we assign classic readings relevant to a particular chapter (see Table 1 for list of readings) to supplement the material and set the stage for in-class discussion. We believe that it is essential for students to read the accounts of the classic fieldworkers to understand that modern fieldwork is really no different from the trials and tribulations reported in past decades. We stress that there are a number of dilemmas within the actuality of fieldwork that defy time, space, and location. In this way students can link the past to their own fieldwork experiences.

We have also found it useful to require students to choose an ethnographic or other in-depth qualitative study to read, write a report on, and present an overview in class. The range of such texts has been quite broad but some of the more common selections have been (in no particular order) Anderson's (1999) *Code of the Street*, Ferrell's (1996) *Crimes of Style*, Jacobs' (1999) *Dealing*

Table 1   Suggested readings[1]

Week 1: What is Fieldwork?
  Geertz (1958/1994): Deep play
  Berg (2009): Chapter 1

Week 2: Problem Selection and Fieldwork Roles
  Jacobs (1977): Participant observation in prison
  Van Maanen (1984): Fieldwork on the beat
  Humphreys (1975): Public settings
  Berg (2009): Chapter 2
  Cromwell (2006): Chapter 1

Week 3: "Getting in" and Establishing Relations
  Whyte (1943): On the evolution of street corner society
  Berk and Adams (1970): Establishing rapport with deviant groups
  Kluckhohn (1940): The participant observer
  Cromwell (2006): Chapter 2

Week 4: Doing Field Research
  Cromwell (2006): Chapters 1, 16
  Berg (2009): Chapters 6, 7

Week 5: Cultivating Informants
  Cromwell (2006): Chapter 21
  Berg (2009): Chapters 4, 5

Week 6: Data Collection, Record Keeping, and Coding
  Lofland, Snow, Anderson, and Lofland (2006): Chapter 5

Week 7: General Problems of Fieldwork
  Wax (1971): Warnings and advice
  Marquart (1986): Doing research in prison

Week 8: The Personal Side of Doing Fieldwork
  Styles (1979): Insider/outsider
  Corsino (1987): Fieldworker blues

Week 9: Specific Concerns: Reliability and Validity
  Vidich and Bensman (2000): The validity of field data
  Becker (1958): Problems of inference and proof
  Cromwell (2006): Chapter 21

Week 10: Theory and Evidence from Field Research
  Berg (2009): Chapters 8, 9, 10
  Cromwell (2006): Chapters 10-16

Week 11: Analyzing Data
  Berg (2009): Chapter 11

Week 12: Writing up Research
  Lofland et al. (2006): Chapter 10
  Becker (1958): Problems and the publication of field studies
  Liebow (1995): Research methods and writing
  Knafl and Howard (1984): Interpreting and reporting qualitative research
  Berg (2009): Chapter 12

Week 13: The Impact of Field Research on the Researcher and Subjects
  Humphreys (1975): Chapter 2
  Hilbert (1980): Covert participant observation
  Bulmer (1982): When is disguise justified
  Berg (2009): Chapter 3

---

[1]Full references to these readings can be found in the references.

Crack, Wright and Decker's (1994) *Burglars on the Job*, Shover's (1996) *Great Pretenders*, and Katz's (1988) *Seductions of Crime*. There are dozens of worthy options for such a project, far too many to list here. However, we have found that the fieldwork project can often monopolize in-class meetings creating a time constraint for this particular aspect of the course. In any case, students will certainly benefit from exposure to contemporary studies of crime, such as those listed here.

Preparing for the Field: Mentally and Logistically

Organizing a fieldwork project for a graduate class is a challenging task, but the process does not have to be burdensome or even difficult. Since the project may have to be organized, approved, and carried out over the course of a single semester, timeliness is critical. More important is the issue of student safety while working in the field. It is critical that students are well prepared to expect the unexpected and be prepared to deal with problems as they arise. We have found it useful to ask students to work in pairs if possible. Another very important concern has to do with the technicalities in arranging for such research to be conducted ethically and in accordance with university policies. In this section, we address each of these issues in detail beginning with the issues surround preparation for the project.

Prior to submitting student applications to the university's institutional review board (IRB) for class-related research, prospective researchers (students and otherwise) must have completed some form of training in regard to the ethics surrounding research with human subjects. Most universities require the no-cost training made available by the National Institute of Health (NIH), though others may differ.[1] In our experience, we recommend that this training be announced during the first class meeting and instructors require that a printout of the certificate be turned in to the professor by the second week of class. This step can easily be overlooked or can result in delays in the IRB process. It is also important to encourage students to hang on to their certificate so they do not have to retake the training course in the future. As surely some readers are aware, NIH has recently updated the training website and old certificates can no longer be retrieved. Thus, if someone has lost their certificate from years past, they will have to retake the training course in order to receive a new one or hope that their institution's human subjects office has a copy on file.

It is also important to consider the workload of your university's research compliance staff. It can be quite overwhelming to such individuals if they are surprised by 15-20 IRB applications over the course of a few days. In being

1. As of 15 September 2009, the link to the training website is http://cme.cancer.gov/clinicaltrials/learning/humanparticipant-protections.asp. Some universities may require certification from a different organization, such as CITI. NIH provides certificates at the close of the course that can be printed out; CITI, on the other hand, may take time to send a certificate. Instructors should keep this in mind when requiring students to become certified under time constraints.

sensitive to this reality, we have found it useful to contact the compliance office and begin a dialog with a key individual during the semester prior to offering the course. A simple "head's up" about the course project can save a lot of time and perhaps keep you in the good graces of your IRB staff. Our IRB staff has been greatly appreciative of this approach. In fact, we have been fortunate enough to have had our IRB representatives willing to visit the class on the first class day to explain the IRB process and what it means to be compliant and how to navigate through the application process as expeditiously as possible. This can be scheduled well in advance. You might find that such individuals have a pre-prepared lecture covering this very topic. In any case, this component is simply a good pedagogy for graduate students (and professors) in general, not just a trick to make a project more doable.

A particular tactic that we employ for our projects is that research designs be tailored so they avoid a full IRB review, which can take weeks to be approved, depending on a variety of factors. We do this by limiting our project to observation only, no interviewing. However, we have found that amending IRB applications to allow for informal interviewing has not been troublesome. Depending on the topic, students may find it useful to engage those whom they are observing to take the project to the next level.

Both authors stress the importance of being open and frank with subjects in the setting were they to be approached by subjects making inquiries as to their intentions. We spent several seminar sessions on the importance of maintaining proper levels of confidentiality and its importance in fieldwork relations. For example, our students were introduced to the work of Laud Humphreys (1975) (public bathroom scene), Joesph Styles (1979) (gay bath scenes), and Adler (1985) (drug dealing scene). As a result of these readings, among others, and in class discussions, our students become well-versed in the relationship between difficult field situations, researcher roles, and the ethical dilemmas confronted by researchers in questionable situations.

Another important milestone that must be tackled early on is locking down topics for the project. This can be tricky since most students will have not yet been exposed to the bulk of the ethnographical and qualitative research literature in the discipline. For this reason, we have had success using a pre-developed list of possible topics that have a proven track record. We outline these topics below but mention them here as a critical step in getting the research applications completed early on; IRB has to know who is going to do what and how the research will impact human subjects before they can approve a study. However, since some criminology/criminal justice graduate students may work full-time for criminal justice, or related, agencies, exceptions should be considered as such individuals may have exclusive access to an important source of data and outsiders may or may not be allowed inside a facility.

In reality, the sky is the limit with regard to generating topic ideas relevant to a criminological qualitative research course. However, many very interesting and potentially fruitful ideas are simply impossible given the realities of the course or are just too risky to attempt. We have found it quite useful to use class time to brainstorm potential observation topics (or allow for the use the internet as a data source, see Holt 2010), but have found several that have proven themselves over the years. For example, some of the more common topics have included observing courtroom workgroups, jail intakes, condom stores, interviewing recently released inmates, drinking behavior at bars, spending a few nights at a homeless shelters, observing tattoo parlors, cop shops, the street racing scene, train stations, sexually oriented clubs for adults, probation departments, and the list goes on.

Once topics have been selected and groups formed, and IRB approval has been achieved, students can get on their way toward gathering data. We attempt to get them in the field as soon as possible. Even for simple observations, it can take time to become attuned to the situation or find the best spot to observe from. From the outset, students should be ready and willing to make adaptations and modifications to every aspect of data collection. At first, we simply have students keep a journal of events. This is done simply for development. As time goes on and observations become more frequent, the goal is for students to develop a coding scheme and adapt their research questions as necessary. Nearly each student project that we have witnessed takes an unforeseen turn or new development that impacts the outcome of the project. Sometimes, the initial observations result in a completely new topic altogether. For obvious reasons, it is much better to get this part of the research project out of the way as quickly as possible, even if students are only beginning to become familiarized with textbook methods of doing qualitative field research.

Danger in the Field

Getting students thinking about the dangers of fieldwork early on is quite important. Indeed, we share with the students that fieldwork is not usually a "clean and sterile" form of data collection. Fieldworkers have been assaulted (e.g., Athens (1997) and Marquart (1986) in their prison research and Jankowski (1991) in his gang research), have been held at gunpoint (e.g., B. Jacobs (1999) in his research with active street criminals), and pressured to take sides in power "games" (J. Jacobs (1977) in his research in Stateville Prison)—for more about dangers to researchers see Jacques and Wright (2010). It is essential that students understand the "ad lib," "anything can happen," dynamic in a fieldwork situation.

Just as study participant safety is important, as required by IRB guidelines, so is the safety of the researchers. It is important to regularly discuss the potential for danger in doing field research, thus we routinely stress the importance of being safe and discuss some simple practices that will enhance researcher safety. We recommend that students select familiar locations so that they can better judge when a dangerous situation may be developing. They need to have exit strategies in place and avoid being in vulnerable spots to prevent someone from sneaking up behind them, for example. Initial site visits should be just as much about scouting the area for safety as it is for how well the location may provide for good data collections. In any case, data should not be collected until the location is adequately understood (e.g., the safest place to park, so that they will not end up blocked in an area when they are ready to leave).

In addition, before each field visit, we tell students that they need to let someone know where they are going, and when they begin and end their research, requiring students to work in groups helps here, but it is a good idea to encourage this type of communication. Groups should always have charged cellular phones on hand and arrange to call someone at a designated time when in potentially dangerous situations. If the student ends up not making the call at the designated time, this "safety person" should be told to call the researcher and/or go to the location of data collection. If the "safety person" cannot contact or locate the researcher in such a situation, they should be informed to contact law enforcement and advise them of the situation (i.e., names, locations, what they are doing, etc.). Code words may also be used in communication between the researcher and the "safety person" if things are not going as planned. The code word/s should be discrete enough to not disrupt the natural setting of the research, or to raise suspicion among study participants. If a code word is mentioned in a call, the safety person should either come to the location or call law enforcement. Finally, we recommend that if at any time the researcher's gut feeling is that something is not right, they should leave the scene immediately.

During each class meeting, we devote a considerable amount of time to allow students to discuss their field experiences and allow for peer review of their situations and the development of their projects. This element of the course is critical to the development of the fieldwork project and ultimately serves as a focus group style critique of the research design. Sharing the experiences of the field research process as weeks pass allows for every student in the class to benefit from the experiences of a single student. Several key aspects that develop during such discussions revolve around the surprises of doing field research and ideas in regard to developing and modifying a coding scheme over the course of the project. It is always surprising what can be accomplished by forcing students to the chalkboard and allowing the rest to serve as a focus group.

Surprises of Fieldwork

Of particular relevance to embarking on such a project are the unforeseeable, and often exciting, events that seemed to occur on a weekly basis in our experience. For example, one student worked as an administrative assistant in a large city courthouse and was interested in observing social interactions between plaintiffs and defendants of family court cases. Her employment position made the project very doable because her office was in the same building as the family court. She had heard from co-workers that the floor of the building where family court was held was eventful on a daily basis. In response to this, she developed a plan to observe violence occurring in the family court main hallway, just outside the actual courtroom. Each week, this particular student would report physical violence between family members going through divorce, girlfriends versus ex-wives, even grandmothers battling granddaughters. Though the stories told by the student were riveting, they highlighted the reality that there was the potential for real danger in doing this type of research. Fortunately for her, she had the proper identification badge so if an entanglement broke out, she could observe from a private attorneys' lounge equipped with a glass window to the main hallway (where the bulk of the violence would occur). Not only did her stories serve as a warning to others but her observations led to a change in focus given that she began to notice that the bailiffs, who were responsible for breaking up entanglements, reacted differently depending on who was involved and the attitudes of the participants. This led to her uncovering a bailiff culture that was molded around daily violence and essentially self-selection of engagement depending on whether the bailiff thought the victim "had it coming." In all, this student learned very quickly that she had to be alert at all times, protect herself first, be mentally prepared to face danger, and think about her role as a witness to violence. She did report having to respond to police officers questions after one particularly bloody incident; unfortunately, encounters with law enforcement as a result of conducting observations were not limited to this particular student.

Another important consideration is how people on the street will react to seeing people make their observations. For example, two other students, one male and one female, choose to work as a team to observe tattoo parlor patrons who visited various parlors in different areas of the city including an uptown area, a suburban tattoo parlor located in a shopping mall, and another located in a trendy, yet economically deprived, high crime, area. The students were interested in exploring differences in appearance and behavior among patrons from varying backgrounds as they shopped for tattoos and ultimately received service. The initial observations were made from a distance, typically from a parked car. After observing the higher crime area tattoo parlor for a few days, they were approached by police officers very suddenly who had been contacted by concerned citizens who had reported their *suspicious* behavior. After all, they were indeed suspicious looking; a man and a women sitting in a parked car for several hours many times throughout the week in a seedy part of town. Fortunately, the officers were understanding, at least after some explanation from a few nervous graduate students. The students were not approached again. A different pair of students wrote this account of their similar experience, one they will remember and retell forever:

> Our non-participant observation project explored the world of modern adult novelty stores in a large city with the goal of gaining insight into this industry. For that reason, we selected a well-known adult novelty store in the city of Dallas ... In addition to identifying the types of customers that were shopping at

adult novelty stores, we also wanted to examine the demeanor of these customers. Studying their demeanor was an effort to determine whether these individuals were uncomfortable shopping at adult novelty shops, thereby suggesting that the activity may be socially stigmatized or taboo. We were to observe Thursday, Friday, and Saturday evenings and later on decided to observe afternoons as well. We parked in the liquor store next door where we could see what was happening at the front of the novelty story location, as well as a partial view of their parking log.

After the first few evening observations, one female worker started to become a little suspicious of our car. The next week we came back and the same worker was there. We were in a different car, but parked in the same spot. We were going about our normal observations when we noticed that the same female employee and a male coworker kept peering out the window at us.

Ten minutes later a police patrol car pulled into the parking lot and parked perpendicular to the passenger's side. The officer got out and we rolled down the window with our IRB information in hand to defend our situation. We told him we were conducting field research and showed him our IRB form stating we were doing non-participant observation and he was said "Okay that is fine." He went into the [store] for a short second and we believed he told the workers that we were there doing research and that we were harmless to them. We decided to stay the full observation time and discussed what we were going to do now that our cover was blown, so to speak. Determined to finish our research without further incident, we felt the best solution was to go in before we start observing the next time and tell the employees that we were parked in the parking lot below and we were conducting research. (Swensen, DeShay, and Horton 2008, p. 5)

Developing a Coding Scheme

Many qualitative scholars would agree that developing a coding structure for synthesizing data is an iterative process and that a researcher should be open-minded about making modifications. The class time devoted to discussing the students' projects has proven to be a tremendous help for such modification for neophyte field researchers. Open discussion and brainstorming sessions specific to individual projects were responsible for making vast improvements to coding schemes and even toward modifying or completely altering research questions. We strongly recommend a loose structure for these discussions as different students will be at different stages of observation and coding. We have found it very useful to use a whiteboard to outline and modified taxonomies of what the students had observed. This forced students to step back and think about what the data is really saying, and hearing the thoughts of fellow students, in addition to the professor, really seemed to stimulate this process. In fact, we have found that such discussions are never dull and quite educational for all of those involved.

In addition, it is critical that students learn to be adaptive to coding and recording data. Qualitative research can be extremely fluid and we teach students to simply be adaptive when required—we use many illustrations of this "i.e., Bill Whyte, Jim Jacobs, Bruce Jacobs, and John Van Mannen." Copes, Hochstetler, and Williams (2008) provide a good example of this. They write:

> When we began interviewing offenders for this project our intent was not to explore the phenomenon of managing social identities, but rather to explore the social world of those who engage in violent street crime ... As the interviews progressed, it became clear that fostering a view of themselves as hustlers rather than crackheads was significant to participants. Upon recognizing this trend we adjusted the interview guide accordingly. (p. 258)

These people began with a research idea and ended with something rather unforeseen, ultimately helping to develop their careers and research further than expected.

Conclusion

Even though both of us have taught this course at different times with different students we have the same goal—to conduct a course that balances the literature with personal experience. Field research is much like learning how to ride a bike or learning how to swim—you just have to do it.

We want our students well-versed in the classics (i.e., to read about researchers' accounts about street corners and urban neighborhoods, tea rooms, cellblocks, drug deals, and police stations). Understanding the distinctive experiences of earlier fieldworkers prepares, to some extent, the modern era student of what to expect in a fluid field situation. Also, given the times, we want our students well-versed in the complexities of IRBs and the importance of completing accurate forms; and yes, we expect our students to be good bureaucrats. Furthermore, requiring students to present their project findings in a format equivalent to that of what might be seen at an annual meeting of a national professional academic organization (e.g., Academy of Criminal Justice Sciences or American Society of Criminology) was an aspect that appeared to help students develop professionally. In fact, several students from the course presented their project findings at annual conferences and hope to turn their work into dissertations and/or research publications. While student and/or course success can be measured in multiple ways, we believe that this class and its organization lent itself to the professionalization of our students, increased their understanding of different methodological designs, and led to their eagerness to present papers at conferences. In short, this course increased our students' adoption of an academic value system (e.g., the collection of data, preparation of results, and presentation of findings to peers for evaluation).

It is also important that prospective instructors consider other challenges that may arise in carrying out such a course. One issue is that some students may falsely assume that the course will be easier than analogous quantitative courses. This fallacy should be addressed the first day of class. Additionally, instructors should be mindful of the fact that the majority of students will have had no prior qualitative training whatsoever, and should consider this as the course is developed. Course projects may extend beyond the close of the semester. Instructors should consider their university's policy on assigning "incomplete" grades as students may need extra time to complete their study. Another issue that may arise, though we have not experienced it, is that departmental barriers in quantitative departments may shed a negative light on the course for some students. Finally, instructors should be mindful of the fact that the course may draw students from other disciplines and should consider being flexible in research topic assignments.

Getting students involved in qualitative field research can be a very fruitful endeavor and can make for a memorable graduate class. As mentioned above, we find that even quantitatively oriented students enjoy they experience of doing field research and that the experience may help to increase the use of qualitative research in criminological research and/or its use in tandem with quantitative methods. Being exposed to field research is fun, inspiring, and enlightening, and is a technique that is as useful today as it has ever been. Nearly a century ago, the famous sociologist Robert E. Park urged his students to:

> Go and sit in the lounges of the luxury hotels and on the doorsteps of the flop-houses; sit on the Gold Coast settees and on the slum shakedowns; sit in Orchestra Hall and in the Star and Garter Burlesk. In short, gentlemen, go get the seat of your pants dirty in *real* research.[2]

This advice from one of the giants of social research is as relevant today as it was in the 1920s, and we expect nothing more or less from our students today.

References

Adler, P. A. 1985. *Wheeling and dealing*. New York: Columbia University Press.
Anderson, E. 1999. *Code of the street: Decency, violence and the moral life of the inner city*. New York: W.W. Norton.
Athens, L. 1997. *Violent criminal acts and actors revisited*. Urbana: University of Illinois Press.
Becker, H. S. 1958. Problems of inference and proof in participant observation. *American Sociological Review* 23: 652–660.
Berg, B. L. 2009. *Qualitative research methods for the social sciences* (7th ed.). Boston: Pearson.
Berk, R. A., and J. M. Adams. 1970. Establishing rapport with deviant groups. *Social Problems* 18: 102–117.
Bulmer, M. 1982. When is disguise justified? Alternatives to covert participant observation. *Qualitative Sociology* 5: 251–264.

2. This is a quote from Robert E. Park quoted in Gomm and McNeill (1982).

Cherbonneau, M., and H. Copes. 2006. Drive it like you stole it: Auto thieves and the illusion of normalcy. *British Journal of Criminology* 46: 193-211.

Copes, H., A. Hochstetler, and P. Williams. 2008. We weren't like no regular dope fiends: Negotiating hustler and crackhead identities. *Social Problems* 55: 255-270.

Copes, H., and L. M. Vieraitis. 2009. Bounded rationality of identity thieves: Using offender-based research to inform policy. *Criminology and Public Policy* 8: 237-262.

Copes, H., and M. Cherbonneau. 2006. The key to auto theft: Emerging methods of auto theft from the offenders' perspectives. *British Journal of Criminology* 46: 917-934.

Corsino, L. 1987. Fieldworker blues: Emotional stress and research under involvement in fieldwork settings. *The Social Science Journal* 24: 275-285.

Cromwell, P. (Ed.). 2006. *In their own words* (4th ed.). Los Angeles, CA: Roxbury.

Ferrell, J. 1996. *Crimes of style.* Boston: Northeastern University Press.

Ferrell, J. 2002. *Tearing down the streets: Adventures in urban anarchy.* New York: Palgrave-Macmillion.

Geertz, C. 1958/1994. *The cockfight: A casebook.* Madison: University of Wisconsin Press.

Gomm, R., and P. McNeill. 1982. *Handbook for sociology teachers.* London: Heinemann.

Hilbert, R. A. 1980. Covert participant observation. *Journal of Contemporary Ethnography* 9: 51-78.

Holt, T. 2010. Exploring strategies for qualitative criminological and criminal justice inquiry using on-line data. *Journal of Criminal Justice Education* 21: 466-487.

Humphreys, L. 1975. *Tearoom trade: Impersonal sex in public places.* Hawthorne, NY: Aldine Transaction.

Jacobs, B. A. 1999. *Dealing crack: The social world of streetcorner selling.* Boston: Northeastern University Press.

Jacobs, J. B. 1977. *Stateville: The penitentiary in mass society.* Chicago: University of Chicago Press.

Jacques, S., and R. Wright. 2010. Dangerous intimacy: Toward a theory of violent victimization in active offender research. *Journal of Criminal Justice Education* 21: 503-525.

Jankowski, M. S. 1991. *Islands in the street: Gangs and American urban society.* Berkeley: University of California Press.

Katz, J. 1988. *Seductions of crime: Moral and sensual attractions of doing evil.* New York: Basic Books.

Kluckhohn, F. 1940. The participant-observer technique in small communities. *American Journal of Sociology* 46: 331-343.

Knafl, K. A., and M. J. Howard. 1984. Interpreting and reporting qualitative research. *Research in Nursing and Health* 7: 17-24.

Liebow, E. 1995. *Tell them who I am: The lives of homeless women.* New York: Penguin.

Lofland, H., D. A. Snow, L. Anderson, and L. H. Lofland. 2006. *A guide to qualitative observation and analysis.* Florence, KY: Cengage.

Marquart, J. W. 1986. Doing research in prison: The strengths and weaknesses of full participation as a guard. *Justice Quarterly* 3: 15-32.

Shover, N. 1996. *Great pretenders: Pursuits and careers of persistent thieves.* Boulder, CO: Westview.

Styles, J. 1979. Outsider/insider: Researching gay baths. *Urban Life* 8: 135-152.

Swensen, M., R. DeShay, and A. Horton. 2008. Non-participation observation of an urban condom shop. *Qualitative Criminology* (CRIM 6340), Spring.

Van Maanen, J. 1984. Making rank: Becoming an American police sergeant. *Urban Life* 13: 155-176.

Vidich, A. J., and J. Bensman. 2000. *Small town in mass society.* Champaign: University of Illinois Press.

Wax, R. 1971. *Doing fieldwork: Warnings and advice*. Chicago: University of Chicago Press.

Whyte, W. F. 1943. *Street corner society*. Chicago: University of Chicago Press.

Wright, R., and S. Decker. 1994. *Burglars on the job: Streetlife and residential break-ins*. Boston: Northeastern University Press.

On the Way to the Field: Reflections of One Qualitative Criminal Justice Professor's Experiences

Mark R. Pogrebin

In this short essay I attempt to summarize my view of qualitative research and delineate a few of the challenges that qualitative researchers working in the field of criminal justice face. I reflect and draw upon my past research to demonstrate my opportunities and challenges in the hope that others can learn from my experiences and mistakes. While qualitative criminal justice researchers have much to be wary of in terms of institutional review boards, increased publication pressures, and highly quantitative journals and departments, there is, nevertheless, hope for the future.

When Heith Copes asked me to write an article focusing on my qualitative experiences for this special edition of the *Journal of Criminal Justice Education (JCJE)*, I enthusiastically accepted his invitation. After all, we qualitative types have argued that our contributions to crime causation and criminal justice policy have a history of being neglected by the discipline. Once I agreed to be a contributing author, I suddenly realized that I did not have a clue as to what I would write about that would be a worthwhile addition to the topic. The task proved to be one that caused me much anguish, perhaps because I have never had the opportunity to stop and reflect upon the research I have conducted during my career. This sounds odd since we all know professors talk endlessly about their research to anyone who will listen, especially students who represent an involuntary and captive audience. It was not until the fifth inning of a Colorado Rockies baseball game, when I found my mind wondering on a lazy Colorado summer's day, that I decided what I would write about for this special issue of the *JCJE*. I have decided to write a condensed version of my experiences conducting a few of the fieldwork projects I have been involved in over my career. I begin this essay by discussing my approach to qualitative research. Next, I outline three challenges that qualitative criminologists must overcome. Finally, I end with an overview of research projects I have conducted using a grounded theory approach. I do this knowing that there are so many other qual-itative works that are more informative and well presented than mine. Still, I hope that the qualitative research examples that I present offer some insightful explanations for the use of a few qualitative approaches that perhaps provide those criminologists who are not that familiar with this type of methodological genre a bit more understanding of why and how my collaborators and I conduct this type of research.

Grounded Theory and Ethnography

The purpose of this brief explanation of the literature is to provide the reader with some background on grounded theory and the ethnographic process because these are two perspectives that have shaped my work over the years. It should be noted that this discussion is in contrast to quantitative research ideol-ogy. Qualitative researchers are often not provided with the opportunity to justify their methods. Instead we have been forced to defend our work, espe-cially in the academic areas of social control and crime causation. Instead of belaboring the differences between qualitative and quantitative approaches to the study of crime and the criminal justice system, I will offer a succinct but meaningful explanation of the perceptions of a few noted qualitative and ethno-graphic researchers who offer comments pertaining to this methodological controversy. For example, Anderson (1999, p. 451) observes that:

> [e]thnographic description always has been and always will be controversial, largely because of the personal familiarity that ethnography requires ... the inti-mate vantage point of qualitative researchers makes ethnographers aware of the challengers of representation in ways that other (positivists) not only do not acknowledge but to which they often are oblivious.

Other researchers such as Gergen (1994) and Bochner and Ellis (1999) argue that there are those qualitative researchers who lessen their credibility when they couch their research in the language of empiricism, and that most often seems to be an attempt to fit their ethnographic study into a scientific framework which only serves to increase the false conception that the majority of qualita-tive researchers usually reject. Perhaps those who organize and produce their qualitative studies in this type of empirical format are attempting to please the status quo of social scientists that overwhelmingly represent the quantitative position on editorial boards. This is especially true in our academic field where very few qualitative researchers are represented as editors, associate editors, or editorial board members.

Grounded Theory

Qualitative research can utilize multiple methods for collecting data (see Pogre-bin 2003). However, I focus my discussion on the grounded theory approach to ethnographic research because this is the research method I have used in the majority of my work and because I am most familiar with this type of analysis. In 1967, Glaser and Strauss published their groundbreaking book, *Discovery of Grounded Theory: Strategies for Qualitative Research*. In that work they explain how their approach is empirical in nature and can be used to study social life. Glaser and Strauss explain that grounded theory means that various themes emerge from the data we collect. The emphasis is on field research that generates those themes as opposed to having preconceived ideas of what to study before entering the field. Glaser and Strauss emphasize that grounded theory bridges the gap between empirical research and theory by grounding the theory in the data. Thus, grounded theory is based on the supposition that theory at various levels of generality is necessary in order to gain more in-depth knowledge of the social phenomenon and that theory should be generated and developed in close relationship with the data. The major proposition is that detailed analysis of the collected data will produce an emerging theory that guides the collection of additional data. Gary A. Fine (1993, p. 274) notes that Glaser's and Strauss' ethnographic approach often means that "not only are [we] unsure of the effects of explaining our plans but often we do not know what we want until well into the research project." In short, Glaser and Strauss (1967) sought to develop an inductive approach to collecting and analyzing qualitative data through field work and attempted to be faithful to the understandings, interpretations, intentions, and perspectives of those whom they were conducting research on in their study subject's own terms as expressed through their words and actions.

The exploration of how people make sense of their experiences is well suited to the narrative process (Clandinin and Cornwelley 1994); moreover, this use of grounded theory really is the key to conducting ethnographic research. Narrative research studies are often utilized to describe and analyze the organizational processes in which people interact with one another within the community (Scott 1989). Natural analysis is a vital component of ethnographic research within social psychology. That is, people's interactions and interpretations of their life experiences in particular settings are necessary to gain an understanding of intergroup processes and individual meanings people give for interactions with others.

Ethnography

Van Maanen (1988, p. 13) points out that "an ethnography is a written representation of a culture. ... [T]he trick of ethnography is to adequately display the culture (or commonly, part of the culture) in a way that is meaningful to readers without great distortion." Van Maanen's description of ethnography as a way researchers convey culture does not suggest how ethnography is to be carried out. It is important to point out that some researchers believe ethnography excludes some qualitative research methods, for example, where the

researcher is not immersed in the day-to-day life of his or her study participants. Without this immersion it is not possible to truly understand their actions
and convey the culture to which those participants belong in any meaningful
way (Glaser and Strauss 1967). In short, this perspective suggests that semi-
structured interviews are not ethnographic. Other researchers such as Kleinman, Stenross, and McMahon (1994) argue that the capacity of the interviews to
elicit discussion should not be underestimated, especially when rapport has
been established. Thus, they argue that in-depth interviews have an advantage
over participant observation for the exploration of participant's feelings and
perceptions. In short, lengthy interviews offer participants an opportunity to
share their perceptions and ideas about daily life that may be neglected or
suppressed in spontaneous conversations with researchers involved in participant observation (McCracken 1988). Moreover, researchers like Spradley (1980)
define ethnography by perceiving it as description. Spradley (1980, p. 132)
notes that it is the purpose of ethnography to understand how people "routinely
behave in everyday life and how they make sense of experience." Spradley
(1977, p. viii) clearly speaks about the benefits for utilizing this form of
research design:

> Ethnography offers all of us the chance to step outside our narrow culture back-
> grounds, to set aside our social inherited ethnocentrism if only for a brief period
> and to apprehend the world from the view point of other human beings who live
> by different meaning systems.

Ethnographic researchers tend to organize their data in an analytic methodological framework. Miller and Sperry (1987, p. 4) claim that what they attempt to
accomplish is a "balance between structure, disciplined by the goal of understanding the informants' point of view." To just describe what one observes in
the field or gains through interviewing is only part of what Geertz (1973) terms
the "ethnographic equation." He further explains that ethnographic researchers
need to attach meanings to the data they collect in their field experiences
through an interpretive process that he defined as "thick description." In short,
while grounded theory is the key to ethnographic research, attempting to
interpret the meaning of the collected data to formulate meaningful and
explanatory theory is a difficult task for ethnographers. Atkinson (1992)
suggests that qualitative researchers should make sure that their study presents
life accounts as accurate and realistic.

An important advantage of the methodological process of conducting ethnographic studies is that the researcher's misjudgments can be corrected during
the investigative process (Eder and Corsaro 1999). Eder and Corsaro (1999,
p. 525) claim that this "is one useful way that ethnographers' gain information
for revising their procedures to better fit their demands of a particular field
situation." In addition, the researchers note that the flexibility and the ability
to correct mistakes permits directional modifications to the actual phenomenon
being studied. This flexibility and the self corrective nature of ethnography
allows for the generation of theory as an ongoing and ever-changing process.

This approach to qualitative methods is how I have conducted my work. My prior research has utilized methods that range from participant observation to semi-structured interviews—both of which I consider to be ethnographic approaches.

Early Beginnings

From the beginning of my doctorate program in a Big Ten sociology department until my first job at a prestigious school of criminology, I endured enormous pressure to get with the program and join my quantitative colleagues. My mentors argued that I should put aside my qualitative instincts until such time as I made a name for myself in the academic arena. One factor that pushed me to remain faithful to my qualitative self can be traced back to a conversation I had with another new assistant professor who seriously suggested that Jerome Skolnick's (1967) *Justice without Trial* (a book I was using for one of my classes) would have been greatly improved had Skolnick quantified all the variables he observed while in the field. My response was one of shock and disbelief at the purely quantitative methodological position. Still, that interaction reinforced my belief in the importance of the qualitative approach. Over the years I have encountered similar subtle (and not so subtle) comments from colleagues that a quantitative approach is superior to a qualitative approach. Even today, despite the enormous contributions qualitative researchers have made in criminal justice, criminology, and other social science disciplines, the qualitative approach is still marginalized in our profession (Miller 2005). Indeed, even the number one ranked department in our field identifies itself as purely quantitative in its job ads.

Doctoral students who choose qualitative methods to investigate social and criminal justice policy in our School of Public Affairs elicit less than receptive (and sometimes even hostile) reactions by my more quantitatively orientated colleagues—even those who have served with me on dissertation committees. Inevitably, they begin their line of questioning at the defense with an attack on the qualitative approach asking "why not study this issue quantitatively?" Normally I would consider this a fair and valid question to ask any doctoral student as part of his or her dissertation defense. However, the group's quantitative bent, combined with methodological questioning, always seems to take a life of its own and grows into the major focus of the defense. After a good deal of careful explanation on the part of the now beleaguered student, he or she inevitably looks to me for help. I have found it necessary on each of these occasions to repeat the valid reasons why a qualitative methodological choice was appropriate for this student's particular research project. Only after I have interceded on the student's behalf did the questions from committee members become more substantive and respectful. The aftermath of these dissertation defense experiences were rapidly communicated to other doctoral students who usually decide to maintain the status-quo and conduct a deductive hypothesis-driven dissertation. Since I am the only qualitative researcher working in the area of criminal justice within our school, I realize it is to the doctoral students' advantage to stay as far away from me as possible. The good news is that there has been one qualitatively oriented dissertation completed within the last year and one being written presently, so all is not as gloomy a picture as I have painted. The current challenge with qualitative research in our university is the same challenge that many universities face: the institutional review board (IRB).

Let me not leave my fellow criminal justice peers with the impression that all is not well for those of us who take seriously the narrative form of research pursuits. Each of us, both qualitative and quantitative, has encountered methodological struggles along the way in our scholarly pursuits; however, it is necessary to mention that it is only in recent years that we have witnessed a more ideological acceptance, to a degree, on the part of funding agencies and journal editors, who have come to value the contributions that qualitative researchers have made to the criminal justice and criminology. While progress has been made, there are still many obstacles to overcome for those who pursue academic credibility for their inductive methodological choices.

Productivity and Qualitative Methods

Those of us who have been granted tenure and promotion at our respective colleges and universities are cognizant of how important our research and publications are for succeeding in this area. Buckler (2008) notes how time consuming most qualitative studies are, and argues that choosing this methodological approach can reduce publication productivity. He interviewed a number of criminal justice/criminology journal editors who provided him with their estimates of the publication rates for quantitative versus qualitative manuscripts submitted to their respective journals. One journal editor provided an insightful observation on the impractical time and effort qualitative fieldwork takes, thus limiting the number of articles that can be published by new assistant professors. A good indication of the amount of time such fieldwork endeavors take is to use my studies as an example. Each of my research projects lasted over one year in duration, and unlike survey studies, I was lucky to produce two publications from each. Most, however, resulted in a single publication. Not a stellar number for the time and effort put into each project, especially when many new assistant professors are publishing five or more articles per year. As far as publication acceptance of my fieldwork projects, I can only disagree with those journal editors who reported to Buckler that they always entertain qualitative manuscripts, but claim that they do not receive too many. My experiences have not been in keeping with their perceptions. On too many occasions I have received negative comments from reviewers concerning the fact that I should have conducted survey research with a large study population or that the entire study is too idiosyncratic to be considered scientific. Miller (2005, p. 71) notes:

For instance, I recently co-authored a paper based on in-depth interviews with African American young men about their negative experiences with the police. The paper was derided by one reviewer as "journalistic," and another reviewer referred to the data—in the case of young men's descriptions of their own encounters with the police—as "hearsay," and—in the case of their accounts of their perceptions of neighborhood policing—as "double hearsay." I give this example not to bemoan a set of negative reviews, but to highlight what I see as dangers to the qualitative enterprise when reviewers drawn from the broader discipline do not appreciate its methodological approach, and thus qualitative studies are expected to adhere to ill-fitting standards that undermine the very strengths and foundations of the methodology.

Recently, a few of my younger qualitative criminal justice/criminology types have published in the very journal outlets I received negative comments from; thus, I am beginning to see positive signs that things are changing for the better for those qualitative-oriented researchers who have their work appear in mainstream criminal justice/criminology publications. Although such articles are few in number, it signals, perhaps, a new day for qualitative-oriented researchers in our field.

The Institutional Review Boards and Ethnography

Another challenge that many qualitative researchers face is the IRB. Eder and Corsaro (1999, p. 525) note that:

> In contrast to positivistic approaches, interpretive analysis of ethnographic data cannot be fully specified in advance. Interpretive analysis is theory generating because the guiding criterion is one of cultural validity. Descriptive categories are not pre-determined.

This fundamental quality of qualitative research presents serious problems for most IRB boards. Because ethnographic research studies are not outlined in advance like the quantitative hypothesis-testing formula, which is deductive in practice and attempts to measure theory from the study's inception, inductive studies face greater obstacles in getting approval from IRBs due largely to the very nature of inductive grounded theory-type approach (see Katz (2007) for complete discussion of this issue).

Qualitative researchers often face serious problems when attempting to gain IRB approval of their study project that quantitative researchers do not face. I will not go too much into my own personal experiences with our university's IRB nor will I take up time describing how our IRB has compromised my doctoral students' dissertation research. The subject of IRB could be a separate manuscript. For now, however, I will simply point out the conflicts and misunderstandings that IRB board restrictions place upon qualitative research proposals. A brief history of how IRB came into existence has been addressed by Katz (2007, p. 801).

In the 1990s disasters in biomedical research provoked federal human subject's protection officials, who had become increasingly suspect that universities were not rigorously implementing oversight in bio-medical research ... Although the oversight problems were with the natural sciences of schools, and even though no new harms had emerged in social science research that would be of concern to regulators, the university research community as a whole was perceived as needing closer scrutiny.

Katz (2006) argues that IRB rules and procedures developed to protect the rights of human subjects have, as a consequence of their restrictions on ethnography, pushed many qualitative research to forgo their research or avoid using IRB by taking their research underground. In short, most IRB boards restrict data collection that involves an interaction with subjects that is not scripted ahead of time. Thus, every time a new subject is broached in conversation, IRB approval is technically required. This requirement places serious limitations on grounded theory which cannot be compatible with such a human subjects approach. This IRB roadblock is well noted by qualitative researchers. For example, Agar (1996, p. 22) shows that it is impossible to satisfy IRB regulators in conducting any ethnographic study using the following approach:

> You learn something (collecting data) then you try and make sense out of it (analysis), then you go back and see if the interpretation makes sense in light of new experience (collect more data) then you refine your interpretation (more analysis) and so on. The process is dialectic not linear.

There are numerous examples of classic ethnographic studies that meet ethical standards in research but would no longer pass IRB approval. For example, William Whyte's *Street Corner Society* (1955) would likely not be allowed by today's IRB. In the appendix of this work (pp. 279-358), Whyte explains how his original research proposal differed from the actual study he ended up conducting, because that initial proposal was conceptualized before he actually spent any time at the research site. Only after a lengthy period of time conducting field work did Whyte become aware that his first research proposal was not appropriate for the community he was studying. It took Whyte years in the field before he was able to conceptualize and then analyze the data he collected into an interpretive set of ideas that became a first-rate study and, to this date, remains one of the greatest ethnographies ever written. Suffice to say, ethnographic researchers will continue to be presented with multiple obstacles in attaining IRB approval for their proposed studies until realistic changes are made in the review procedures and regulations of university IRB boards that understand and respect the research methodology that qualitative researchers propose in their field work projects.

My personal examples with IRB are similar to what other qualitative researchers have faced, especially those described by Katz (2006). Five years ago I was fortunate to receive a Project Safe Neighborhoods Grant from our US Attorney (see Pogrebin, Stretesky, and Unnithan 2009). I wanted to talk with gun offenders in Colorado and designed a proposal to submit to the IRB. I believed there was hesitation on their part to approve the study and so I asked to go before the board to explain my study and, thus, help alleviate the board's anxiety. I spent nearly two hours being repeatedly questioned about hypothetical statements my participants may give if they were to go off protocol. This questioning then led a few of my academic colleagues on the board to become seriously concerned about the problems the University might face if an inmate disclosed that he was going to kill his father, once paroled. Their fears for this type of violence were for naught as none of 117 inmates on our list were likely to be paroled in the next 20 years. Retrospectively, I believe that these questions were meant to provide obstacles to my research as opposed to helping me find ways to better protect my participants' confidentiality. Moreover, the physicians' representative (my university is attached to a medical school) who favored quantitative approaches to research could not understand why I did not have control group protocol and use that group as if I were testing a drug during a medical trial. I found myself defending my methodological approach and sample and tried to assure him that there were no placebos given out, but that I was interviewing a random sample of people using a weapon in the commission of a felony in Colorado. My experience before the IRB was frustrating and shocking. At one point during my hours of questioning I even asked the committee if it would be better if I gave the grant monies back to the US Attorney. In the end they seemed to draw upon my past experiences in the field as opposed to my protocol and methodology to find a reason to pass my proposal. They felt that because I spent two and a half years working as a counselor in an adult reformatory for men and that because I was a parole officer in New York City for over three and a half years that I would be suited to conduct this research. In short, I can now see why many qualitative researchers go underground.

My Confessional Tales

I cannot think of a better way to describe my field work experiences to my non-qualitative peers than to begin this with Van Maanen's (1988, p. 95) insightful explanation of what he believes constitutes the confessional tale. In short, I use Van Maanen's work as an illustration of the unknown world of participant observation and interviewing in an attempt to gain insight into the world of criminal justice and criminal behavior utilizing a grounded theory of approach.

> The confessional tale attempts to represent the fieldworker's participative presence in the study scene. The fieldworker's rapport and sensitive contact with others in the world describe something of the concrete cultural particulars that baffle the fieldworker while he learns to live in the setting. It is necessarily a blurred account, combining a particular description of the culture alongside an equally partial description of the fieldwork experience itself.

Perhaps no words can better describe my intentions than the following stanza of the song by the late singer and songwriter Harry Chapin, *Greyhound* (1972), when he relates that "stepping off this dirty bus, first time I understood it's got to be the going not the getting there that's good."

Humor in the Briefing Room: A Study of the Strategic Uses of Humor among Police

On the way to the field is what retrospectively I have come to consider the most fascinating part of the field experience. One research project that shows how this might occur was conducted over 20 years ago by Professor Eric Poole and me (Pogrebin and Poole 1988). I was working for a suburban police department as an organizational consultant studying the degree to which administrative policies were actually enacted by uniform officers working in the community; that is, to what extent were officer discretionary practices on the street modifying administrative decisions downward through the ranks in their interactions with the public? In order for me to gain a perspective to the extent that organizational policies were or were not enacted by street patrol, I spent nine months with three patrol shifts observing their interactions with the public. I also attended briefing room sessions with each shift before and after every shift. It was during these briefing room sessions that I became aware of the discussions as odd that they included the type of humor could be best described as black humor. These tales would not be humorous to most people looking in from the outside as they were often directed at women, minorities, department administrators and the public. Still, they appeared especially funny to the shift patrol. At first, the fact that I failed to recognize the humor made me believe that I was simply an outsider and thus not part of the in-group who were reacting to the jokes as exhibited through their laughter and comments. However, I had been at the department for over six months by this time, enough to be perceived as non-threatening to those officers. After all I have spent a great deal of time in patrol cars with my participants so it had to be more than that. It was at this point that I elicited the help of Professor Eric Poole, my colleague and close friend, to join me at the police department and observe police on patrol and at briefing sessions. Simultaneously, I began to read everything I could find on humor in organizations to better get a grasp of the role humorous behavior played for those lower-level participants in their everyday functions on the job. One particular article by Rose Coser (1959) focused on hospital patients interactions with hospital staff helped me begin to grasp the meanings of joking behavior in organizations in general terms. Coser's qualitative research on hospital staff and patients set the stage for the thematic study of humor and its strategic meanings for police patrol officers. Coser's article among others offered a behavioral trail for our observations and the eventual interpretative role that humor played within the context of its importance as an organizational method of communication among the rank and file of workers in highly structured authoritative work settings as a means for various types of expression, both internally within the department and externally toward the community.

The actual study of humor among police took over one year for the field work to be completed. The important point to be made here is that I had no idea that briefing room humor among patrol officers played any significant role in their everyday interactions among themselves in what Goffman (1959) termed backstage areas (the briefing room). Nor had I any idea that this type of social interaction phenomenon among police would be something I felt compelled to study. It did not become noticeable until well into my time spent observing patrol on a daily basis. Hopefully, this reporting of a confessional tale has provided a clear example of the inductive research process.

Accounts of Professional Misdeeds: The Sexual Exploitation of Clients of Psychotherapists

This particular research project is representative of a more focused study in that we gained an interest in the deviant activities of psychotherapists who have had sexual relations with their clients by way of an informal discussion with the Director of the Colorado Mental Health Grievance Board (Pogrebin, Poole, and Martinez 1992). During our conversations we discovered that sexual offending by clinical therapists was part of the board's oversight.

Under Colorado law sexual relations with a client in treatment is a felony. After more in-depth discussion of the topic I became intrigued with this deviancy among professional mental health treatment types (e.g., social workers, psychologists, counselors, and marriage counselors) that the grievance board agency had regulatory authority over. I was even more interested when I learned that after a client in treatment writes a letter of complaint to the grievance board, the psychotherapist—by state law—has to write a letter of response within 10 days of having received the complaint. Each complaint by a client who is receiving therapy against the therapist is answered in written form and then is investigated and results in a disposition by the appointed mental health grievance board. The board was comprised of four professional therapists and four lay community members. All were appointed by the Governor and all were ratified by a legislative committee.

Being knowledgeable that the grievance board was recently legislated to constitute all four of the above mentioned treatment professions into one single board as opposed to four single boards as was the case for many years prior, I seized at the opportunity to study this newly created regulatory agency, knowing that I could have access to all the 10-day response letters from therapists who were complained about by their clients. In short, I learned early on that the majority of letters from therapists consisted of guilty confessions and that there would be a short window of opportunity to study the required letters before lawyers would be attained to represent them, which became the practice approximately one and a half years into the newly formed grievance board's existence.

Once again, I elicited Professor Poole to join the research project. Although a bit hesitant at first, Poole became my research partner in this project and we decided to conduct a content analysis of 35 letters written by accused therapists who were explaining their professional behavior. We had no access to their names, demographic data, and so forth. We only had access to the complainant and therapists letters. We separately read each therapist's letter multiple times over a four-month period and then developed a coding scheme, which resulted in our utilization of neutralization theory as an explanation for their deviance (Scott and Lyman 1968; Sykes and Matza 1957; see Maruna and Copes (2005) for a review of this literature). We then exchanged letters and each of us coded the remaining letters individually. We then used a large room and placed separate coding schemes for each therapist on the wall in order to see the number of similarities and differences we found with all the letters. Because neutralizing theory's criteria of excuses, justifications, and sad tales were clearly defined, it was not difficult to code each therapist's letters into one or more definitional categories. After categorizing major and minor themes found within each letter for the accused therapists' behavior by using a content analysis methodology, we disregarded a few letters that were either too ambiguous for us to understand or were unable to clearly discern their content. Suffice to say, we agreed on the themes for the vast majority of our sampled letters and for those few where we differed in its content we disregarded. We ended up producing an article for publication based on this study.

The use of qualitative content analysis proved to be the best route method-ologically for this study. We would have liked to interview the therapists whose letters we analyzed, but were prohibited from doing this due to issues of confidentiality. The tradeoff for attaining the letters was that I agreed to be nominated for grievance board membership. I served on the Colorado Mental Health Grievance Board for five years and learned the hard lesson that I should never trade my time for access to data.

In a great deal of qualitative research, access to subjects that one wants to study is often difficult. In *Accounts of Professional Misdeeds* we discovered how important an informant (e.g., a person who can provide entry to the group) can be. In this particular study we were lucky enough to have the Director of the Colorado Mental Health Grievance Board providing access to the letters in response to complaints by clients of psychotherapists. Without the Director we would not have been able to gain access to these data, and the study would have never been conducted. Often, conducting qualitative research in public agencies (e.g.,, criminal justice) can be quite difficult because gatekeepers can prohibit and thwart access. Even though these common wheel agencies are thought to be transparent and provide access to researchers, my experiences have shown that this is rarely the case.

Natural Deaths and Unknown Persons: The Process of Creating an Identity

This particular study was an offshoot of a larger study I was conducting in a police department in a southern city (Pogrebin, Poole, and Regoli 1986). Two relevant factors have to be explained from the outset. First, I did not know what I was observing in natural death investigations until approximately five months into the larger study. Secondly, this research is indicative of a symbolic interaction approach, which comes under the sociological rubric of social psychology.

I conducted my participant organizational research in a state where investigators had to attend all natural deaths to determine if any foul play was involved. Usually two detectives inspected the dead person's dwelling and the deceased body order to decide if there were any unlawful events that occurred before a natural death report could be produced. After being called to the death scene in order to investigate the death of those who died at their residence, I began to notice that many of the deceased were not well-known to anyone in their neighborhood. Neighbors often knew who they were, but really did not know any more about them than their name and where they lived. In short, the deceased who were not well known appeared to have lived fairly solitarily lives. No immediate relatives living near the dead person's city and no close acquaintances who could provide us with any biographical information. After being part of six natural death investigations of unknown persons, I began to observe my senior investigative partner gather information and making notes while looking at objects in the dead person's dwelling. It took me months to grasp the meaning of the objects each detective I worked with identified to define just who this dead person was and how he or she fit into the larger community. The objects in the home became the major source of impressionistic definitions for detectives in cases of unknown people who die of natural causes. Fine (1999, p. 534) describes what I was observing into an understandable framework stating that "those scholars linked to the symbolic interactions perspective recognized that the meaning of objects was constrained and shaded by the responses of those who were viewing the scene."

By detectives' interpretation of objects of the deceased (i.e., medicine, clothes, photos, jewelry, etc.) an identity was created for them. The need to classify and characterize people in our society is an ongoing social process that lets others know one's status and how to respond to people through social interaction. The same definitions are utilized for the dead, more so if they are unknown. In these cases of natural deaths, it is the on-site investigator who attaches meaning to objects found in the deceased's home. Investigators interpret and define the value of the deceased for the world of the living. The final police death investigation report becomes the created identity for the unknown dead individual.

After working on 12 natural death scene investigations I began to reflect on my experiences with the four different investigators I worked with. I could never interview them for a more in-depth explanation of why they conducted their procedural use of material objects to define the unknown, because it would have caused a distance between us that I had worked so long to overcome and maintain. The conceptual theory came to me after many months of observing and listening to their verbal rationale for the meaning of objects in the home in order to define just who the dead person was and what identity was formulated for the unknown dead by each detective.

Years later I was joined by two other criminal justice/criminology professors who were fascinated by my description of the investigation of natural deaths. They added to my research by observing natural death cases in other police departments and together we published an article based on our findings. Perhaps, no other methodological genre could have described and analyzed the interaction between detectives and objects in the home than the trained eye of the social scientist; it brings into focus important understandings of symbolic meanings that are produced by all of us in everyday life. In this particular study of natural deaths I received a summer research grant provided by the Florida Board of Regents so that I could work for a state agency. I had the opportunity to join and study the Tallahassee Police Department as a commissioned detective in the Persons Division. This opportunity was permitted because a fellow professor was working in the patrol division for over one year which opened up the department to others who wished to conduct research. For a professor to join a police department and gain acceptance is a long and tedious process in which trust and compatibility had to be developed over a long period of time. This research was based on an ethnographic grounded theory approach because I really had no idea what I would be looking for and it was months before I noticed that police were creating identities for those who died of natural causes and were on the margins of surrounding community. This study is an example of data collected based on observations because to interview the detectives I worked with at natural death scenes would make them aware of the fact that I was really an outsider who was there for a relatively short time. I believed that asking too many questions while working on these scenes may have damaged the working and personal relationship that I established over many months of being with the department. It was absolutely necessary that I fit into the detective culture and not ask questions that would place me outside of the department milieu.

Advanced Placement—Pressures for Academic Dishonesty among Elite High School Students

Elite high school students who attend advanced placement courses and those accepted to the international baccalaureate programs (i.e., demanding programs of study that emphasizes other cultures and where students can earn college credits while still in high school) in high school are considered the best and the brightest of our nation's secondary school students. Our study of their participation in "cheating behavior" was the result of my discussing high school pressures to succeed with my friend's children and some of their peers who all were participants in one of the two mentioned elite academic programs (Taylor, Pogrebin, and Dodge 2002).

Professor Lyn Taylor, a professor of math education at the graduate level and also my wife, agreed to collaborate on a research project focusing on academic dishonesty among a sample of students in the two programs. Although Lyn was reluctant to involve herself in what could prove to be a study of deviance among this elite group, she conceded after much cajoling. Lyn's interest was in collaborative learning styles, which when instituted in math class should lessen the need for competitive grade-seeking and result in the main goal of learning, which would considerably reduce the degree of academic dishonesty.

We recruited six experienced high school math teachers who taught in advanced placement courses and the international baccalaureate program and were students in Lyn's graduate course at the time to participate in the study. We had each math teacher interview high school students at schools where they did not teach. The six high schools were evenly divided between urban and suburban locations. Also, we requested that the teacher collaborators introduce themselves as graduate students conducting a study for their math education course and only to inform the sample of students of their math teacher occupation if asked by the subject being interviewed. Further, we requested that all elite student interviews be conducted off campus in a public place (i.e., restaurants, coffee establishments and the like). In order to recruit our sample of secondary high school participants, we framed our study within the context of academic pressures to achieve good grades. Each of the study participants interviewed was recommended by high school math teachers who were known to one or more of our six teacher interviewers.

The 32 elite students had to be currently enrolled in advanced placement classes and international baccalaureate programs. Participants were both juniors and seniors and considered to be in the top 10% of their respective classes. Further, the teachers who selected the voluntary study participants were extremely cooperative and interested in learning more about the relationship between pressures to succeed academically and the possible use of dishonest means to achieve good grades.

Our findings suggest elite students were under constant strain to succeed in a highly competitive environment. The emphasis to achieve and maintain good grades, which had a direct bearing on class rank, seemed to be the most important academic pressure.

For this endeavor it was the "going there" as opposed to the "getting there" that is the most important thing to convey. This research project provides a good example of a more structured, pre-determined study that utilized graduate student math education teachers who, under our guidance, conducted the interviews. In the end, the participating teachers were quite understandably devastated by the findings. However, the study results offered many classroom policy changes that could prove to aid math teachers to emphasize learning over that of individual grading pressures for these—the best and the brightest—high school students. If nothing else was accomplished, we were able to bring to the attention of the teachers the nature and extent of the academic dishonesty employed by these students as a means to achieve good grades and high class ranking that were directly linked to the institutional competitive strains fostered in their respective schools. In addition, Professor Taylor's collaborative math learning theory could prove to be applicable in teacher development for a classroom teaching-learning environment which could possibly change the ultra competitive culture of these elite programs for those participating students who perceived deviant methods to meet the high achievement expectations placed on them by parents, teachers, and their fellow students.

This particular study is an example of bringing two differing academic subjects together for purposes of data collection. Math education and the sociology of deviance are quite different from one another. And since Professor Taylor and I (a wife/husband team) come from disparate academic disciplines, we had to overcome the differences in our scholarly interests to conduct this study. Getting there was difficult. This is an issue that can be prevalent in conducting research with academics from various disciplines with conflicting theoretical approaches. That is, we tend to perceive our interests within a particular study as being more interesting and important. So in these instances the research team has to accommodate each other's interests into the study.

The Sexualized Work Environment: A Look at Women Jail Officers

The original conception for this research study came from my graduate course in corrections. Three female jail deputy sheriffs were enrolled who were more than willing to share their working experiences with me during the break of our evening three-hour weekly seminars (Pogrebin and Poole 1997). I encouraged them to collectively prepare a class presentation on their experiences as female jail employees in a male-dominated occupation. As it turns out, county jails and detention centers employ more women than any other criminal justice agency. This fact by itself made their struggle for equality within the work setting much more relevant. Their class presentation revealed many obstacles they attempted to overcome in their daily responsibilities as jail officers. They spoke of a very masculine-charged work environment that appeared far more unequal and unfair in every way compared to the plight of female police officers described in Poole and Pogrebin (1988). This is not to dismiss the gender issues that women police officers also face on the job; rather, it is to point out how the structured closed environment of jails can exacerbate the stereotypical perceptions and differential treatment of female deputies by many of their male peers and ranking staff.

After much discussion with Professor Poole, we decided to conduct a study based largely on the knowledge that three female deputies informed the class about. We then interviewed separately each of the three deputies in order to elicit their individual thoughts about their chosen career as well as gain some insight for the direction our research should follow. We decided that an interview format would be the most revealing path to undertake because it would allow other female jail deputies in various county jails and detention centers to address the issues related to women working in a masculine-centered work environment. Admittedly, there existed numerous studies of women employed in male-dominated organizations, but nothing had been published on female jail officials. Still, the literature about women professionals in private and public organizations offered us many applicable findings that provided us a direction to follow that would prove useful to us in our research.

Four county jails and three adult detention centers located in four counties in the Denver Metropolitan area were selected for our study. These local correctional facilities were managed and staffed by personnel from four sheriffs' departments. Using personnel rosters of deputy sheriffs provided by the respective facilities, we drew systematic random samples of all female officers from each institution ($N = 135$). We contacted sampled female officers individually to inform them of the purpose of the study, requested their participation and obtained their informed consent. A total of 119 women agreed to participate. Due to work schedule conflicts, sick leave, vacation, transfer, and other related issues, we were able to complete face-to-face interviews with 108 women deputies. It is important to note that in all seven facilities, women officers were assigned to supervise both male and female inmates. Their job required duties that were the same for both male and female officers.

Our findings were gender-based, and a pervasive sexualized work environment was documented in all seven facilities. We further found a variety of adjustment strategies utilized by female officials to cope with the various problems stemming from sexism and sexual harassment directed at them by their male co-workers. The impact of and the response to these work-related issues were analyzed and categorized by us.

The vast majority of the women deputies were open and candid with us, even though they were relating very sensitive feelings to two male professionals. It seemed our interest in their occupational plight offered a rare opportunity for them to vent many pent-up feelings regarding their job-related problems caused by male staff for a long period of time.

As one can see, this qualitative study exposed us to some sensitive gender-based issues; yet, the interviewed women officers were forthcoming and were quite explicit in describing the nature of the problems they faced daily while serving on their various sheriff departments. Further, we utilized a random sampling technique to acquire our study respondents, something I rarely have done due to the small participant size of most of my past ethnographic research. At the time this study was conducted in local jails, a male-dominated work culture prevailed. This is important to point out because it exacerbated the difficulties female deputies were experiencing at the time. This sexualized work environment was largely unknown to either the public or to many researchers in criminal justice. Because jail administrators had not framed our study in terms of gender issues, we believe we were given access to study participants. Perhaps if the sheriffs or jail directors realized that women's treatment by their male peers was so incredibly problematic, they would not have been so willing to offer the names of the women deputies we interviewed. When the results of this study were made public, Dr. Poole and I were inundated by the media, mainly newspapers, to reveal the names of the jails and the women deputies who participated in the study. We, of course, provided no additional identifying information in order to preserve the confidentiality of our study subjects. The issue of subject protection and access that can lead to the discovery of potentially sensitive problems within criminal justice agencies is one that qualitative researchers often face when studying sensitive topics in criminal justice.

Qualitative Research and Criminal Justice/Criminology Doctoral Programs

The studies I have just discussed represent how I approach my research and the problems and issues that I have encountered. As I previously noted, I was pushed to be quantitative in my research approach while a graduate student and early in my career. I believe the reason for this is simple: my professors were trained in quantitative methods and this was the approach they believed was the appropriate method by which to study sociological phenomena. So one important question that has to be asked is where do qualitative criminal justice/criminology researchers come from? That is, in what types of academic disciplines have they attained their doctoral degrees, and what number of qualitative-oriented graduate courses did they take while they were pursuing their degree? If one were to list current professors whose academic specialty is criminal justice or criminology, one would be hard pressed to name qualitatively trained researchers who received their degree from a Ph.D. program in our field. Most notable academics who are considered the new generation of qualitative-type criminal justice/criminology researchers have come out of sociology departments that offered qualitative courses and studied under professors whose research publications were qualitative in nature. This is not meant to be misleading, for it is well known that all but a few sociology graduate programs emphasize quantitative methods proficiency in their research requirements. As a result of a much longer history of sociology graduate programs compared to the more recent development in doctoral programs in criminal justice and criminology, it is understandable that there are many more senior sociology professors who specialize in the area of deviance, social problems, criminology, delinquency, and corrections.

The issue that needs to be discussed has to do with the part that a qualitative orientation currently plays and will play in the future for doctoral students in these fairly young graduate criminal justice/criminology programs. For initial answers to this pressing issue, I turn to Kevin Buckler (2008) who conducted a study of a qualitative/quantitative divide in criminal justice/criminology doctoral programs. Buckler (2008, p. 390) provides an overall picture of just how few of these programs offer qualitative courses at the graduate level:

> Across all 25 Ph.D. programs there are a total of 90 methods-oriented classes that are required. Of these required methods courses, only five (5.5%) of the

courses focus specifically and exclusively on qualitative methodologies, whereas 35 (35.5%) of the courses focus exclusively on quantitative methods. The gap becomes larger if required data analysis courses are added to the number of classes focusing on quantitative methods. There are a total of 44 courses dedicated to either quantitative methods or data analysis (48.8%) ... The same basic pattern emerges with respect to the methods-oriented elective courses. There are a total of 139 methods-oriented elective courses offered by the 25 Ph.D. programs. Only 22 (15.8%) of these courses focus on qualitative methods, whereas 76 (54.6%) focus on quantitative methods.

It is obvious, as Buckler's (2008) study attests to, that there remains a genuine void in the inclusion of qualitative-type course work offered in the 25 criminal justice/criminology doctoral degree-granting programs as either required or elective methods courses. If graduate students in these programs are not offered the opportunity to experience the qualitative research imagination, then they will not be able to understand that there are other legitimate methods in which to study social phenomenon. Further, by focusing a student's entire graduate education largely on a quantitative approach to the study of criminology and criminal justice, a disservice is rendered to graduate students who have no choice but to employ quantitative methods. Without multiple methodological orientations, graduate students leave their graduate training having acquired only a limited background in alternative research methods in which to view the world. In short, by focusing a doctoral criminal justice/ criminology curriculum with only a deductive format, students are never offered the choice of deciding for themselves which research approach they wish to utilize for their dissertation.

A Final Note

I do not wish to end this presentation on a negative note, especially for those new to criminal justice/criminology graduate programs or for recently hired assistant professors. Yes, it is true that qualitative field work studies are very time consuming and do require a great effort in the field whether one's study requires participant observation or interviewing subjects outside of one's academic institution. However, an academic's research findings should be judged on the quality of the work produced and not only on the quantity of articles resulting in publication. If your fellow faculty, as well as the evaluating committees above the departmental level, are of this thought process, you are in luck. If not, one has to decide if the opposite is true. Do you want to be at a university that does not appreciate the quality of your work? I realize this is a difficult decision, but remember, you did not suffer the "pains" of a doctoral program to give up the type of research you love doing once you become a member of the faculty. There is more than enough room for all methodological approaches in a field of study such as ours, where there is so much we do not know and so much more research needed to better understand both crime and the criminal justice system.

Perhaps I have pointed out too many challenges for qualitative researchers so let me end on a positive note and suggest worthwhile steps that may be (and have been) taken to ensure the acceptance and value of inductive research. Importantly, as I previously pointed out, there are a growing number of very talented criminology/criminal justice qualitative researchers who have published their work in some of the highest ranked journals in the field. This fact alone is extremely encouraging and certainly should provide graduate students with solid and important examples of excellent qualitative studies that have been conducted. I believe these young researchers provide qualitatively oriented graduate students with the necessary hope that their work can too be published in respected academic outlets. Moreover, the accomplishments of these young qualitative researchers demonstrate that at least some change in methodological thinking has occurred among journal editors and reviewers in recent years.

Despite the hopeful signs that the field is taking qualitative research more seriously, far more needs to be done on the part of qualitative types if we are going to see the kind of changes we want to occur in the future. I suggest that those of us who have complained for too long about the value placed on our contributions to criminology and criminal justice need to formulate a more aggressive posture by getting ourselves appointed as journal editors, editorial board members, and IRB board members. We also need to serve on graduate program review teams that evaluate the curriculum of criminology/criminal justice courses that are offered by various programs. During these reviews the idea of offering qualitative research methods courses should be argued. Of course, any qualitative courses would necessitate the hiring of faculty who are proficient in qualitative research and methods. Who knows, we may see a qualitative academic revolution in our graduate programs in the not too distant future.

Acknowledgments

I owe a great deal of gratitude to my colleagues Eric Poole and Paul Stretesky for their help and thoughtful suggestions in improving this manuscript and to Heith Copes for providing me with the opportunity to contribute my thoughts to this special edition of the *Journal of Criminal Justice Education*.

References

Agar, M. 1996. *The professional stranger: An informal introduction to ethnography*. San Diego, CA: Academic Press.
Anderson, L. 1999. The open road to ethnography's future. *Journal of Contemporary ethnography* 28: 451–459.
Atkinson, P. 1992. *Understanding ethnographic texts*. Newbury, CA: Sage.

Bochner, A., and C. Ellis. 1999. Which way to turn. *Journal of Contemporary Ethnography* 28: 485-499.

Buckler, K. 2008. The quantitative/qualitative divide revisited: A study of published research, doctoral program curricula, and journal editor perceptions. *Journal of Criminal Justice Education* 19: 383-403.

Chapin, H. 1972. *Greyhound.* New York: Electra Records.

Clandinin, D. J., and F. M. Cornwalley. 1994. Personal experience methods. In N. Denzin and Y. Lincoln (Eds.), *Handbook of quantitative research* (pp. 413-427). Thousand Oakes, CA: Sage.

Coser, R. 1959. Some social functions of laughter. *Human Relations* 12: 171-180.

Eder, D., and W. Corsaro. 1999. Ethnographic studies of children and youth: Theoretical and ethical issues. *Journal of Contemporary Ethnography* 28: 520-531.

Fine, G. A. 1993. Ten lies of ethnography: moral dilemmas in field research. *Journal of Contemporary Ethnography* 22: 267-294.

Fine, G. A. 1999. Field labor and ethnographic reality. *Journal of Contemporary Ethnography,* 28, 532-539.

Geertz, C. 1973. *The interpretation of culture.* New York: Basic Books.

Gergen, K. J. 1994. *Realities and relationships: Soundings in social construction.* Cambridge, MA: Harvard University Press.

Glaser, B. G., and A. C. Strauss. 1967. *The discovery of grounded theory: Strategies for qualitative research.* Chicago: Aldine.

Goffman, E. 1959. *The social psychology of everyday life.* New York: Doubleday.

Katz, J. 2006. Ethical escape routes for underground ethnographies. *American Ethnologist* 33: 499-506.

Katz, J. 2007. Toward a natural history of censorship. *Law and Society Review* 41: 797-810.

Kleinman, S., B. Stenross, and M. McMahon. 2004. Privileging fieldwork over interviews: Consequences for identity and practice. *Symbolic Interaction* 17: 37-50.

Maruna, S., and H. Copes. 2005. What have we learned from five decades of neutralization research? *Crime and Justice: A Review of Research* 32: 221-320.

McCracken, G. 1988. *The long interview: Sage university qualitative research methods series, vol. 13.* Newbury Park, CA: Sage.

Miller, J. 2005. *The status of qualitative research in criminology.* Proceedings from the National Science Foundation's Workshop on Interdisciplinary Standards for Systematic Qualitative Research. Retrieved from http://www.wjh.harvard.edu/nsfqual/Miller%20Paper.pdf

Miller, P., and L. Sperry. 1987. The socialization of anger and aggression. *Merrill-Palmer Quarterly* 33: 1-31.

Pogrebin, M. 2003. *Qualitative approaches to criminal justice: Perspectives from the field.* Thousand Oakes, CA: Sage.

Pogrebin, M., and E. Poole. 1988. Humor in the briefing room: A study of the strategic uses of humor among police. *Journal of Contemporary Ethnography* 17: 183-210.

Pogrebin, M., and E. Poole. 1997. The sexualized work environment: A look at women jail officers. *The Prison Journal* 77: 41-57.

Pogrebin, M., E. Poole, and A. Martinez. 1992. Accounts of professional misdeeds: The sexual exploitation of clients of psychotherapists. *Deviant Behavior* 13: 229-252.

Pogrebin, M., E. Poole, and R. Regoli. 1986. Natural deaths and unknown persons: The process of celebrating an identity. *Social Science Journal* 23: 391-396.

Pogrebin, M., P. Stretesky, and N. P. Unnithan. 2009. *Guns, violence, and criminal behavior: The offender's perspective.* Boulder, CO: Lynne Rienner.

Poole, E., and M. Pogrebin. 1988. Factors affecting the decisions to remand in policing: A study of women officers. *Journal of Police Science and Administration* 16: 49-55.

Scott, D. 1989. Meaning construction and social work practice. *Social Service Review* 63: 474-480.

Scott, M., and S. Lyman. 1968. Accounts. *American Sociological Review* 33: 46-62.

Skolnick, J. 1967. *Justice without trial*. New York: Wiley.

Spradley, J. 1977. Forward. In R. Weppner (Ed.), *Street ethnography* (pp. vi-viii). Beverly Hills, CA: Sage.

Spradley, J. 1980. *Participant observation*. New York: Holt, Rinehart and Winston.

Sykes, G., and D. Matza. 1957. Techniques of neutralization: A theory of delinquency. *American Sociological Review* 22: 664-670.

Taylor, L., M. Pogrebin, and M. Dodge. 2002. Advanced placement-advanced pressures: Academic dishonesty among elite high school students. *Educational Studies* 33: 403-421.

Van Maanen, J. 1988. *Tales of the field: On writing ethnography*. Chicago: University of Chicago Press.

Whyte, W. 1955. *Street corner society*. Chicago: University of Chicago Press.

Index

INDEX

feminist scholarship 48, 56; fieldwork 62–4, 66–7, 71, 75; gangster discourse 72; genres 55–6; identity, narrative as a shaper of 55; inconsistencies and missing parts 54; indicators as criminal behaviour 64; individualism 60, 75; institutions, fieldwork in 62–3, 65; interpersonal interaction between interviewers and participants 52; interpretation, narrative as 47, 56, 64; intertextuality 67; interviews 44, 49, 51–2, 55, 58, 61–75; intuition 51–2; knowledge creation 56; labelling 46, 48–9; language 50, 52–3, 64, 68; literary genres, borrowing from other 67–8; methodological criticism 74; narrative psychology 67, 70; natural analysis 155; neutralization techniques 47, 65, 69–70; objectivity 44; observation 62–7, 71–4; offenders 44–58; outsiders 62, 66; pain, causing 49; perceptions of participants 61; positivism 47, 51, 60, 64–5, 74–5; postmodernism 67; post-structuralism 47, 67; prompts 49–50; rationality 69–71, 75; reality, narrative as shaper of 50, 52, 57, 65; record, narrative as 47, 56, 64; repetitions 53–4; routine activities theorists 51; self-narrative 55, 64–6, 68–9; social context 62, 68, 70–1, 75; speech acts 68; standard plots 55–6; standardization 74–5; street culture 70, 72; subcultural narratives 61, 64, 71, 73–4; subjectivity 44; symbolic interactionism 69; talk as action, analysing 68; text analysis software 52; themes of interest 52; time, events across 51–2; truth 44–5, 60–76; whole life stories 51
National Institute of Health (NIH) 143
natural analysis 155
natural death investigations 164–6
Neuman, L 26, 33
neutralization techniques 47, 65, 69–70, 164
newsgroups 80–3, 95
Nuyorican cocaine dealers in Puerto Rico 54–5

objectivity 28–9, 44, 64, 67
observation 62–7, 71–4, 107–8, 110, 145–8
O'Connor, PE 53–4
on-line data, strategies for using 79–96: anonymity 81–2, 91–2, 93–4; blogs 85–6, 88, 92, 95; bulletin boards 80–3, 95; classroom, application in the 94–5; credit card fraud 94; culture 89; data collection 87–95; data loss 90–1; data sources 80–6; data triangulation 86–7; email 79–80, 83–7, 91, 95; ethics 91, 92–4; ethnography 82; focus groups 84; forums 80–3, 87–90, 92–3, 95; fraud 83; gangs using MySpace 88; Google 88; hacking 84, 86, 87, 93; harassment 93; identification 92; identity theft 94; instant messaging 83–5, 87, 88, 95; international data collection 88–9; Internet 79–83, 87–95; interviews 84–5, 87, 91, 94; male escorts 85–6, 88, 91; methodological concerns 87–91; MySpace 88; newsgroups 80–3, 95; privacy 92, 93–4; representative nature of information 87–8; researcher identification 82, 92–3; response rates 91; risk, protection from 93; saving websites 91; screenshots 91; search engines 88–90, 92; security software 93; snowball samples 89; social networking 79–80, 95–6; spam 83, 91; spider programs 89; subculture 80, 83–4; text messages 85–6; threats 93; transcription 84; undercover operations 90; universities, risk to 93; viruses and malicious software 80–1, 85–6, 93; websites 85–6, 88–93, 95
Onwuegbuzie, A 31
opportunism 112, 119–20, 133
outsiders 62, 66

pain, causing 49
Park, Robert E 150
Pasko, L 48
Pearson, G 63
peer review and discussions 146
philosophy 26–8, 101–2
Pierce, JL 51
Pogrebin, Mark R 14, 162, 168–9
police: humour, use of 162–3; natural death investigations 164–6
Polkinghorne, DE 46–7
Poole, Eric 162–4, 168–9
positive social sciences (PSS) 28
positivism: ethnography 154; mixed qualitative-quantitative methods research 28–9, 31–2, 34, 40; narrative research 47, 51, 60, 64–5, 74–5; qualitative-quantitative dichotomy 102–3; subjectivism 101–3
postmodernism 67
post-structuralism 47, 67
pragmatism 26, 31–2
Pratt, T 1, 27
predation 118–19, 121–3, 129–31, 133
presentations 149
Presser, L 55, 60, 64–5, 66, 72, 75
prison see jail
privacy 92, 93–4, 108, 111
productivity 103, 158–9
prompts 49–50
ProQuest Digital Dissertations 9
prostitutes 80–3, 90, 105, 107
Pruitt, MV 86, 91
psychology 12, 13–14, 67, 70, 165
psychotherapists, sexual exploitation of clients of 163–4
publications 31 see also journals, prominence of qualitative research in CCJ